ENDORSEMENTS FOR WALKING THROUGH THE FIRE—STEVE KING

"Steve King is an American patriot—a man of great faith, unassailable character, and unwavering grace. *Walking Through the Fire* recounts his life story, from his family-centered Midwestern upbringing to his grass-roots political campaign, to his championing of traditional values and America First nationalism. In this candid and invaluable memoir, King calls out the race baiters, media liars, Democrat defamers, and RINO smear merchants who work together to cancel defenders of Western Civilization. In a world of phonies and cowards, Steve King is the real deal. If you want to know what a modern 'Horatius at the Gate' looks like, read this book and make your children read it too!"

—**Michelle Malkin**, investigative journalist and
best-selling author of *Invasion, Culture of Corruption*,
and *Open Borders, Inc.*

"Congressman Steve King writes this no-holds-barred account for all the world to see exactly what has been going on in Congress. Unlike many today who write a book to cover up the things that evoked criticism, Steve lays out all the facts for the world to see and judge for themselves, without the deceptions and fabrications the Alt-Left media created. For the few Leftists who still admire people who speak very candidly, whether agreeing or disagreeing, you will find plenty upon which to base admiration. Steve believes in our country, warts and all, but knows America is the greatest gift of a nation God ever gave a people. Readers will be very pleasantly surprised."

—**Louie Gohmert**, U.S. Congress (2005–present), chief justice,
Texas Court of Appeals (2002–2003), district court judge (1993–
2002), Baylor University, juris doctorate (1977),
Texas A&M, B.A. 1975

"Is Steve King an American hero, or does he embody a thousand vile accusations hurled by the *New York Times* and the DC Ruling Class? You, dear reader, have the luxury of learning politics as it really works in State Capitols and in our Washington, D.C. Capitol. In this easy-to-follow new book, you'll join Steve King on a guided tour of how and why American school children went from honoring our sacred heroes, like Washington, Lincoln, or Jefferson, to despoiling their statues and memorials in public squares across our nation. To many of the events in this book, I serve as an eyewitness affirming the accuracy of Congressman King's experiences. Steve King narrates a riveting description of the tumultuous changes of our times; he brings you into the story of how a nation destroys itself by destroying those who are the strongest defenders of its foundational values. Read this book and you'll go from bewildered to thanking heroes like Steve King for fighting to maintain your liberties!"

—**Michele Bachmann**, former member of the U.S. Congress, Minnesota, former 2012 Republican Presidential candidate. Now serving as Dean of the Robertson Graduate School of Government, Regent University, Virginia Beach, VA

"Truth matters a great deal. However, it seems that in politics, truth and facts matter little. The 'facts,' as manipulated by the media, undermine the foundation of the American republic. And Steve King, at the hands of the media's 'facts,' has suffered the indignity of having people lie about and to him because he dared to speak the truth. And now, with truth on his side, he is fighting back. Within these pages, you will get an insider view of all that is wrong with American politics. If Steve King's account represented an isolated case, it would be of little value. But cancel culture cut its teeth on Representative King, and now, conservatives are under attack everywhere.

"After reading *Walking Through the Fire*, you will know the truth. You may find it more disturbing than liberating, but you will no doubt know truth defends Steve King at every opportunity."

—**Sam Clovis** Jr., BS, MBA, DPA, past national co-chair and chief policy advisor, Trump for President Campaign

"Steve King experienced the quagmire of the Washington Swamp first-hand and fell victim to its toxicity. Having been there for many years, in Congress and even now with Conservative Partnership Institute, I know well what Congressman King went through and why. We the People must work harder than ever to purge our government of its deeply rooted corruption. I highly recommend an objective read of *Walking Through the Fire* for needed insight in this fight."

—**Jim DeMint**, former U.S. Senator, chairman of Conservative Partnership Institute, and best-selling author of *Satan's Dare*

"This book is a page-turner. It is an insider look at the back stabbing, plotting, betrayal, and deals at the highest levels in government. A must-read."

—**Brigitte Gabriele**, founder and chairman of Act for America, *NYT* best-selling author, political commentator

"*Walking Through the Fire* is the inside story of how a man of integrity was taken out by corrupt politicians on both sides of Washington's 'aisle,' revealing how truth is despised by government elites. 'Fragging' is a term coined in the military during the Vietnam War referring to soldiers assassinating their own. Congressman Steve King's character was fragged by his own colleagues in collusion with fake media. This book is a must-read wake-up call to us all who want a return to America's First Principles."

—**LtCol Oliver L. North** (USMC ret.),
CEO of Fidelis Publishing, LLC, and
best-selling author of *The Rifleman* and
We Didn't Fight for Socialism

"I was honored to serve with Steve for eight years in the Halls of Congress and witnessed him *Walking Through the Fire*. Steve is an individual who loves America, the Constitutional principles and opportunities provided for all regardless of one's background. He is an individual who does not bend his principles to appease the leadership of either party. Steve spoke the truth unabashedly and the Republican leadership—caving into political correctness and wokeness—turned the flames of the fire up to get Steve to back down, but he never did. He survived the walk through those flames and, like tempered steel, has become stronger and, in the process, made this Nation better. I am proud to call Steve my friend and fellow patriot."

—**Ted S. Yoho**, DVM, former member of Congress,
Florida 2013–2021

"Congressman Steve King could always be found on the hottest part of the battlefield, speaking out clearly and regularly on all the hot-button issues where the establishment gets most ruthless in enforcing its speech codes. It's a miracle Steve King survived there for eighteen years. Republicans who show courage on those issues don't have a long political 'life expectancy.' The media and Democrat money wound them and eventually Republican operatives and leadership pile on too. I've seen this happen repeatedly to good men in Congress. King's eighteen years of fearless frankness on immigration, life, religious freedom—it's a remarkable run!"

—**Capitol Hill Chief of Staff** (former), name withheld
to protect his congressman

"*Walking Through the Fire* is an apt description of the political career of my friend Steve King. His brilliant defense of Western Civilization is what put him in the crosshairs of those trying desperately to erase the reality of a civilization that attracts millions. They seek something—dare we even say it—BETTER. Mass migration of every color of humanity is a one-way street to the West. Steve King forces the 'woke vampires' of the Left to face the crucifix of the allure of Western Civilization. They recoil against it and try to kill the messenger. Modern despots on the Left can't let the knowledge of a civilization based on Judeo-Christian morality and one that brought enlightenment and the Rule of Law to a world in desperate need of both, be passed on to another generation. So books will be banned, statues torn down, speeches will be censored, careers will be destroyed, and history will be rewritten in order to, as Obama described his dream, 'thoroughly transform America.' Steve King stands, as did Horatius, against the onslaught of barbarians. It is a lonely vigil that has earned him the derision of his foes and the undying admiration of those who love liberty."

—**Tom Tancredo**, U.S. Congress 1999–2009,
presidential candidate 2008, candidate for governor
of Colorado, 2010, 2012, 2014, author of
In Mortal Danger: The Battle for America's Border (2006)

"Steve King has been through 'Hell on Earth.' I have joined with and also followed many of his cultural battles to reclaim the American heart and soul. King's resilience is supernatural. *Walking Through the Fire* edifies why Steve King was a threat to political elites as a U.S. Congressman. His story must be told. Too many complain without leading; Steve has led without complaining, and now, in this book, he provides a solution—a call to action—with reasoned arguments that will lead us out of the swamp. His solution? Tell the truth, espouse the principles of Western Civilization, and fight against the abandonment of our American ideals. Starting with our time together in the Iowa State Senate, I have enjoyed our friendship as we fight for the grandest 'American Traditions.'"

—**Neal Schuerer**, Iowa State Senate (1997–2005),
National Article V Movement, and executive director
of Path to Reform.Org

"I have been blessed in my life to know, work with, or work for, a few American heroes whose selfless service to this great nation never appears to end. Congressman Steve King is one of those few, and his *Walking Through the Fire* sets a high standard for us all. It is a must-read for those who want to know how the 'sausage' is made, yet it's written for the common man. King's book is threaded with uplifting narratives, but the real meat is his factual first-person account of the backstabbing, double dealing, and dishonesty of Washington, D.C.—even within his own party. King slugged it out with Leftists and RINOs for eighteen years in the United States Congress in a battle for the soul of our nation. It's a story all Americans need to know. Stand and Fight or Live on Your Knees! Nice Shot, Congressman!!"

—**Kim L. Herzfeldt**, congressional staff for Congressman Tancredo,
congressional campaign staff, presidential campaign staff
planning commissioner for Colorado counties

Walking Through the Fire

My Fight for the Heart and Soul of America

By

Steve King

FIDELIS
PUBLISHING

FIDELIS PUBLISHING
ISBN: 978-1-7366206-4-9
ISBN (eBook): 978-1-7366206-5-6

Walking Through the Fire
My Fight for the Heart and Soul of America

Cover Design by Diana Lawrence
Interior Design by Xcel Graphic – www.xcelgraphic.com

For information about special discounts for bulk purchases, please contact Bulk-Books.com, call 1-888-959-5153 or email – cs@bulkbooks.com

(RSV) Revised Standard Version of the Bible, copyright © 1946, 1952, and 1971 the Division of Christian Education of the National Council of the Churches of Christ in the United States of America. Used by permission.

(ESV) The Holy Bible, English Standard Version. ESV® Text Edition: 2016. Copyright © 2001 by Crossway Bibles, a publishing ministry of Good News Publishers.

(NLT) Holy Bible, New Living Translation, copyright © 1996, 2004, 2015 by Tyndale House Foundation. Used by permission of Tyndale House Publishers, Inc., Carol Stream, Illinois 60188.

Fidelis Publishing, LLC Sterling, VA • Nashville, TN
fidelispublishing.com
Manufactured in the United States of America
10 9 8 7 6 5 4 3 2

DEDICATION

To my family, staff, and friends—those who actually know me and know me best.

Each of you stood your ground, facing vicious political attacks, personal harassment, and relentless revilement. You were subjected to despicable, iniquitous assaults on your character and on mine. Your will and restraint, provoked by denigration and threats, demonstrated unflinching courage. Not one of you walked away during two and a half years of an unrelenting, remorseless siege. You walked toward the fire. You walked into the fire. You walked through the fire with me. We all came out the other side stronger, wiser, and grateful to our Lord and Savior for walking through the fire with us. God bless you all.

"When you walk through fire you shall not be burned." (Isaiah 43:2 RSV)

CONTENTS

FOREWORD

Never before, in my nearly thirty years as a conservative journalist and proud American, have the forces of evil converged so insidiously to sabotage our freedoms and destroy our great country. Big Tech, Big Pharma, Big Business, Big Media, and Big Government are all working together to tear down the pillars of our sovereignty. It's not a "conspiracy theory." It's the truth.

The radical Left is, and always has been, out to Cancel America. It's a perpetual campaign waged on a mountain of lies. Cultural Marxists have nurtured generations of aggrieved young minds to believe these falsehoods to be self-evident: that all white people are inherently "privileged," all black people are inherently oppressed, the police are an irredeemably racist and oppressive force, and America is an incorrigibly racist, sexist, fill-in-the-blank-phobic nation in need of transformative dismantling and reimagining.

Throughout his life, Steve King has battled valiantly against all these forces of evil. I've been blessed to know him and stand beside him on the issues that matter most—our families, our faith, our history, and our borders. He speaks unapologetically about America's enemies, who will not rest until the foundations and monuments of Western Civilization crumble. Like me, Steve has been called every ad hominem and slur in the Alinskyite playbook for his vigilant defense of America—racist, nativist, homophobe, anti-Semite, white supremacist, bigot, wash, rinse, and repeat.

I call Steve an American patriot—a man of great faith, unassailable character, and unwavering grace. He championed strict immigration enforcement for years before President Trump embraced the agenda. And as Steve points out, "Trump did indeed adopt many of my policies, including the building of a wall, the ending of birthright citizenship, the rejection of sanctuary cities, and even some of the more specific policies like basing congressional redistricting on the population of documented citizens."

Walking Through the Fire recounts Steve King's life story, from his family-centered Midwestern upbringing to his grass-roots political campaign, to his championing of traditional values and America First nationalism. In this candid and invaluable memoir, King calls out the race baiters, media liars, Democrat defamers, and RINO smear merchants who work together to cancel defenders of Western Civilization.

In a world of phonies and cowards, Steve King is the real deal of integrity and courage. If you want to know what a modern "Horatius at the Gate" looks like, this book vividly paints that portrait for you and hopefully for the generations in your wake!

Michelle Malkin
www.michellemalkin.com

PROLOGUE

Walk toward the fire. Don't worry about being
called a racist, a homophobe, a sociopath, a violent
heteronormative xenophobe with fascistic impulses.
They say all those things about you because they're
keeping you inside the Complex, forcing you to
respond to their playbook.[1]

—Andrew Breitbart

Before his untimely death in March 2012, I had the great fortune of being able to call Andrew Breitbart a close personal friend. I also had the profound honor to deliver his eulogy at his memorial service in Washington, D.C.

Andrew had an instinct for where the battle should be fought and an intellect that informed him as to how. In the eulogy, I described him as Horatius at the Gate. Here is my favorite excerpt, as I delivered it, from the poem by Thomas Babington Macaulay:

> *Then out spake brave Horatius,*
>
> *The Captain of the gate:*
>
> *"To every man upon this earth*
>
> *Death cometh soon or late.*
>
> *And how can man die better*
>
> *Than facing fearful odds*
>
> *For the ashes of his fathers*
>
> *And the temples of his [god].*[2]

Andrew Breitbart was a man who, in walking toward the fire, always walked point. The "point" is the one who takes the lead, sounds the warning, and makes it safer for those who come behind. In military combat, walking point takes keen instincts and steely physical courage. Lives are at stake. In political combat, walking point takes instincts and conviction but little physical courage. There are risks, great risks but no one has died from being stripped of a committee assignment, losing a primary, or getting canceled.

I began my political career years before I met Andrew Breitbart. Although we had superficially little in common—he from Hollywood, I from Iowa—we clicked when we met. The reason was simple enough. We each believed to fight the corruption of our culture, you could not, in the memorable words of Barack Obama, "lead from behind." You had to take point.

Among the messages Andrew preached was this one: "Telling the truth is fun." As the introductory quote suggests, however, Breitbart also knew telling the truth came at a cost. The cost part of the equation is more obvious than the benefit. It almost always is. "They want to stop you in your tracks," said Andrew.

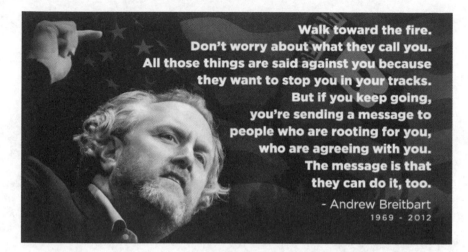

Andrew Breitbart: The inspirational theme of Andrew Breitbart's best seller, "Righteous Indignation."

In the following pages you will get a real sense of just how costly it can be to speak honestly in a political environment that has little use for truth. "But if you keep going," Andrew promised, "if you tell them you can stop their verbal bullets and keep walking, you'll send messages to people who are rooting for you, who agree with you."[3] The message I hope to send is this: their bullets aren't real but the truth always is.

CHAPTER ONE

RUNNING RISKS

On the final weekend of May 2020, violent mobs of entitled young Leftists, black and white, raged through the streets of nearly every major city in America, burning, looting, and defacing all vestiges of Western Civilization they could get their hands on. Statues of Washington, Jefferson, Teddy Roosevelt, Christopher Columbus, Andrew Jackson, Robert E. Lee, and even Abraham Lincoln were tagged, toppled, or beheaded. In England, rioters went after the statues of Winston Churchill, George Washington, and anyone even remotely linked to the slave trade no matter their other virtues or accomplishments. When the mobs toppled the statue of black abolitionist Frederick Douglass in Rochester, New York, everyone should have known the mobs were attacking Western Civilization writ large.

Not a single Democrat of note protested the madness. If anything, they sang the praises of these anarchists and their mindless acolytes. The Democrats were banking on the mayhem to fire up their base for the November elections. Few Republicans were speaking out with any measure of force or purpose. Most had long ago been cowed into submission, not by the voters, but by a hostile media and the leadership of their own party.

If elected Republicans needed a reminder of the price they might pay for defending Western Civilization, they got it on the Tuesday following this unhinged weekend of broken glass. With the full-throated support of the media and the Republican establishment, an off-the-shelf state senator named Randy Feenstra bested me in the Republican primary for an Iowa congressional seat I held since 2003. My crime: warning my constituents and my colleagues that Western Civilization was under assault.

I was the Republican's Czechoslovakia. GOP leaders figured if they just surrendered me and a few others to the Left, they could appease the beast and hold on to their own seats. They had no more luck than Chamberlain did at Munich. The brown shirts were on the march. If these GOP leaders did not know it when they launched the campaign against me starting years back, they know it now. Today, maybe even in the eyes of their own children, *they* are all white supremacists.

I got a taste of what was to come on January 10, 2019. That was the day the *New York Times* revealed something to the world no one who has known me would have ever suspected. For sixtynine years—including twenty-five years swimming with the sharks, eighteen of them in the D.C. swamp—not one person in a huge and ever-growing circle of friends, enemies, family, and colleagues ever witnessed or reported even a whisper of me saying or doing anything meriting the devastating allegation the *Times* reported as fact. To their surprise and to mine, I had become a "white supremacist."

Intrepid *Times* reporter Trip Gabriel, former *Sunday Styles* editor, won the hearts of his bosses, Democrats, NeverTrumpers, globalists, and elitists by showing he could race-bait with the best of them. My own Republican leadership, Kevin McCarthy and others, should have responded with outrage. Instead, they urged Gabriel on. One would think with a name like McCarthy the House minority leader would have shied from the tactics he deployed if only to avoid the obvious comparison. The truth is, though, it was far less damaging to be labeled a communist, even at the height of the Cold War, than it is to be labeled a white supremacist today. And unlike the current witch hunters, *Joe*

McCarthy was pursuing *real* witches, and I was dealing with a classic narcissistic abuser.

To speak candidly today is to run risks. I know that. On sensitive subjects, illegal immigration most prominently, progressives have neutralized the effective use of language in advance by declaring it offensive, even racist. They insist Republicans speak softly and mildly about controversial issues as a way of ensuring no one hears them. I have refused to play their game. In my nine terms in Congress, I have never shied from strong language. The Irish blood in me rebels against that. I believe there is a place in our rhetoric for immoderation. Some issues demand it.

William Lloyd Garrison certainly thought so. In launching his newspaper, *The Liberator*, in 1831, here is what he had to say on the emancipation of enslaved African Americans: "On this subject, I do not wish to think, or speak, or write, with moderation. No! No! Tell a man whose house is on fire, to give a moderate alarm; tell him to moderately rescue his wife from the hand of the ravisher; tell the mother to gradually extricate her babe from the fire into which it has fallen;—but urge me not to use moderation in a cause like the present. I am in earnest—I will not equivocate—I will not excuse—I will not retreat a single inch—AND I WILL BE HEARD."[4] To be heard, Garrison had to speak immoderately to an audience largely hostile to his message. I fully understand.

The Democrats were, of course, on the wrong side of the slavery issue just as they are on the issue of illegal immigration. In fact, Democrats have been on the wrong side of many race and ethnic issues. Democrats started the Ku Klux Klan. Democrats presided over a century of Jim Crow. Democrat governors stood in the doorway of schoolhouses and universities and blocked the entrance of would-be students, and they did so not all that long ago—I am old enough to remember.

Today, as the Democrats see it, everyone else in America is racist but themselves. I wish I were kidding. "We have a racist society from top to bottom," Bernie Sanders said at the February 2020 Democratic debate in New Hampshire. He added, our "racist society" is "impacting health care, housing, criminal justice, education—you name it." The criminal justice system was particularly bad. "What we have got to do is understand the system is broken, is racist."[5]

No one on the stage disagreed with him. Said Joe Biden, as only Joe Biden could say it, "The fact is that we in fact there is systemic racism." Elizabeth Warren insisted, "We need race-conscious laws in education, in employment, in entrepreneurship to make this country a country for everyone." Andrew Yang argued, given the depth of the problem, "You can't legislate away racism." Said Tom Steyer, an open champion of reparations, "Anyone who thinks that racism is a thing of the past and not an ongoing problem is not dealing with reality."[6] And this was all said before the George Floyd mania made even these unhinged accusations seem restrained.

One major reason the Left is keen on branding their political opponents as racists is so racial minorities will overlook the hardcore racist roots of a party whose two prominent standard bearers are Thomas Jefferson and Andrew Jackson. For all their many virtues, both of these men did own slaves, and every prominent Democrat in America has attended many a festive dinner in their honor.

Let me give you a quick example of how the media help the Democrats play the race card. In 2008, Nixon-era Secretary of Agriculture Earl Butz died. Butz was a Republican. In 2010, U.S. Senator Robert Byrd died. Byrd was a Democrat. The *New York Times* headlined Butz's obituary, "Earl L. Butz, Secretary Felled by Racial Remark, Is Dead at 98."[7] The *Times* headlined Byrd's obit, "Robert C. Byrd, a Pillar of the Senate, Dies at 92."[8] From the perspective of the *Times*, Butz would seem to be the one haunted by a racist past.

Earl Butz's sin? In an otherwise blameless life, Butz, the most consequential secretary of agriculture since the Depression, told his seatmate a joke. Sitting behind Butz on this Gerald Ford campaign plane was professional snitch John Dean of Watergate fame. Butz could have told this joke just as readily about any rural male, but he told it instead about "coloreds," saying they wanted little more out of life—as the *Times* politely phrased it—than "satisfying sex, loose shoes and a warm bathroom." Butz promptly apologized, but it did no good. That one joke, privately told, cost Butz his job and his reputation. Thirty-two years after he told it, the media still would not forgive him. In fact, they all but etched the joke on his tombstone.

Robert Byrd had real sins to atone for. In the 1940s, while America was at war, so was Byrd. He recruited one hundred fifty of his friends and associates to form a Ku Klux Klan "klavern" in West Virginia. The new Klansmen, in turn, made Byrd the "Exalted Cyclops" (chapter president). In 1944, Byrd sent a letter to segregationist Mississippi Senator Theodore Bilbo. "I shall never fight in the armed forces with a negro by my side," wrote Byrd. "Rather I should die a thousand times, and see Old Glory trampled in the dirt never to rise again, than to see this beloved land of ours become degraded by race mongrels, a throwback to the blackest specimen from the wilds." Now there's a white supremacist!

In running for Congress, Byrd tried to distance himself from his Klan past, but he did not exactly embrace the cause of civil rights. In 1964, as a U.S. Senator, he personally filibustered the Civil Rights Act for fourteen hours and voted against it. He joined twenty other Democratic Senators in opposing it. Only six Republicans opposed it and they did so on libertarian grounds. In the House, a higher percentage of Republicans than Democrats voted for the bill's passage as well.

Yet it was not until the *fifteenth* paragraph of Byrd's glowing obituary when the *Times* even mentioned his racially troubled past. Upon his passing, the *Times* quoted then-president Barack Obama as saying, "America has lost a voice of principle and reason." For Byrd, a reliable Democratic vote, all was forgiven.

I cite these examples to show the reader right upfront how uneven is the playing field on which we are forced to compete. It gets more uneven by the day. Take the case of Virginia Gov. Ralph Northam. In February 2019, Northam confessed to being one of the two men in a medical school yearbook photo of a Klansman and a man in blackface. The next afternoon Northam, according to the *New York Times*, "suddenly recanted," saying he was neither of the men.

A four-month investigation resulted in a fifty-five page report that proved bizarrely inconclusive. Said the investigators, "No one we interviewed told us the governor was in the photograph, and no one could positively state who was in the photograph."[9] Northam skated. Of course, it helped that the black lieutenant governor Justin Fairfax was accused of sexual assault in the interim and the Attorney General Mark Herring acknowledged that he too had worn blackface in college. So they all skated. Do you think Republicans would have? Not on your life.

The Left has to keep the playing field uneven to maintain power. In the years before the Civil War, the fear keeping slave owners awake at night was the thought the men and women they kept enslaved might rebel and slaughter them in their beds. Today, what keeps Democratic operatives awake at night is the fear blacks will see through their crippling paternalism and leave the progressive plantation. When that happens, the "Party" is over. Literally.

To prevent minorities from quitting the Democratic Party, Leftists in and out of the media have had to create and sustain an environment of fear. To accomplish this, they constantly remind their base that Republicans are fundamentally evil. Sometimes they even own up to the strategy. In an unusually honest moment, the Leftist former chair of the U.S. Commission on Civil Rights, Mary Frances Berry, discussed in a *Politico* chat session why it was essential to brand the emerging tea party movement as racist. After admitting there was "no evidence" of the same, Berry argued such branding was nonetheless an "effective strategy for Democrats." Said Berry in the midst of the economic doldrums of 2010, "Having one's opponent rebut charges of racism is far better than discussing joblessness."[10]

In 2010, Barack Obama was president. In 2020, Donald Trump was. Once again, leftists did not want minorities discussing joblessness but now for the opposite reason. Pre-Covid, there was close to none. It was getting harder and harder for the media to deny Trump the credit for reviving an economy floundering for eight long years under President Obama. Once again, it became an effective strategy for Democrats to have Republicans, especially the president, rebut charges of racism rather than talk about joblessness or the lack thereof.

And so in Minneapolis, when one police officer *appeared* to suffocate a black man, Black Lives Matter and its allies used the opportunity to denounce the 800,000 other police officers in America as racist. A complicating factor, of course, was Democrats controlled every major city and their police forces. In its get-out-to-vote video, BLM ignored this inconvenient fact and shifted voter wrath to, yes, "the oppression of white supremacy." This, of course, was nonsense. At a congressional hearing in 2019, conservative black activist Candace Owens observed had she made a list of a hundred things troubling black America, "white supremacy and white nationalism . . . would not be on it."[11]

BLM could resurrect this phantom only because establishment Republicans have all but encouraged them to do so. This concession gave BLM a pretext to channel donations received to the Democratic Party. Ideally, the Democrats could then drive the white supremacists out of the White House, out of Washington altogether. In November 2020, they succeeded in doing this, and too many Republicans refused to protest the unholy way they pulled it off.

CHAPTER TWO

SHARING THE TRUTH

If you can bear to hear the truth you've spoken/
Twisted by knaves to make a trap for fools.

—Rudyard Kipling, *If*

I knew the Left's strategy well. I was roughed up by the imagination of one Trip Gabriel who was acting, by his own admission, under the specific direction of his editor. The *Times* was assaulting the president by proxy while setting me up for the political lynch mob to be unleashed by their story. There is some irony at work here. During the 2016 primary campaign, I did not stump for Trump. As history will note, I was Ted Cruz's national campaign co-chairman.

As the first state to register its formal support for a presidential candidate through its famed Iowa Caucus, Iowa matters. It is the most important early contest in the country because it's the first test of a candidate's strength. It requires grassroots activism, and each caucus season Iowans prove they cannot be bought with big money and high-dollar campaign ads. Don't believe me? Ask Jeb Bush.

The Iowa caucus must be earned with shoe leather and hand-shakes. For example, in the 2012 campaign Rick Santorum had a low budget but a lot of energy. Riding from event to event in the "Chuck Truck," named after its driver, Chuck Laudner, my first chief of staff, Santorum gave 385 speeches in Iowa and beat Mitt Romney and his expensive consultants and ever-present entourage. Elitists don't like to lose, especially to those whom they regard as their cultural inferiors.

Given I always took an active role in presidential politics, I had a higher profile than a Midwestern Congressman might have oth-erwise—and a bigger bull's-eye on my back. I wasn't batting a thousand with my presidential picks but I was successful enough to see Ty Cobb's lifetime average in my rearview mirror. Then the long knives started to come out.

In 2016 I traveled with Texas Senator Ted Cruz and his entou-rage on his campaign bus. In town after town we hosted rallies and

King, constituent Rosie Osterberg and Senator Ted Cruz, on the Iowa Caucus, first in the nation, campaign trail. Spirit Lake, Iowa—January 6, 2016

delivered speeches to enthusiastic audiences. Early on, establishment Republicans failed to take Trump seriously and directed much of their fire at Cruz, the most consistent conservative in the race.

One day, a corn-wrapped Winnebago motor home showed up at a Cruz rally even before we got there. This became a routine. As I learned, Governor Terry Branstad's errant son, Eric, hired young people to stand on each side of the entrance doorway handing out anti-Cruz literature and promoting ethanol, which I have championed even before the first gallon was pumped.

Television commercials blanketed the airwaves. My face was featured next to Ted's in the attack ads. We soldiered on. It was clear Governor Branstad, the very epitome of the Republican establishment, would never support the most principled conservative in the race. Although he took the pledge not to endorse a candidate, two weeks before the caucus Branstad called for Cruz's defeat. Even a former Democrat Congressman, Dave Nagle, was put off by Branstad's gesture. "We don't blackball people," Nagle said of his party, but Republicans could make no such claim. Branstad blackballed Cruz and let everybody know who the establishment feared. He put Iowa's first in the nation caucus status at great risk. Why?

Establishment Republicans may dislike Democrats, but they reserve their hate for serious conservatives. They lose their ability to reason when challenged by those who take seriously the fundamental principles of Nature's God and our Founding Fathers. An Iowa governor needs to encourage all the candidates and ensure a level playing field. If the top-tier candidates refuse to compete in Iowa, that would be the end of Iowa's first in the nation status. Terry Branstad apparently did not care. If Branstad had the political capital to defeat Cruz, from that day forward candidates would be reluctant to campaign in Iowa for fear that, after more than a year on the ground, a governor might kill off their candidacy in a thinly veiled gambit to advance himself or another candidate.

Had Branstad gotten his way, if his political capital were sound enough, Cruz would have dropped in the polls like a rock. Branstad struck the hardest blow he could against Cruz and by far the hardest ever delivered against his own state's first in the nation status. In both cases, they turned out to be feeble and glancing blows.

Cruz won Iowa. It was a happy time, and Cruz gave a long and rousing victory speech. I was on the stage the entire time. By now, I knew Cruz's applause lines and delivered some of them myself as the crowd cheered. I saw the video. I actually looked too happy for my own good. I was happy partly out of sheer joy, partly out of *schadenfreude*. I confess to taking pleasure knowing how glum our happiness made Branstad and his deep-pocketed allies watching TV at their "victory" parties.

The next day, these guys launched their campaign to recruit a primary challenger to run against me. I knew this was a favorite tactic because Bruce Rastetter, a former Iowa ethanol magnate and a top Republican donor, tried to recruit me to challenge my senior Senator, Chuck Grassley, in a primary. I also knew what he used for bait because he served it up to me.

Glenn Beck of *The Blaze*, Steve King, Phil Robertson of *Duck Dynasty*, and Ted Cruz who was only two days away from winning the Iowa Caucus. Sioux City, Iowa — January 30, 2016

The attempt was an insult to my intelligence and an example of Rastetter's poor judgment. As hatchet man, he used former Congressman Tom Latham's notorious son-in-law whose stock-in-trade was "scorched earth" campaigns against his political targets. I also knew Rastetter had a relationship with billionaire vulture capitalist Paul Singer, who later that year took down Cabela's and pocketed more than one hundred million dollars. It's worth noting, Singer is Kevin McCarthy's top donor, and his name came up multiple times in my research. I cite Rastetter's involvement because it is not an anomaly. As we saw during the 2020 election, he and self-entitled gaslighters like him haunt Republican politics nationwide, willing to shake hands with the devil while thinking they got the better part of the bargain.

I began to get calls from Rastetter's chosen potential candidates. The first to contact me was well positioned in the Trump administration and will remain anonymous. Being an honorable man, he called me to let me know what the establishment was attempting to do.

"You need to primary King," the party bosses told him, and I paraphrase here. "We have budgeted five million dollars in our super PAC, and we will use it to burn King to the ground. Within a week of your announcement, Governor Branstad will endorse you. Within two weeks, we will have one million dollars deposited in your campaign account. You can use all of it for name ID and sweetness and nice. Don't worry. We'll take care of the negative attacks."

The bosses' chosen candidate then made a recommendation as to where they could deposit their ideas and dollars. He called me right after and let me know he would be supporting me. I thanked him and typed his name into my iPhone notes where another five names would soon be listed. The establishment finally found its man; after at least six rejected attempts, the establishment elitists finally recruited a primary opponent to run against me. I didn't spend a dime on advertising in that primary or the general. In fact, I won the next three elections, two primaries and a general, while spending zero on advertising.

In 2016, as it happens, I may have had as much or more influence on the Trump campaign as I did on the Cruz campaign. Trump's first hire in Iowa was my former chief of staff Chuck Laudner. Chuck called me one day during the campaign to tell me he was assigned the job of building an immigration policy for his candidate. He wondered if he could borrow some of the immigration policies I had been promoting for the previous fourteen years. I was flattered Trump was interested and consented saying, "Copy and paste, liberally!"

Trump did indeed adopt many of my policies, including the building of a wall, the ending of birthright citizenship, the rejection of sanctuary cities, and even some of the more specific policies like basing congressional redistricting on the population of documented citizens.

A few months into the president's first term, he met with me and a handful of other congressmen in the Oval Office. In the spirit

Ernst, Branstad, King, and Reynolds ham it up with happy confidence, two days before Trump won Iowa and the presidency. Sioux City, Iowa — November 6, 2016

of fun, Trump boasted of having raised more money for my campaign than anyone else. This was not technically true but true enough. What was also true was the response I delivered in the same spirit, "I market-tested your immigration policy for fourteen years, Mr. President, and that ought to be worth something." Immigration was one of the issues on which I took point. We all had a good laugh.

Trump's help proved valuable in 2018. Sensing opportunity in what they suspected would be an off year for Republicans, Democrats poured millions into northwest Iowa to put their candidate over the top. In their minds, by beating me they would beat Trump and his immigration policies. Angry Democrats far and wide chipped in for this anticipated upset. We were outspent by something like fourteen-to-one and if social media and earned media were included in the mix, the real numbers would be something like seventy-five-to-one. By the end of August, we were up in our

One-on-one with President Trump in the Oval Office. Over the course of seventy-five minutes, the discussion covered a myriad of topics including, King's HeartBeat and immigration bills, and King's Chinese pirating of U.S. intellectual property bill. —October 2, 2018

polls by 22 percent. The Democrats opened the spigot and pounded me even more with attack adds. But again, in the first days of October, we were up 21 percent.

National media salivates over the prospect of defeating a conservative and in 2018 I was their number one target. The *New York Times, Washington Post, Huffington Post,* the *Weekly Standard*, and *Esquire* all hounded me in person and print like a pack of hungry junkyard dogs. Thirteen days before the election, we polled again and learned we were up 18 percent, an insurmountable lead especially given they used up all imagined negatives or so I thought.

Democrats ran ads and got "earned media" support for accusations that I was an anti-Semitic neo-Nazi. Where did this come from I wondered? My record with Israel is 100 percent. What kind of neo-Nazi supports Israel? As it turns out, I did an interview with a newspaper in Vienna in which I criticized George Soros. Part of the strategy of reputational rehab for the sinking image of Soros was to attack anyone who criticized him as an anti-Semite.

I was also attacked in the *Washington Post,* in the *Huffington Post* and in Bill Kristol's now deservedly defunct *Weekly Standard* among others for attending a meeting with Austria's Freedom Party, supposedly an ultra-right wing party with "Nazi roots." It's worth noting every party formed in Austria or Germany post–World War II has "Nazi roots." In short, if a man was to survive the war, he survived either as a Nazi or a very quiet resister. Therefore, all the parties forming in the political vacuum after the fall of the Reich had Nazi roots somewhere in its past, an inconvenient fact willfully ignored by partisan Leftists and NeverTrumpers.

But there was no such meeting. I accepted an invitation to a dinner during that trip to Austria requested by a friend who wanted me to meet some people. There were five new faces around the table. In that pause awaiting the first to speak, the gentleman on my right opened with this statement, "Congressman, I think you should know that you are seated here with two homosexuals and a Jew." Immediately, the man across the table shot out, "Who's the Jew?" Everybody laughed. For those who missed the joke, he was telling us he knew who the other homosexual was. I never did learn which of my dinner companions it was and didn't care. That was the last reference to either Judaism or homosexuality for the duration of the dinner meeting. Suffice it to say anti-Semites and neo-Nazis do not plot against homosexuals and Jews with half the table occupied by one or the other.

Current events multiplied the effects of the false allegations of anti-Semitism and neo-Nazism. On October 22, a pipe bomb was conveniently placed in Soros's mailbox. Although no one claimed responsibility, the *New York Times* promptly reminded its readers that Soros was a "focus of right-wing vitriol" and "the target of anti-Semitic smears."[12]

On October 25th, the *Washington Post* hit piece on the Austrian Freedom Party came out. Two days later, the ghastly slaughter at the Tree of Life Synagogue in Pittsburgh saw eleven members killed in an actual anti-Semitic attack. We now had a boiling cauldron of fear and loathing fueled in part by a relentless media as the Left sought to blame the violence on the Right. With Trump not on the ballot, I made for a ripe proxy target.

Into this intense situation stepped the chairman of the National Republican Congressional Committee, Steve Stivers. As committee chairman, Stivers's sole responsibility is to reelect incumbent Republicans and unseat Democrats. On October 30, 2018, one week out from the election, Stivers sent this tweet: "Congressman Steve King's recent comments, actions, and retweets are completely inappropriate. We must stand up against white supremacy and hate in all forms, and I strongly condemn this behavior."[13] In this case, incredibly, "white supremacy" turned out to be my criticism of George Soros. Fragged* by my own party leadership.

The Stivers tweet raised one and a half million dollars for Democrat J. D. Scholten in the last week and unleashed an even bigger and louder media onslaught. When a high-ranking Republican attacks a standard bearer of conservatism, that attack serves to validate all the Left and the media have been saying. To frag a fellow Republican in this way is an act of party treason. I disagree with

---

*Fragging and frag is military slang for using a fragmentation grenade to attack a fellow unit member or superior.

those who think Stivers is good for nothing. It is a fact he is good at something—aiding, abetting, and raising money for Democrats.

Less than four hours after his boss's initial tweet, Stivers's communications director, Matt Gorman, piled on. He said in an interview, "We believe Congressman King's words and actions are completely inappropriate, and we strongly condemn them. We will not play in this race."[14] Gorman was acting at the direction of his boss, Stivers.

The NRCC was never going to "play in this race." It was a very long time since I had any help from the Republican Party. I released this statement: "Americans, all created equal by God, with all our races, ethnicities, and national origins-legal immigrants & natural born citizens, together make up the Shining City on the Hill. These attacks are orchestrated by nasty, desperate, and dishonest fake media. Their ultimate goal is to flip the House and impeach Donald Trump. Establishment NeverTrumpers are complicit."

I think my words hold up pretty well. The Democrats did flip the House and impeach Donald Trump, twice as it turned out. Stivers and the House leadership were complicit, at a minimum, in setting the stage and encouraging future assaults on traditional American values.

To this day, I don't specifically know which of the pack of lies they were reacting to. I don't know if Stivers ever knew either. I only know the press reported he responded after he "had been briefed." At the time he was busy pumping tens of millions of dollars into the unwinnable races of squishy RINOs who were a drag on the conservative agenda. Had that money been spent on the close races we lost, Republicans may well have retained the majority. As it was, Stivers, with his upside-down priorities, was at the helm when our majority was lost. This colossal blunder facilitated the return of Speaker Pelosi, the continuation of the Russia-Russia-Russia investigation, and the impeachment fiascos. I'm glad I don't have all that on my conscience.

I was at a rally in Sioux Center, Iowa, the night before the 2018 election. The rally included Iowa governor Kim Reynolds and Iowa

Senator Joni Ernst, all happy and collegial. My cell phone rang and I stepped away to take a call from Kevin McCarthy. Strange he would be calling me the night before the election. There were 434 other congressional races and he couldn't be calling them all. He was fishing. Kevin inquired about my race. I told him it was tightening up and the reason was Stivers's attack on me. McCarthy said he was surprised to learn what the chairman of the NRCC did to me. I soon had it directly from Speaker Ryan and Whip Steve Scalise that they were also unaware of what Stivers did, and each insisted they had no conversations with him on the subject. Okay, sure, and I have a mountaintop villa to sell you in the Iowa Alps.

Despite their relentless and baseless attacks, I won anyway but only by a 3.4 percent margin. Still, I was beginning to feel like the "just one" in the Book of Wisdom. "With revilement and torture," say his enemies, "let us put the just one to the test that we may have proof of his gentleness and try his patience." My patience was indeed being tried.

When an election is over the attacks stop, even from Democrats who need a rest too. I didn't expect the next attack to come within a week of victory and I didn't expect it to come from the leader of my own Iowa party, Governor Kim Reynolds. At a press conference in Ottumwa, in response to a question, Reynolds said, "Congressman King needs to decide what he wants to do. Whether he wants to represent the values of the 4th District or do something else."

The following day, the *Sioux City Journal* posted on its front page a picture of a Reynolds note card. On it, in her handwriting, was "Steve King" underlined and beneath it the words "Needs to decide if he's going to represent the people and Values of the 4th District or Do Something Different."[15] The response was obviously planned. I strongly suspect the question was planted as well. She delivered her response virtually verbatim. Her statement declared open season to all establishment Republicans. She said, in effect, "Steve King is now fair game." I was being fragged by my own party leadership.

Steve King
- Needs to Decide if he's going
to Represent the People and
Values of the 4th District
or Do Something Different

Lt. Governor Adam Gregg watches the audience as Governor Reynolds, with aides, prepares herself to make the remarks that, in effect, declared "open season" on Congressman King for elitist Republicans. Her note card reads: "STEVE KING Needs to decide if he's going to represent the People and Values of the 4th District or Do Something Different." Ottumwa Job Corps Center, Ottumwa, Iowa—November 13, 2018 (Kelsey Kremer, Des Moines Register)

The next week, Dave Kochel, the president of Red Wave communications and a long-time ally of Branstad's, said in an interview on "Iowa Press" that I would not be on the ballot in 2020. As you can imagine, that caught my attention. I knew instantly, the only reason Kochel would make such a statement was to take credit for the plot when and if it came to pass. Kochel not only wired himself in with Ernst but through Branstad, with Reynolds too. In fact, Sarah Craig Gongol, Kochel's former CEO, is, as I write, the chief of staff for Governor Reynolds. There are no coincidences in politics, at least not in Iowa. The 2018 campaign was rough.

The day before Thanksgiving 2018, I got a heads-up about a plot against me by a high-level political operative. Jeff Roe, founder of Axiom Strategies and manager of Ted Cruz's presidential campaign, advised me about an impending viral media and internet campaign to force my "resignation" from office. At first, I didn't take the warning seriously because it sounded too conspiratorial. I wondered, "On what possible grounds could I be forced to resign right after an election and even before I took the oath of office for the next Congress?" What angle of attack could my political enemies possibly use? Having no skeletons in my closet, I was able to be candid and outspoken throughout my career. Virtue offered immunity, or so I thought.

The enemies of full spectrum constitutional Christian conservatism must have figured everyone was as corrupt as they were. I imagined them rummaging through my metaphorical closet looking for that elusive skeleton. They must have presumed I had something to hide they could expose and exploit through their allies in the media. *Bring it!* I thought. *Just bring it!*

Roe brought the subject up a second time, I discounted it, and then a third time. Now he had my attention, and this is what I learned in paraphrase: "They have chosen a messenger who has the ear of the president. They will convince the messenger to go to the president and get him to send out a negative tweet against you. That will be the trigger that launches an all-out media blitz designed to force you to resign. The messenger will likely be someone like Senator Joni Ernst. She has the president's ear and can convince Trump to act."

I was skeptical. I met Joni in Iraq when she commanded the 1168 Transportation Company. Back in Iowa, I helped her run for county office, then state senate. Roe advised me to preempt this initiative at the White House and with the messenger. I did both.

It took until January 8, 2019, to get a meeting with Joni. I left her office at 4:40 p.m. that day feeling pretty good. I have a twenty-four-minute tape of my thoughts recorded immediately after the private meeting which makes clear my belief Joni remained loyal and would not encourage President Trump to unload on me. I didn't know then Joni and her chief of staff were likely in real-time communications with Dave Kochel. Kochel, you will recall, was the fellow who predicted I would not be on the ballot in 2020. As I later learned from the FEC records, Kochel received tens of thousands of dollars in consulting fees from Ernst.

I did expect if Joni were the designated messenger to President Trump, she would warn others that I knew about the plot and was prepared to blow it up in the media. If she were not the messenger, I hoped and believed she would have my back. The conspirators were bolder and more decisive than I expected. The Ernst meeting was January 8. The next day, January 9, at 11:23 a.m., Iowa State Senator Randy Feenstra announced on Twitter—*Twitter?*—he would challenge me in the primary. Feenstra had no rollout plan. He had no website. He had no media plan. He was scheduled to take his oath of office for the next General Assembly in the Iowa Senate the following Monday.

From any traditional perspective, Feenstra's timing made no sense. Who called him, I wondered, to tell him he needed to announce his unprepared candidacy immediately? Kochel? McCarthy? Rastetter? In any case, someone advised him to scrub his Twitter account of all prior posts dating back to 2009. Why? I speculate here, but I don't think posts attacking Donald Trump would play well in Iowa's 4th.

Kochel was the "horse whisperer" of this orchestrated plot to take down a guy who had been walking point on most key hot-button conservative issues. Kochel was positioned to whisper in the ear of all the primary players in the drama to come.

Kochel and Liz Cheney, the vice president's daughter and the third ranking Republican in the House, worked together as senior policy advisors to Romney. Kochel was senior policy advisor to Jeb Bush, Governor Branstad, Governor Reynolds, and Joni Ernst.

A long-time advocate for same-sex marriage, Kochel signed on to an amicus brief with Liz Cheney's sister Mary, a prominent lesbian activist, in 2007, when even Obama was still championing traditional marriage.

In addition to gay marriage, Kochel was passionate about granting voting rights to felons and encouraging high schoolers to take a knee in solidarity with Black Lives Matter long before BLM was fashionable. He emerged as a prominent "Trump skeptic" who turned on the insidious Lincoln Project only after it targeted Republican senators like Ernst. What else might he have been whispering into the ear of those listed above and others?

Now, during the 2018 campaign it was particularly difficult having to see ad after ad claiming I was ineffective and had little or no influence in Congress. I knew better, of course, and was looking for an opening to set the record straight. So when Trip Gabriel texted me asking for an interview I was more interested than I should have been. The way I figured, I needed to have a voice in the media to keep my leverage in Congress.

In our initial communication, Gabriel explained he was given an assignment by his editor to write a story about the immigration policy in the United States, specifically how it was President Trump who adopted almost verbatim the immigration policy I advocated over the previous sixteen years. I thought this might be a useful opportunity to show there are more ways to measure influence than having one's name on a bill. I also thought this was an opportunity to get credit for something I did deserve. I believed the *New York Times'* target was Trump, not me. As it turned out, I was the intended prey, and I walked right into the trap.

I responded to him it was best to go through my communications director, John Kennedy, but it appeared I would be open after 8:30 a.m. the following day. I then sent John a text to advise him to expect a call from Gabriel requesting an interview.

The following morning Kennedy's response came at 7:48 a.m. while I was in the shower. It read, "I think it's a trap. I also killed a December story about you he wanted to write. He's out to get you." I did not see the email in time. Gabriel called right at

8:30 a.m. Thinking the interview was cleared rather than nixed by Kennedy, I took the interview.

I just had the one phone at my disposal and did not have a chance or the means to tape the interview. An oversight, but I was not concerned; I spoke to the media many times. I assumed Gabriel would insinuate the president was racist. Imputing racism to the president was standard procedure at the *Times*, and Trump would shrug off or rebut the slander at his discretion. For my part, I hoped to get enough real information on the record to compensate for the slams and to influence the few fair-minded people who still read the *Times*. To prevent new attacks against me, I determined I would not say anything to Gabriel I hadn't already said in the press elsewhere. It turned out that wasn't protection enough.

The conversation lasted fifty-six minutes. I have no reason to believe Gabriel taped the conversation as we went over the issues more than once. On occasion, he asked me to repeat a sentence so he could capture it verbatim. At the end of the discussion, I felt good about it. Our conversation was friendly and long enough for me to make my case. I anticipated an article giving me substantial credit for Donald Trump's immigration policy without taking away anything from Trump. He acknowledged and drove these issues home as only a president can do. That I acknowledged. Of course, I hoped the article would answer in an honest way those Democrats who insisted I was irrelevant. If I hoped to remain effective in Congress, I could not let that charge stand.

Gabriel's article was published on January 10. The headline was reasonably straightforward and pretty much what I hoped it would be: "Before Trump, Steve King Set the Agenda for the Wall and Anti-Immigrant Politics."[16] Of course, the *Times* used "immigrant" where any fair-minded journalist would have used "illegal immigrant" or the legal and correct term, "illegal alien," but the media committed itself wholesale to this deception long ago.

Gabriel's language was predictably loaded as well. "Trump demonized immigrants," he wrote, conflating "demonized" with "described." The president made "demeaning" remarks, inspired "fear" and used "misleading" statistics. My behavior was even worse. I used "racist language" in the past, "promoted neo-Nazis" on Twitter, and was denounced by one "Republican leader" as a "white supremacist."

Before going further, let me show you what these terms mean in *Times* world. The link about racist language leads to a *Salon* article detailing comments I made using the common metaphor "pick of the litter." I used the phrase to describe how the image of America attracts the sibling with the greatest ambition, giving our country a unique and vibrant vitality, regardless of race. Legal and ambitious immigrants select themselves as the pick of their litter. I have for years said, "We need an immigration policy designed to enhance the economic, social, and cultural well-being of the United States."

The Leftist *Salon* editors had no intention of being fair. They headlined the article, "Rep. Steve King: Immigrants are like dogs."[17] As to the neo-Nazi reference, I retweeted a *Breitbart News* article objectively headlined, "Vast majority of under-35 Italians now oppose mass migration." It turns, out, however, the British fellow who tweeted the *Breitbart* article had something of a check-ered history. I had no idea who the guy was. In his posting he made no comment on the article. "It's the message, not the messenger," I told Gabriel. Whatever the guy's background, he at least never served as the Exalted Cyclops of anything, and his facts were straight.

As to the "Republican leader" who called me a white suprem-acist, Gabriel did not tell the reader who it was who made such an accusation. Gabriel did cite a "former state senator" who lumped Trump and me in the "same subset of white nationalists." That is mighty fine sand on which to build a slanderous accusation like "white supremacist." But for the *New York Times*, as I was about to be reminded, slander is the name of the game.

CHAPTER THREE

KEEPING YOUR HEAD

If you can keep your head when all about you are losing theirs and blaming it on you / if you can trust yourself when others doubt you yet make allowance for their doubting too.

—Rudyard Kipling

Gabriel sabotaged my career with one sentence. He set it up with a fairly accurate summary of my stance on immigration, writing how I supported "immigrants who enter the country legally and fully assimilate because what matters more than race is 'the culture of America' based on values brought to the United States by whites from Europe." If you will note, Gabriel quoted me on the phrase, "the culture of America," but did not quote me on the phrase, "whites from Europe." The latter was Gabriel's paraphrasing of what he wanted me to say and wanted you to believe was what I said. The fact is Europe was the fount from which Western Civilization flowed into the United States. That fact does not require a reference to skin color.

It was the next sentence that caused me a world of headaches. "'White nationalist, white supremacist, Western Civilization—how did that language become offensive?' Mr. King said." The following quote should have clarified the preceding sentence, "Why did I sit in classes teaching me about the merits of our history and our civilization?" When I said "that language" I was specifically referring to "Western Civilization." Had I meant to lump all three phrases together I would have used a plural pronoun and said "those words" not "that language." The pronoun "that" is definitively singular as is my reference to the culture of Western Civilization. Besides, no one sat in a class being taught about the merits of the odious ideologies, White Nationalism or White Supremacism. Gabriel knew that and he heard what I said and knew what I meant.

On January 18, Mark Steyn, filling in for Rush Limbaugh on his radio show, did a good job explaining the game the *Times* was playing. The mistake I made, said Steyn, and I agree, was giving an interview to the *Times* in the first place. "They're only asking you . . . to stitch you up. To talk to you for three hours and get you to use one phrase in there that they can lift out and kill you with."

The *Times* routinely stitches Republicans up. As I was taking a last pass at this text, the *Times* ran a hit piece on Sen. Mike Lee. Appearing on a Fox Newsroom show during Trump's second impeachment, Lee tried to strike a conciliatory note. After being shown clips of three Democratic members of Congress making inflammatory statements, Lee said, "Look, everyone makes mistakes. Everyone is entitled to a mulligan once in a while. And I would hope, I would expect that each of those individuals would take a mulligan on each of those statements because in each instance they're making it deeply personal." Here is how the *Times* headlined its article on Lee, "Mike Lee Suggests Trump Should Get a 'Mulligan' for Jan. 6 Speech."[18] Lee was not referring to Trump when he talked about a mulligan.

Conservatives in the media defended Lee in part because they could see the interview and judge for themselves. There was no recording of my interview with Gabriel. I could not unequivocally state I did not say those words in the interview. Later, Gabriel admitted he fed those words to me in his question. But I knew—and he knew—if I stated those words at all, I paused after "white supremacy" and started a new thought with "Western Civilization." He knew too a Republican who defended white supremacy could be elected to no office higher in this land than Exalted Cyclops in the late Democratic Senator Robert Byrd's old Klan klavern—that is, if the klavern accepted Republicans. Republican leadership knew the power of that accusation too and they knew it in advance, Kevin McCarthy in particular.

The media did what they always do when they catch a Republican saying something that sounds "controversial." They rushed to other Republicans looking for critical sound bites. By late afternoon on January 10, the same Thursday the *Times* article was published, the Associated Press had rounded up a few. Liz Cheney told *The Hill* my remarks were "abhorrent and racist and should have no place in our national discourse."[19] You would think Ms. Cheney would know better. The media routinely branded her father as a racist and later in 2019 the *Daily Kos* headlined an article about her, "Liz Cheney tries to prove she can be just as racist and petty as Trump."[20] Her sin was referring to Elizabeth Warren as "Pocahontas." When Cheney voted to impeach Trump in the second go-round, she showed what side she was playing on.

Now, you will never catch Kevin McCarthy tweaking Elizabeth Warren with "Pocahontas." Had McCarthy said what Cheney did, there would have been a round of calls for DNA tests of his family and in-laws. His family members are currently the beneficiaries of at least $7.6 million in mostly no-bid government contracts based upon their claimed membership in the Northern Cherokee Nation, a tribe not recognized by state or federal governments. One has to have a lot of *chutzpah* to cash in as an undocumented Native American.

The no-compete contracts put McCarthy's family in the same category as Elizabeth Warren. The family also claimed to be victims of discrimination at the hands of a banker, justifying their

Vice President Dick Cheney, freshman Congresswoman Liz Cheney, and chairman of the Conservative Opportunity Society and host, Congressman King. Washington, D.C.—February 14, 2017

registration as a minority contractor. They registered as a disadvantaged business enterprise in 1998, the same year they supposedly learned of the lucrative family tree opportunity from a now deceased cousin.[21] I'm sure Senator Warren would recommend DNA tests from all the McCarthy's and in-laws. I'm confident I will be selling my real estate in the Iowa Alps first.

The Associated Press also cited a tweet from Rep. Justin Amash. Few on the national scene had heard of Amash until, relying on reports about Russia collusion in the major media, he called for Trump's impeachment as early as April 2017. Again relying on reports in the major media, Amash tweeted about my remarks, "This is an embrace of racism, and it has no place in Congress or anywhere."[22] For Amash, I served as a Trump proxy. I was fair game. On January 11, smelling blood in the water, Gabriel came back with another article boldly headlined, "Steve King's White Supremacy Remark Is Rebuked by Iowa's Republican Senators."[23]

At a minimum, Joni Ernst knew of the plot against me from our meeting just two days before. That did not stop her from unloading on me with this tweet: "I condemn Rep. Steve King's comments on white supremacy; they are offensive and racist—and not representative of our state of Iowa . . ."

Senator Chuck Grassley had been around long enough to understand he was being played by the *Times*. He endorsed me in 2018 and took some heat for doing so. Gabriel pointed this out as a way of scolding Grassley. Curiously, Gabriel made no reference to what Grassley said. If Chuck called out the *Times* for its chicanery, the *Times* did not report it.

I had seen these media cycles before. What I learned is they can't last forever. They inevitably die off. That said, a political lynch mob was formed and its blood was up. I had to let it cool before making any major decisions. The Democrats in Congress were making noise about censuring me, but I knew they could not remove me from office. As Rudyard Kipling suggested in *If*, it is not just about keeping your head when others are losing theirs, it is also about understanding why others might doubt you. The *New York Times* is the paper of record. Some sensible people still take its reporting as gospel. And yes, I know the "woke" crowd now routinely denounces Kipling, the *Jungle Book* author, as a colonialist but in my book, he like Gunga Din, is a "better man than I am," and a better man than most in the media will ever be.

The next day, January 11, I made a statement on the floor of the House echoing my published rejection the day before. The Associated Press quoted it: "I reject those labels and the evil ideology that they define. Further, I condemn anyone that supports this evil and bigoted ideology which saw in its ultimate expression the systematic murder of 6 million innocent Jewish lives. Under any fair political definition, I am simply a Nationalist."[24] You would think a flat-out rejection of these ideologies as "evil" would carry more weight than a twisted misquote but not in Washington, not if you're a Republican, not when the guns were already loaded and aimed at me *before* the triggering event by the *New York Times*.

I flew back to Iowa that Friday hoping this controversy would bleed out but fearing it wouldn't. My fears were justified. The media piled on, tying me to the notorious David Duke, the former Klan leader whom I am convinced is being subsidized by the Left to create mischief for the right. In fact, when Steve Scalise, the second-ranking Republican in the House publicly rebuked me, several major media outlets, here and abroad, reminded America, "in 2002 [Scalise] addressed a conference backed by former Ku Klux Klan leader David Duke."[25]

In 2002, Scalise was a state representative in Louisiana. In 2014, when Scalise was on the verge of assuming a House leadership role, the *Washington Post* did a deep dive into his past and came up with the gem, twelve years earlier, he spoke at "a gathering hosted by white-supremacist leaders." I believe I'm the only one who stood up for Scalise when the story surfaced in 2014.

This is what I said unsolicited in his defense, according to the *Washington Post*: "Jesus dined with tax collectors and sinners. It's not the healthy who need a doctor, it's the sick. Given that piece of Scripture, and understanding Scalise probably wasn't staffed thoroughly, I could understand how something like this happened. But I know his heart. I've painted houses with him post-Katrina and I know he is a good man."[26] Scalise had my cell phone number. He had an example to follow and a favor to return. He did neither.

In 2019, I became a center of international attention in a way as never before and hope never to be again. The press hounded me. Wherever I went, there were fuzzy microphones hanging all around my head. Reporter gaggles were camped outside my office. I remember one reporter shouting out, "How will it feel to be just the twenty-fourth person to be censured in the United States House of Representatives?" Said I, "That's not going to happen," but who could be sure given the media feeding frenzy.

For a misquote, I was getting the kind of treatment Rep. Gary Condit got as a suspect in the murder of his intern and alleged mistress, Chandra Levy. How surreal is that? Although Condit left office the same day in 2003 when I first took office, I was in Washington early enough to see my first pack of press hounds clustered outside Condit's office. Condit, a California Democrat the media took pains to declare a "conservative" Democrat, saw his life fractured when Levy went missing, come apart when her body was discovered, and destroyed as he emerged as the chief media suspect of her death. He was innocent, at least of Levy's murder, but no one wanted to believe that. It took months and competing events to push Condit off the front pages and dispatch the media scrum I saw clustered outside his door in the Cannon Building.

Most readers of this book will remember Chandra Levy, but few, I suspect, know who was convicted of killing the unfortunate young intern. For the record, in 2010 a Washington D.C. jury convicted Ingmar Guandique of Levy's murder. The conviction got almost no media attention, not because people forgot about Condit and Levy but because in the age of Obama the media routinely suppressed stories of crime committed by illegal aliens, even members of the murderous MS-13 gang like Guandique, who years later was released by a judicial decision. When the truth got in the way of the Democratic agenda, the media no longer had much use for it.

On Sunday, January 13, three days after the *Times* article was published, Republican wheels started to turn. At 6:30 a.m. my chief of staff, Sarah Stevens, was contacted by the chief of staff of Kevin McCarthy. The purpose of the call was to set up a meeting with McCarthy for Monday, January 14. If you are wondering if congressional staffers routinely set their schedules before the sun rises on the Sabbath, the answer is no, they don't. McCarthy, I suspected, was going on the Sunday morning talk shows, and he wanted to be able to say he had a "come-to-Jesus" meeting set for Monday with King, and some form of discipline will be coming down.

On CBS's *Face the Nation* that Sunday morning, Margaret Brennan grilled McCarthy about my future. To be fair, it was not the top item on Brennan's agenda but it did seem to be her favorite one. The media like nothing better than seeing Republicans throw one of their own under the bus. Brennan led by paraphrasing Jeb Bush to the effect, "it's not enough to condemn" me, "party leaders actually have to do something." Bush suggested either censuring me or supporting a primary challenge against me.

Jeb Bush? Why Jeb Bush? He had not been in the news for nearly three years since his humiliating defeat at the hands of Donald Trump in the 2016 primaries, starting with Iowa. Like other elected officials in Iowa, the state with the first in the nation caucus, I have more influence in party politics than I would if I represented any other state, especially when there is a contested Republican primary. In 2016, I backed Ted Cruz. By supporting one candidate I risked alienating the others, but I considered it a risk worth taking.

Cruz won the Iowa caucus with 27 percent of the vote. Trump came in second with 24 percent. In the process, some very high-powered and delicate egos were badly bruised. Bush, the establishment favorite, came in sixth with an embarrassing 3 percent of the vote despite spending a huge chunk of his campaign's $139 million in Iowa.

Jeb's is the voice of the establishment. Low energy or not, he gave his all in Iowa with Dave Kochel, his senior policy advisor, at his side and the political elite cheering him on. But money and title can't buy a ticket into the top tier in the Iowa caucus, at least not as long as we conservatives are in the front lines defending our platform.

McCarthy was not about to be one-upped by Jeb Bush. "First, and foremost, I came out at the very moment—that language has no place in America. That is not the America I know, and it's most definitely not the party of Lincoln," he told Brennan. When she asked if I should be punished, McCarthy was quick to respond, "I have a scheduled meeting with him on Monday."[27] Yes, he nailed that down. "I've watched on the other side that they do not take action when their members say something like this," McCarthy added and he was right, at least half right.

Democrats are not misquoted saying offensive things. They are quoted accurately as saying offensive things and almost always with impunity. Leadership's fear of the racist label is one reason they were so quick to condemn. Without evidence, and without giving me an opportunity to defend myself, they pounced immediately. They refused to accept the reality that Leftists will repeat their tactics until no one has the guts or will to stand up to them.

A month after my dust-up with the *New York Times,* in explaining congressional support of Israel, Congresswoman Ilhan Omar of Minnesota tweeted, "It's all about the Benjamins." She was trading on the old stereotype of Jews buying their way to power. A month later, Omar accused American Jews who supported Israel of "having allegiance to a foreign country." In response to Omar's comments, described by many as flagrantly anti-Semitic, the Democrat-controlled House twice passed resolutions denouncing anti-Semitism and other forms of bigotry but did not mention Omar by name in either of them. Nor did Democratic leaders strip Omar of committee assignments. "The controversy has split the Democratic Party and clouded their agenda," said NPR's Cody Nelson,[28] but not for long and not with any lasting damage to Omar. She and her fellow "Squad" members remained rock stars in the world of the Left.

Republicans play by different rules. "I'm having a serious conversation with Congressman Steve King on his future and role in this Republican Party," McCarthy told Brennan. "I will not stand back as a leader of this party, believing in this nation that all are created equal, that that stands or continues to stand and have any role with us."[29] I wasn't exactly sure what McCarthy meant, but whatever it was, I was pretty sure it was not going to be good news for me. I didn't know it at the time but McCarthy was quoted off mic saying he might kick me off all my committees. This statement showed his hand and further exposed their plan.

On Monday afternoon, I made my way to the designated meeting spot in the basement of the Capitol, somehow avoiding the press along the way. McCarthy's staff met me at the elevator and escorted me, not to McCarthy's office but to an ornate meeting room on the third floor. The meeting was awkward. It began with a kind of stilted silence. I broke the ice.

"Well, you know we're in a heck of a shape right now," I said.

McCarthy insisted I brought my troubles on myself—he was half right—and something had to be done. I told him in turn, "This quote does not reflect any thoughts that I've ever formed in my head." I explained there had to have been a gap between what I called the "two odious ideologies" of white nationalism and white supremacism on the one hand and Western Civilization on the other. I was not about to back down in my defense of Western Civilization.

I laid down a copy of the quote on a table and zeroed in on the offending ideologies, drawing a double-ended red ink arrow on the page and explaining there should have been a hyphen or period after "White supremacist" and before "Western Civilization." McCarthy was not buying. In that room, it became very clear to me McCarthy took on the role of prosecutor rather than a fact finder. Even though there had never been a credible challenge to my veracity in twenty-two previous years of public life, McCarthy determined, before he went on the air the previous day, the *New York Times* quote and punctuation was the only "factual evidence" necessary. It was the trigger substituted for an unattainable Trump tweet. I was the target from the beginning.

McCarthy insisted Trip Gabriel was a reliable and reputable reporter. "He's been at this a long time," McCarthy explained. "He is highly respected and wouldn't make a mistake like this."

I was not at all sure it was a mistake. Later that year, as I mentioned earlier, the *Times* editor would say out loud what those paying attention did not have to be told: The *Times* was going after Trump and the people around him "who peddle hatred." To score points in the newsroom, reporters were prepared to define "hatred" down. As commentator Mark Steyn has said, only half in jest, "Even when you have no idea you're committing a hate crime, chances are you still are." If the "hater" could be linked to Donald Trump, as I obviously could, that made for a juicier story still.

In July 2020, *Times* op-ed writer and editor Bari Weiss penned a public resignation letter that shook the media world and erased all doubt about the oppressive state of affairs at the paper. Wrote Weiss, "A new consensus has emerged in the press, but perhaps especially at this paper: that truth isn't a process of collective discovery, but an orthodoxy already known to an enlightened few whose job is to inform everyone else."[30]

One of my quotes in a New York Times story has been completely mischaracterized. Here's the context I believe accurately reflects my statement.

In a 56 minute interview, we discussed the changing use of language in political discourse. We discussed the worn out label "racist" and my observation that other slanderous labels have been increasingly assigned to Conservatives by the Left, who injected into our current political dialog such terms as Nazi, Fascist, " White Nationalist, White Supremacist, Western Civilization, how did **THAT** language become offensive? Why did I sit in classes teaching me about the merits of our history and our civilization?"..just to watch Western Civilization become a derogatory term in political discourse today. Clearly, I was only referencing Western Civilization classes. No one ever sat in a class listening to the merits of white nationalism and white supremacy.

When I used the word "THAT" it was in reference ONLY to Western Civilization and NOT to any previously stated evil ideology ALL of which I have denounced. My record as a vocal advocate for Western Civilization is nearly as full as my record in defense of Freedom of Speech.

The original document King used to show the *NYT's* misquote to Kevin McCarthy during the intense one-on-one meeting in the Capitol at 4:00 p.m., Monday, January 14, 2019. King drew the double-ended ink arrow so McCarthy could see he was defending only Western Civilization. McCarthy insisted the *New York Times* was honest and would not make such a mistake.

Jewish and a self-described "centrist," Weiss was called a "Nazi" and a "racist" for challenging that orthodoxy, however gently. "Some coworkers insist I need to be rooted out if this company is to be a truly 'inclusive' one," she wrote, "while others post ax emojis next to my name. Still other *New York Times* employees publicly smear me as a liar and a bigot on Twitter with no fear that harassing me will be met with appropriate action." Welcome to the club, Bari. This one is very "inclusive." Today, even centrist Jews get to be white supremacists.

What was obvious to everyday conservatives about the *Times* was apparently not obvious to McCarthy. He chose to take Gabriel at his word. I asked McCarthy if he talked to Gabriel. He had. I asked if there was a tape of my conversation with Gabriel. There wasn't. I asked if there was a transcript. There wasn't. Sarah and I talked to Gabriel twice earlier that day. We knew the answers before I asked them. I just wanted to confirm McCarthy knew what I knew. McCarthy countered that Gabriel kept precise notes. I told him no one could type—and punctuate—with precision as fast as I talk, given I talk faster than a political guy from rural Iowa really ought to talk. Still, McCarthy continued to defend Gabriel.

I later talked to a stenographer on the House floor and these people are the best in the business. On a keyboard, this particular stenographer can type 130 words a minute. On a steno keyboard, she can type 280 words a minute. "When you're on a roll," she told me, "I can't keep up with you even at 280 words a minute." Gabriel is no stenographer. Without supporting audio, it was reckless of him and his editors to insert a quote they knew could damage my career, if not kill it outright. But in 2019, smoking out "haters" was the stated mission of the *Times* newsroom, whether they were real haters or not. McCarthy was far more trusting of the *Times* people than he should have been. Too many Republicans are. When things don't add up in politics or business, there is always a reason, and over the next months I learned why.

When Sarah and I talked to Gabriel we asked him which particular question prompted the potential career-killing answer I gave. I was just hoping to establish the context for what I was alleged to have said. Gabriel wouldn't or, more likely, couldn't tell us. In fact, during the initial interview, when I asked him to repeat a question, he was unable to, at least with any precision. I got the sense he was improvising as he went, basing his questions on my answers.

I conveyed all this to McCarthy, but he continued to press. He asked me if I said the words attributed to me. For him, the question I answered, the context and the punctuation were utterly irrelevant. For McCarthy, the words alone were enough to hang me. Refusing to lie my way out of the jam, I told him I could not say with perfect confidence whether those actual words came out of my mouth or not. I did say if those words came out in that sequence I was likely repeating the question Gabriel asked me but I assured McCarthy the only thing I was defending was Western Civilization.

This answer did not satisfy him. To McCarthy, the *New York Times* was the Bible, and I was a troublesome congressman from fly-over country, a guy who could not remember word-for-word, dash-for-dash, what I told a reporter more than a week earlier in a fifty-six-minute interview. McCarthy claimed he could remember everything he said in every interview for the previous six months. I didn't say it but I was thinking, "Who is this guy? Rain Man?"

If I explain my predicament in detail, it had no effect. Today, we are all vulnerable to the kind of thought control the Left imposes. Yes, as a Republican and as a Congressman I was more vulnerable but no one is immune. During the Obama presidency, everything was racialized, and even innocent, apolitical people could be struck down for a simply misunderstood word.

In his bold new book, *The Age of Entitlement*, Christopher Caldwell describes the new reign of censorship being imposed top down not just on America but on the Western world, with political correctness being our most successful export:

> *Americans in all walks of life began to talk about the smallest things as if they would have their lives destroyed for holding the wrong opinion. And this was a reasonable assumption. Over the decades, one hapless white after another would see his career brought to a sudden stop when a tantrum, a drunken slip, or some imperfectly calibrated phrase revealed wrong attitudes about race, gender, or sexuality. Cant was the only way a sensibly self-protective person would talk about race in public—and when it came to civil rights, every place was public.*[31]

I could cite any number of examples, but one comes quickly to mind as it parallels my own case. Although ESPN tennis commentator Doug Adler, a southern Californian with close family ties to the film community, has no obvious political sympathies, he got caught up in the mania surrounding Trump's election. In fact, ESPN fired Adler on Inauguration Day 2017. Adler was calling a match in the Australian Open between Stefanie Voegele, who is white and Venus Williams, who is black. "She [Voegele] misses a first serve and Venus is all over her," said Adler. "You see Venus move in and put the guerilla effect on. Charging."

The Trip Gabriel of this story was Ben Rothenberg, a tennis writer for—you guessed it—the *New York Times*. Upon watching a clip of Adler's commentary, the trip-wire sensitive Rothenberg heard "gorilla" not the "guerilla" Adler obviously intended. Instead of contacting Adler and determining what he actually said, Rothenberg decided to ruin Adler's career. If he couldn't ruin Trump, he could at least ruin someone like Trump who "peddled hatred." Trump Derangement Syndrome (TDS) has that effect on people. "This is some appalling stuff. Horrifying that the Williams sisters remain subjected to it still in 2017,"[32] tweeted Rothenberg with the full force of *Times* blue Twitter check mark assuring his credibility.

As Rothenberg had to know, Nike once prominently ran an ad featuring Andre Agassi and Pete Sampras called "Guerilla Tennis." Ironically, the *Times* was running an ad campaign at the time, claiming, "The truth is hard to find. The truth is hard to know. The truth is more important now than ever." Rothenberg, like Gabriel, did not bother to go look for it. Like Gabriel, he was too busy hunting for racists, preferably real, but imaginary would do in a pinch.

On January 19, a day after Adler's comments, ESPN demanded Adler apologize. Adler knew exactly what he said, but he went along with the ESPN brass to keep his job. The following day, January 20, with the Twitter storm still building, ESPN fired Adler anyway. "During an Australian Open stream on ESPN3, Doug Adler should have been more careful in his word selection," read

ESPN's public statement. "Because the words gorilla and guerrilla are pronounced similarly, it's impossible to say for certain which word Adler spoke."[33] Fired and disgraced, Adler suffered a massive heart attack weeks later. Said Rothenberg in full Pontius Pilate mode, "I've been surprised at how much I become a part of the story of Doug Adler's comment/ESPN's decision to part with him, which was ESPN's own."[34]

Said Adler, who successfully sued ESPN, "What made no sense to me whatsoever was that anyone would think that just because Venus is African-American, I would call her a 'gorilla'!! It took a twisted, even racist mind to impute such a thought to me." Adler should have sued the *New York Times* as well. Imputing racist thoughts to others seems to be part of their business model.

CHAPTER FOUR

FORCING YOUR HEART

If you can force your heart and nerve and sinew/ To serve your turn long after they are gone/ And so hold on when there is nothing in you/ Except the Will which says to them: "Hold on!"

—Rudyard Kipling

Republican leader McCarthy wasn't through with me after that endless Monday, January 14. After dissecting the *New York Times* quote, he pulled out his iPhone already cued up to a twenty-second clip, a clip served up to him and narrated by none other than Trip Gabriel, of a conversation between me and Dave Price, the publicly non-partisan centrist political director of WHO Channel 13 in Des Moines. My comments to Trip Gabriel were part of a pattern, McCarthy insisted, a pattern evidenced in the October 2018 interview I did with Price.

Out of the blue, Price asked me, "What is a white nationalist?" I had never been asked that question before and I don't traffic in white nationalist circles, so I was caught without having a pre-packaged answer. "Well, I'm not sure of that. First of all, I think you have to be white," I answered, wandering around, looking for a way to answer a question this loaded, "but then we've got Rachel Dolezal who didn't have to be black to be black so it's a derogatory term today. I wouldn't have thought so a year or two or three years ago, but today they use it as a derogatory term, and they imply that you are a racist."[35]

My tone in answering the question was calm and dispassionate as I tried to give form to the definition. McCarthy, however, took my answer to mean I did not think the term "white nationalist" was derogatory "one or two years ago." For whatever reason, he kept dropping "three years" from my hastily improvised statement. He was holding the video up as he spoke to me, mischaracterizing what I said in the hope I would somehow agree with his mischaracterization.

With reflection, I could have given Price a clearer answer. What I intended to convey was that just a few years earlier, before the emergence of Donald Trump, almost no one spoke of "white nationalism" in an American context. In my long history in politics I did not have any recollection of the term being used in our political dialogue. In the literally thousands of Republican and conservative gatherings I attended over the years, I am not sure I ever met a white nationalist, let alone a white supremacist.

Now, as I explained to McCarthy, the phrase was showing up repeatedly. This was not by chance. The Left introduced "white nationalist" and weaponized it to silence critics of illegal immigration, Trump most notably, me and others secondarily. The passage of Brexit in Great Britain gave the international Left an excuse to apply the "white nationalist" slur to its political opponents as well. As British author and philosopher Roger Scruton observed before his recent death, "I have been as astonished as everyone else by the mass denunciations and targeted character assassinations that enforce prevailing orthodoxies today."[36] McCarthy wasn't listening to me or to people like Scruton. He was convinced the Price interview confirmed the racism Gabriel attributed to me.

I told McCarthy, "I can prove the *Times* story to be false but I need time." I was calculating a Lexis/Nexis search on my use of these words and their emergence in the everyday American vocabulary. I wanted to prove to him how the Left used these words to suppress honest discourse on issues like Brexit, affirmative action, diversity, and immigration, legal and illegal.

McCarthy responded, "How much time do you need?" I knew the train was rolling down the tracks and picking up speed. I didn't have bargaining leverage so I gave him the absolute minimum, all-hands-on-deck, all-nighter, possible time. I said, "I need twenty-four hours."

"You've got one hour!" said McCarthy. He gave me one hour to do what would take days and, even then, I would have no platform from which to make my case. His mind was made up. The die was already cast. Instead of defending me or even ignoring me, Republican leadership was prepared to make an example of me. I didn't know it at the time, but McCarthy scheduled a House Steering Committee meeting for an hour after our meeting. McCarthy handpicks the Steering Committee, which in turn makes the official Republican committee assignments, giving McCarthy control of all those assignments. I didn't get to make my case before the committee. I didn't get to go before the conference.

The only forum I had available was the House floor. On the following day, I stood in front of a packed House and spoke truth and facts into the Congressional Record in response to an empty resolution already set in stone. The resolution's only reference to me was Gabriel's misquote in the *New York Times*. The balance of the resolution rejected the "odious ideologies," as I called them, albeit with substantially less vigor than I used.

In my statement on the floor of the House, I announced to the chamber I would say to them the words attributed to me in the cadence I would have delivered them, if I actually did deliver them. I pointed out there would be a pause, which can be punctuated by a hyphen or a period to delineate my separate thought questioning how Western Civilization became an offensive ideology.

Ironically, the excellent professional stenographers of the House printed my statement in the Congressional Record with exactly the same punctuation error as the *New York Times*! One would think that would have made my case but in this arena, facts don't matter to the mob. I would not be cut down from the hanging tree. The virtue signalers would leave me to dangle from the bough. A political lynch mob cannot admit its guilt.

Shortly after the Monday evening Steering Committee meeting, when McCarthy successfully stampeded the committee decision to strip me of my committees, the *New York Times* happily reported my fate. Trip Gabriel and colleagues Jonathan Martin and Nicholas Fandos shared my undoing with their readers before my supporters even knew.

"House Republican leaders removed Representative Steve King of Iowa from the Judiciary and Agriculture Committees on Monday night," they gloated, "as party officials scrambled to appear tough on racism and contain damage from comments Mr. King made to *The New York Times* questioning why white supremacy is considered offensive."[37]

The reporters' strategic use of the word "appear" insinuated Republicans were not really tough on racism. They just wanted the public to think they were. That one word sabotaged whatever Republican leaders hoped to achieve by punishing me. Interestingly, too, Gabriel and pals misquoted Gabriel's original article to strengthen the case against me. Here he has me questioning why "white supremacy" is offensive. In the original, he quoted me wondering how "that language" became offensive. This is not a small point. It is also a selective use of the most odious of the three ideologies.

The media have a way of persuading Republicans a circular firing squad is a good idea. For the firing squad with me at the center, all the usual suspects signed up. Senate Majority Leader Mitch McConnell suggested I should find "another line of work." Senator Mitt Romney said I should quit. Rep. Steve Stivers, the by now failed former chairman of the National Republican Congressional Committee, was publicly condemning me and, I was told, privately recruiting primary opponents to run against me. And Lord knows McCarthy wanted me gone.

"He's not a white supremacist. He's not a white nationalist. It's all stupid talk," said Mark Steyn to the Republicans who just sacrificed me on the altar of political correctness. "So you've just surrendered the phrase 'Western Civilization.' I don't get that. I don't see what's in it for conservatism in surrendering that phrase, in accepting the leftist's view that the term 'Western Civilization' is beyond the pale."[38]

Not all Republicans believed in surrender. Throughout the ordeal, I received any number of heartening messages like this one from Kimberly Fletcher, author and founder of Moms for America: "Apparently people can't handle thought-provoking conversations or even factual truths. Stay strong, my friend. The battle is long and hard but truth wins in the end, and we will be on the right side of the issue." I responded, "I am only troubled if I believe I have troubled God. The rest is just stress and manageable because of Him."

Although we got the results too late to do any good, the Lexis-Nexis research confirmed my point. I had been quoted in print using the term "Western Civilization" 276 times dating back to the year 2000. But in the same period of time, I had not been quoted saying "white nationalism," "white nationalist," "white supremacist," or "white supremacy" even once before the *New York Times* misquote in January of 2019.

The Lexis-Nexis results reaffirmed what I speculated about Gabriel's motives. Members of my legal team summarized the finding of the Lexis-Nexus audit: "It appears unlikely that King spontaneously used the phrases 'white nationalist' and 'white supremacist' in his discussion with the *Times* reporter, as they were never common elements of his speech. It suggests that King was repeating terms fed to him by the *Times*." The results revealed there was a huge spike in the media's use of the phrase "white nationalist." Over the previous twenty years, "white nationalist" or "white nationalism" was virtually unused, meaning 100–200 times a year in all print media. Then, abruptly after Trump's election and a Soros Democrat meeting in Washington, the phrase was used 10,000 times in two months and 30,000 times in 2017, classic statistics revealing the weaponization of the term.

> *The contention that King reacted to the Times reporter's use of the phrases "white nationalist," "white suprema-cist," and "western civilization" as pejoratives is sup-ported by the body of the Times article itself. The article contains the following passage, likely written prior to the King interview: "Elected to Congress in 2002, Mr. King attracted the attention of hate-watch groups like the Anti-Defamation League as he spoke increasingly about pre-serving 'Western Culture' or 'Western Civilization.' The groups consider those buzzwords that signal support to white nationalists, along with an obsession with birth-rates and abortion rates among different ethnic groups."*[39]

I'm nothing if not stubborn. Even before I saw the results of the Lexis-Nexis search, I knew if I walked away the media would promptly write my political epitaph, and there would be no way for me to get the microphone again to amend it. The last word would be theirs. Then thirty years down the road they would bury me as they did Earl Butz, "Steve King, Iowa Congressman Who Championed White Supremacy, Dies at 100." I wasn't about to let that happen. I wasn't about to quit.

History buff that I am, I found myself reflecting on the Battle of the Bulge. Unlike me, the American Army faced real bullets and real bombshells, and the blitzkrieg came from the Nazis, not the media. (It is easy to confuse the two, I know.) German tanks were rolling, American lines were sagging, and the German high com-mand offered Brig. Gen. Anthony McAuliffe a way to save his own skin—surrender. McAuliffe had his response typed up and sent to the Germans. It consisted of one word, "Nuts." If the Germans did not quite get it, McAuliffe's troops did, and they rallied behind him.

I said repeatedly to the press, "I will not resign. They will have to shoot me down in the middle of Main Street at high noon with

The four of us stood together many times, serving the people of Iowa. That would change immediately after the November 6, 2018, election. Senator Joni Ernst (2nd from left), Lt. Governor Kim Reynolds, Governor Terry Branstad, and Congressman King discuss plans to repair flood damage. Clarksville, Iowa—September 24, 2016

everybody watching!" I told my staff they had a job at least until January 2021. They would keep working on behalf of our constituents, and their checks would keep coming. I was prepared to tough this out. Even if the media complex, NeverTrumpers, Republican elitists, and Leftist mob never relented, I was not going to betray the people who voted for me and surrender my seat.

There would be no capitulation. The reasons why were pretty clear to me. McCarthy, Gabriel, and their co-conspirators failed to influence the one man who could have forced my hand, President Trump. When asked about my predicament, Trump blew off the media, saying cagily, "I haven't been following it."[40] It wasn't quite "Nuts," but it was close enough.

CHAPTER FIVE

MANNING UP

*If you can fill the unforgiving minute/ With sixty sec-
onds' worth of distance run/ Yours is the Earth and
everything that's in it/ And—which is more—you'll
be a Man, my son!*

—Rudyard Kipling

"House Resolution 41: Rejecting White nationalism and White supremacy"[41] might better have been called "House Resolution 41: Chastising conservatives who challenge progressive thought control, especially Steve King."

White supremacy was easy to denounce. Relying on FBI intelligence assessments, the resolution read, "White supremacists believe that the white race is superior to all other races and was created to rule them. They view non-whites as subhuman and usually refer to them in derogatory terms." You have to ask yourself how many Americans actually believe this? I've never met one. Not since Sen. Robert Byrd died has any American of any influence ever publicly advanced ideas anything like this. I am not even sure David Duke has. To call someone a "white supremacist" who is not—me, for instance or Donald Trump—is an act of pure and reckless defamation.

"White nationalist" is trickier. The resolution again cited the FBI definition: "To be a white nationalist is to be pro-white. The domestic white nationalist movement seeks to promote, honor, and defend the white race." If, at this point, we substituted the word "black" for "white," no one would bat an eye: "To be a black nationalist is to be pro-black. The domestic black national-ist movement seeks to promote, honor, and defend the black race." A black nationalist invented the holiday called "Kwanzaa." Muhammad Ali was a black nationalist. So was Malcolm X. Just about every university African American studies program fits this description.

The resolution continued with much more detail about white nationalists: "They believe the white race is under attack from Jew-ish interests that dominate the government (referred to as the Zion-ist Occupied Government, or ZOG), the media, banking, and entertainment industries and act to the detriment of the white race." This definition is almost crazily specific. I am sure someone believes this stuff. I just don't know who these people are. According to the resolution, white nationalists see "race mixing as akin to genocide." I had no problem rejecting any of this. I have long been a champion of Israel and have argued—long, relentlessly, and publicly—in favor of assimilation and intermarriage. When one of my sons was single and uncommitted, I tried unsuccessfully to play cupid between him and a very cute and bubbly young black lady. The same son who later pointed out to me the press declared me a racist precisely for advocating for interracial marriage. How? The press imputed to me an alleged belief that interracial marriage would eventually absorb blacks into the white population. My genetics courses taught me enough to call that theory bogus. My theory is interracial mar-riage erases racial friction a generation at a time.

By focusing on white supremacy and white nationalism, the media and the government consciously overlook the dangers posed to American Jews by anti-Semitic thugs who are motivated by Black Nationalist rhetoric—many of whom happen to be black. In December 2019, black nationalists launched two horrific attacks on Jews in metropolitan New York and a dozen or more of random black-on-Jewish attacks in New York City alone.

In the first incident, a black couple carried out, in the words of the *New York Times*, "an anti-Semitic rampage at a Jersey City kosher market in what officials later declared an act of domestic terrorism."[42] The terror attack left six dead, but the *Times* made no effort to tie the attack to black leaders like Louis Farrakhan or Rev. Jeremiah Wright, both of whom have been preaching anti-Semitism for decades, let alone to Barack Obama who has been chummy with each of these men. Obama, in fact, participated in Farrakhan's so-called "Million Man March" and attended Wright's church for years. Wright even officiated at Obama's wedding and baptized his daughters. Evidently, guilt by association doesn't apply to Leftists. In fact, it seems to me guilt in any form doesn't apply to Leftists.

Less than three weeks later another "anti-Semitic rampage" left five injured, one severely, at a rabbi's house in the suburban New York town of Monsey. Incredibly, in a lengthy *Times* article written after the suspect had been caught, the reporters failed to identify his race. In the same article, they refer to the Jersey City mass shooting, an earlier anti-Semitic attack in Monsey, and "a string of anti-Semitic crimes" in Brooklyn and fail to mention the race of these perpetrators even though all of them, like the Monsey assailant, were black.[43] Worldwide, of course, Jews suffer most from attacks by Islamic terrorists of all races, but that fact is inevitably downplayed as well.

Wrote Seth Frantzman in the *Jerusalem Post*, "In American society there is generally only place for one kind of racism. There are far-right white supremacists and everyone else. This Manichean worldview of antisemitism and racism means we are only comfortable with one type of perpetrator. An angry white man."[44] True to form, when Congresswoman Rashida Tlaib first heard of the Jersey City massacre, she blamed "white supremacy" for the attack. "Her tweet was deleted," Frantzman notes. "When it wasn't white supremacy and there was no one to condemn, it didn't fit the narrative and was less important."

This context is important to understand why the Left relentlessly attempts to equate conservatives like myself with white nationalists. Not only does this tactic suppress dissent on subjects like illegal immigration, it also conceals the fact it is the Left's own allies who are terrorizing Jews here and abroad.

A week before the 2018 election, a man named Robert Bowers murdered eleven people at the Tree of Life synagogue in Pittsburgh. I was appalled as was every rational American. Bowers fit the definition of a white nationalist but he was no fan of Donald Trump. "Trump is a globalist, not a nationalist," he posted days before the shooting. "There is no #MAGA as long as there is a kike infestation." In the darker corners of the white nationalist movement, Bowers's take on Trump was commonplace. I have to wonder whether Bowers timed his attack to damage Trump and Congressional Republicans.

The media refused to take people like Bowers at their word. To offset Bowers's anti-Trump remarks, the *Washington Post* promptly published an op-ed by Julia Ioffe headlined, "How much responsibility does Trump bear for the synagogue shooting in Pittsburgh?"[45] In the editorial, Ioffe labored to turn the most pro-Jewish, pro-Israel president in memory into a closet anti-Semite.

Across the nation, Democratic activists worked to turn the shooting by a Trump-hater into a shooting inspired by Trump and others who shared his opposition to illegal immigration. At an event in Iowa a few days later, a smug young man asked me during the Q & A, "The terrorist who committed this crime, he was quoted as saying, 'They bring invaders and they kill our people. I can't sit back and watch our people get slaughtered.' You, Steve King, have been quoted as saying, 'We can't restore our civilization with other people's babies.' You and the shooter both share an ideology that is fundamentally anti-immigration."

I stopped him in his tracks. "No, don't you do that," I said. "Do not associate me with that shooter." He then asked me what distinguished my views from those of the shooter. "No, you're done, you crossed the line," I said. "It's not tolerable to accuse me to be associated with a guy that shot eleven people in Pittsburgh."[46] I continued, "I am a person who has stood with Israel from the beginning and the length of that nation is the length of my life. And I've been with them all along and I will not answer your question and I'll not listen to another word from you." The man was clearly a plant. "Do you identify as a white supremacist?" he asked. "Stop it!" I said. "Why did you meet with a white supremacist group in Austria?" he persisted.

The fellow accomplished what he set out to accomplish, splashy coverage on CNN. "Steve King erupts at comparison to Pittsburgh suspect: 'Do not associate me with that shooter,'" read the CNN headline. CNN expanded on the fellow's disinformation adding more false detail about the "white supremacist" meeting in Austria. You will recall two of the five people I met with were gay and one was Jewish. This confrontation took place five days before the 2018 election. The media and the Democrats work hand in glove to disparage serious conservatives, and with their feeble responses, establishment Republicans allow the strategy to succeed. When you walk point in Congress, you get sniped at by all sides.

This growing dynamic thrust me into center ring in this bizarre media circus. I do not exaggerate my importance to say the white supremacy resolution was about me. Here is how the resolution began: "Whereas, on January 10, 2019, Representative Steve King was quoted as asking, 'White nationalist, white supremacist, Western Civilization—how did that language become offensive?'" My colleague Tlaib never had her name mentioned in the resolutions her anti-Semitic comments inspired, but I got top billing for comments I was "quoted" as saying. Washington is a strange place.

CHAPTER SIX

FINDING MY VOICE

I am occasionally asked why of all the people in Congress I am the one to crawl furthest out on the limb of controversy. When I think about it, I guess I have to credit my dad. He was the best critical thinker I've ever met and I've engaged in debate with far more than my share. When I was a boy, he constantly challenged me to be prepared to rebut any argument. If I said something stupid or just plain wrong, he wasn't the kind of guy to pat me on the head and tell me I was entitled to my opinion. No, he wanted me to come ready to back up my arguments with facts.

One time, for instance, Dad and I argued for three days about whether you could convert watts to horsepower. I said you could and he said you couldn't. I suspect for a lot of people in Congress a discussion like this might as well be in Greek, but in rural Iowa, at least in my generation, it was Greek this kid thought he understood.

So after a couple of days of empty jawing, I went to the high school library and found an old, dog-eared physics book. Eureka! In the book, I found the answer: 745 watts equals one horsepower. I could not wait to get home to show it to Dad. That night I slipped the book to the supper table and balanced it on my knees with the Eureka page bookmarked.

As Mom served dessert, I found an opening and raised the question once more about watts and horsepower. "I thought we settled this," said Dad slapping the table in frustration. "You cannot convert watts to horsepower." In anticipation of my first win over my always-right Dad, I egged him on, then dropped my bombshell. "If I showed you a formula that proves how many watts equal one horsepower," I asked with all the cockiness a sixteen-year-old could muster, "would you still tell me I'm wrong?"

Dad answered, yes, he would tell me I was wrong *because* I was wrong. With that, I pulled the book off my knees and triumphantly opened it to the magic formula. There it was, in print: 745 watts equals one horsepower. Triumph! Dad was going to have to concede his firstborn son finally bested him in debate.

As the Romans say, "*Sic transit gloria*" (Thus passes worldly glory). Without hesitation Dad shot back, "That's not what I'm talking about. A watt is a measure of electrical power. Horsepower is a measurement of mechanical power. You'll look foolish if you equate the two!" I tried to argue back. I tried to convince him we were both right, but Dad wasn't buying, and in my heart of hearts I knew he had me pegged. Even today, when I googled the question, the first hit is still Dad's, in paraphrase, "You can't equate the two." The second is the formula. I looked up to heaven and said, "You're still teaching me how to think."

In the long run, though, I was the winner. I had the privilege of sitting at a dinner table where the discussions were often deep and intense. My father did not graduate from college. Neither did I for that matter, but I would put up my dinner table education against anyone's college degree. He and Mom were both skilled in any number of practical arts and wise in the ways of the world. We didn't have very much money, but my home was as close to perfect as a home could be. It's not every kid who gets to go to church with his family each Sunday and have a pot roast waiting at home. Was this heaven? No, it was Iowa. My parents created a family life right out of the *Dick and Jane* primers of my childhood.

Mom was as good a teacher as Dad. When I gave the eulogy at her funeral, I recounted how she instructed me on the value of charity. She preferred the *King James* version of the apostle Paul's famed letter to the Corinthians, which used the word "charity" where some modern versions used "love." Love has a connotation of a reciprocating agreement, which is why so many people have this passage recited at their wedding.

For Mom, charity meant giving without any expectation the gift was going to be returned. She was charitable: "Charity suffereth long, *and* is kind; charity envieth not; charity vaunteth not itself, is not puffed up." That was Mom. She gave with no expectation of receiving and in doing so, she taught me to live a life of service, to give of myself without expectation of reward in this life.

My education did not end at the dinner table. As a boy, Dad took me hunting for rabbits and squirrels, ducks, pheasants, and deer. Whatever we shot, we ate, including two jackrabbits so tough they had to be put through the grinder. I never shot a jackrabbit after that. We raised a lot of our own food as well. We had a garden in the backyard and raised feisty banty hens and a few roosters. It took a determined kid to gather the eggs from the nest of a banty hen. Maybe some of their scrappiness rubbed off on me. We killed and prepared the chickens we ate just as we killed and prepared the wild game. You learn a lot of common sense when you put your own food on the table.

Another thing Dad taught me was we all had a civic duty to help out our community. At the time we were living in Goodell in North Central Iowa. According to the 1960 census, 231 people lived there including us. One day, Dad was speaking with the mayor in front of the town hardware store when an elderly woman, confusing forward and reverse on her car, drove the mayor into the plate glass window of the store. He survived but he was banged up enough to step down from his lofty post as town mayor. Feeling the need to do his part and resolved to be nowhere near this lady when she was parking her car, Dad took over the job.

Dad had a high-intensity, relentless Midwestern work ethic. The duties of his job always came first and then the work at home. Everything else had to be managed around work responsibilities. When I was in the sixth grade, he took a job as the manager of the state police radio station in Denison, a bustling meat packing plant town of five thousand good souls. He didn't believe in missing work. Every day, my mom packed his lunch in a classic black lunch bucket, and he headed off to the job. If he wasn't feeling well, he'd go anyhow. He would say, "I can be sick at work just as good as I can be sick at home."

Afraid of us getting soft in the "city," Dad bought a house and twenty-six acres south of town, right in the middle of a four-mile stretch of timber known as Coon Grove. We kept a flock of sheep. Managing them took work. So did cutting thistles by hand and fence posts with a two-man crosscut saw.

More memorably, I could roam on my own all the way up and down the full stretch of Coon Creek for miles in either direction. Before I was old enough to carry a .22 rifle, I proudly brought home two squirrels taken with only a pocketknife. I enjoyed the kind of freedom most kids today could not even imagine. Daniel Boone and Davy Crockett were not just my heroes when I was a kid. They were my role models.

"I am at liberty to vote as my conscience and judgment dictates to be right, without the yoke of any party on me," said Crockett when elected to Congress. "Look at my arms, you will find no party hand-cuff on them!" You grow up with that independence of spirit, and you are not inclined to ask party leaders permission to go where you choose and say what you think.

CHAPTER SEVEN

UNDERSTANDING TRUMP

There is no understanding my predicament without understanding that of Donald Trump. The media targeted me because of my consequential role in the presidential nomination process. They also targeted me because I refused to let them dictate the terms of the debate. With Trump, who did the same on a much larger platform, they had all the target they could ever hope for.

During the Obama years, journalists coordinated their strategy through a private chat room called "JournoList." *Politico* described it as a site where "Left-leaning bloggers, political reporters, magazine writers, policy wonks and academics" could share insights and story ideas.[47] By 2008, when Obama was campaigning for president, "Left-leaning" described just about every salaried journalist in Washington and New York. To protect Obama from criticism, many of these journalists were happy to play the race card.

In one case, Spencer Ackerman, then with the *Washington Independent*, recommended a strategy for his colleagues on how to defuse Obama's ticking time bomb known as Reverend Jeremiah Wright. "If the right forces us all to either defend Wright or tear him down," wrote Ackerman, "no matter what we choose, we lose the game they've put upon us. Instead, take one of them—Fred Barnes, Karl Rove, who cares—and call them racists. Ask: why do they have such a deep-seated problem with a black politician who unites the country? What lurks behind those problems? This makes "them" sputter with rage, which in turn leads to overreaction and self-destruction."[48] The difference between Ackerman and his peers is he was willing to say out loud what the others took for granted.

No Republican was safe from a race-based attack. For instance, after being elected president in 1988, George H. W. Bush unexpectedly found himself being called a racist for running the infamous "Willie Horton" ad. In the way of background, Bush's opponent in 1988, Massachusetts Gov. Michael Dukakis, championed a totally insane furlough program allowing the convicted murderer Willie Horton an un-chaperoned weekend furlough despite having stabbed a teenage gas station attendant to death just twelve years prior. Without permission, of course, Horton extended his weekend for about a year or so. It ended only with his arrest in Maryland after a vicious crime spree.

The furlough program was so conspicuous an example of liberal insanity even Al Gore talked about Horton during the 1988 primary season. In the general election campaign, the Bush people criticized the program in a TV spot showing prisoners, almost all of them white, walking through a revolving door. The spot did not mention Horton by name or show his picture. Late in the campaign, an independent group in New England ran a spot on the furlough program that did show Horton's mug shot. Horton was black. The Bush campaign had nothing to do with this second spot, racist only to the degree it showed Horton's picture. The media did not care whether the ad was racist or whether Bush commissioned it. They called him out as a racist for running the ad even though he didn't and it wasn't.

In 2008, the *New York Times* scolded Sen. John McCain for a TV ad in his campaign against Barack Obama. "The presumptive Republican nominee has embarked on a bare-knuckled barrage of negative advertising aimed at belittling Mr. Obama," wrote the *Times* editorial board. "The most recent ad . . . gave us an uneasy feeling that the McCain campaign was starting up the same sort of racially tinged attack on Mr. Obama that Republican operatives ran against Harold Ford, a black candidate for Senate in Tennessee in 2006."[49]

Romney got the same treatment in 2012. In fact, progressives judged his campaign so racist they denounced Romney not just in the daily media but in academic journals, wrote Charlton McIlwain and Stephen Calliendo in *American Behavioral Scientist,* "We focus our attention on a particularly salient form of racist appeal, one based on the long-standing stereotypes of black laziness and taking advantage. . . . We then demonstrate how Romney and the right wove these underlying stereotypes into a seamless racist narrative."[50]

You would think given their treatment in the media Romney, the McCains, the Cheneys, and the Bushes would be a little more discerning in their attacks on people like Trump and even me but they have not been. Headlines such as "Meghan McCain and the 'The View' rip Trump's overt racism" or 'Romney worries Trump is promoting racism' are commonplace. George W. Bush has handed the media even more ammunition. In 2017, he gave what the *Washington Post* called "an unexpected and rather eloquent speech against Trumpism." Said Bush, with his sights obviously on Trump, "Bullying and prejudice in our public life sets a national tone, provides permission for cruelty and bigotry, and compromises the moral education of children."[51] The speech was "unexpected" because the media had been accusing the Bush family of racism since they first emerged as a political dynasty.

One nice speech, a virtue signal for the entire Bush family, was not about to stop the media. On the occasion of the elder Bush's Washington funeral in 2018, the *Washington Post* rewarded his grieving family for its stand against bigotry with an article headlined, "How the Willie Horton ad factors into George H.W. Bush's legacy." The writer accused the late president of creating "one of the most infamous political ads in history, one stoking racial stereotypes that continue to shape criminal justice policy years later."

The fact Bush had nothing to do with the ad did not seem to bother the *Post* editors. Nor did the fact the late president's sons had been attacking Trump to curry the media's favor. Political theorist Roger Scruton spoke to this very subject. "The archive of your crimes is stored in cyberspace," wrote Scruton, "and however much you may have confessed to them and sworn to change, they will pursue you for the rest of your life, just as long as someone has an interest in drawing attention to them."[52]

Don't get me wrong. The Bushes are good people, but as long as they and the likes of Mitt Romney are willing to attack other Republicans for imagined racial offenses, the media are going to keep pulling their own imagined crimes from cyberspace and exploiting them. This trick only works if Republicans fall for it, and fall for it they continue to do.

Donald Trump, however, wasn't about to play that game. In 2011, he showed he was a different kind of cat when he publicly asked to see Barack Obama's elusive birth certificate. He made the request to see it on the Left-leaning daytime TV show, *The View*. Said Trump, "I want him to show his birth certificate! There's something on that birth certificate that he doesn't like." The black cohost Whoopi Goldberg, who is allegedly a comedian, angrily responded, "That's the biggest pile of dog mess I've heard in ages. It's not 'cuz he's black, is it?"[53]

In fact, the multiracial Obama's "blackness" had nothing to do with the questions about his eligibility. The Constitution requires both the president and vice president to be "a natural born Citizen" because our Framers wanted to ensure they be raised with an American experience by American parents with American values in the new American civilization. No one ever questioned Al Sharpton or Jesse Jackson when they ran for president or pretended to. Their roots run deep into the American experience, as do most blacks.

Trump asked about Obama's birth certificate because Obama spent a good deal of money on lawyers determined to conceal it. Obama is the only American president whose parents spent most of their adult lives outside the country. His African father was not a citizen, and his white absentee mother exhibited little fidelity to her son or to her country.

In *Dreams from My Father*, Obama's 1995 memoir, he told a tale about this happy multicultural family, and none of it was true. His parents never even lived together. Obama repeated this story often, especially at the conventions. To challenge it was to be called a racist. Trump did not seem to mind.

"We have a president, and I say this without any joy in my heart, who is a racist," said Sen. Bernie Sanders on the campaign trail in April 2019. When asked why he made this accusation, Sanders said Trump "was one of the leaders of the so-called 'birther movement,' which sought to portray Barack Obama as an illegitimate president, someone not born in the United States."[54] Sanders and Whoopi were apparently on the same wavelength. Despite the fact Obama's African father had zero to do with his upbringing and Obama was raised by his white grandparents in the least black state in America, the media imagined Obama to be as culturally "black" as the son of a black Mississippi sharecropper.

Unlike most Republicans who would have gone into hiding by this time, Trump seemed unfazed. From the June day in 2015 when he and Melania descended the escalator at the Trump Tower and announced his intentions to the world, Trump has been rewriting the rulebook for Republican candidates and office holders.

"When Mexico sends its people, they're not sending their best," he told those assembled in one part of his unscripted remarks. "They're not sending you. They're not sending you. They're sending people that have lots of problems, and they're bringing those problems with us. They're bringing drugs. They're bringing crime. They're rapists. And some, I assume, are good people."[55]

The media, of course, flipped out but not immediately. Reporting the next day, Alexander Burns of the *New York Times* did not mention the "rapists" comment until deep in the article, and even then he put it in its proper context. Wrote Burns, "On Tuesday, [Trump] vowed to build a 'great wall' on the Mexican border to keep out rapists and other criminals, who he said were sneaking into the United States in droves."[56]

Then too, Burns wrote off Trump's chances to be elected president as "remote." As Trump started showing strength in the polls, however, he became—in the media's eyes—more and more of a racist. Check out these quotes emerging in the days and weeks after Trump announced.

> *New York Times:* "Trump's claim that illegal Mexican immigrants are 'rapists."

> *Time Magazine:* "Trump's comment that Mexican immigrants are 'rapists.'"

> *Associated Press:* "Trump called Mexican immigrants rapists and criminals."

> *CBS News:* "Trump defends calling Mexican immigrants 'rapists.'"

> *L.A. Times:* "describing Mexican immigrants as 'rapists.'"

> *Fortune:* "in a speech branding Mexican immigrants as criminals and rapists."

> *Hollywood Reporter:* "he referred to Mexican immigrants as 'rapists.'"

> *Huffington Post:* "He called Latino immigrants 'criminals' and 'rapists.'"

> *The Washington Post:* "He referred to Mexicans as "rapists."

Democratic vice-presidential candidate Tim Kaine went even further in his slander of Trump. "The thing that amazes me is the depth of his trash talking with Latinos," said Kaine, "saying all Mexicans are rapists and going after Latino immigrants."[57] Democratic presidential candidate Martin O'Malley echoed Kaine: "When Donald Trump says all Mexicans are rapists and murderers, that's not being a leader."[58]

Writing in *Salon* six months after Trump's speech, liberal professor Alberto Martinez tried to set the record straight. "You might well dislike Trump's words. I did," wrote Martinez. "But let's not make it worse. He did not say that all Mexicans are rapists. Yet that's what many commentators did."[59] Martinez then went on to cite the staggering number of crimes committed by illegal aliens just in Texas where he lives. He is a brave fellow.

One comment Martinez made needs further explanation. "Many people think that Trump is racist against Mexicans," he wrote without comment. The fact is, though, "Mexican" is no more a *race* than "American." There is, for instance, much more African DNA in the American population than in the Mexican. Along the same lines, "Muslim" is no more a race than "Catholic." Like Catholics, Muslims come in all colors. Like Americans, so do Mexicans. This did not matter to the media. To challenge illegal immigration or even Muslim terrorism was now officially "racist."

In June 2018, the Supreme Court upheld the Trump administration's decision to ban travel from several predominantly Muslim countries. Chief Justice John Roberts wrote that the ban was "expressly premised on legitimate purposes: preventing entry of nationals who cannot be adequately vetted and inducing other nations to improve their practices." The Left did not see it that way. "Too many Muslims have been intentionally targeted, discriminated against, separated from their families and denied opportunities solely based on their faith. Straight up racism!" tweeted Congresswoman Rashida Tlaib. The New York mayor's office called the ruling an "institutionalization of Islamophobia and racism." The Action Network launched a petition drive, "Sign the petition: End the racist Muslim Ban, support the NO BAN Act."[60]

For the record, the seven countries affected by the original ban include Iran, Iraq, Libya, Somalia, Sudan, Syria, and Yemen, all of them hotbeds of terror. The citizens of these countries span the whole racial spectrum from white to black. The ban did not include the most populous Muslim-majority countries in the world, such as Indonesia with its 267 million people or Egypt with its 100 million people. If Islam is not a race and the great majority of the world's Muslims are unaffected by the ban, by what bizarre logic can the ban be considered "racist"? It can't be, but that does not stop the Left from making the charge over and over. "Repeat a lie often enough and it becomes the truth," Nazi propagandist Joseph Goebbels is reported to have said.

In his novel *1984*, George Orwell made a similar point. "And if all others accepted the lie which the Party imposed—if all records told the same tale—then the lie passed into history and became truth," wrote Orwell. "'Who controls the past' ran the Party slogan, 'controls the future: who controls the present controls the past.'"[61] This is a lesson our progressive friends seem to have taken to heart.

Perhaps no incident during the Trump presidency generated more lies than the "Unite the Right" rally in Charlottesville, Virginia, in August 2017. The rally was sparked by the City of Charlottesville's decision to remove a statue of Robert E. Lee and rename the park where the statue was located. Many of those who came to Charlottesville to protest were unaware Neo-Nazi groups would try to seize the spotlight. Similarly, many of the counter-protestors were unaware violent Antifa groups and armed members of the Redneck Revolt would use the occasion to foment violence. The resulting chaos led to one death and nineteen injuries.

Upon learning of the melee, Trump tweeted, "We ALL must be united & condemn all that hate stands for. There is no place for this kind of violence in America. Lets come together as one!" This led to a firestorm of criticism because Trump did not specify the white nationalist and neo-Nazi groups in attendance. When he spoke to the press that day, Trump said, "We condemn in the strongest possible terms this egregious display of hatred, bigotry, and violence on many sides—on many sides."[62] This caused more outrage in the media because again Trump did not list specifically the groups on the right that inspired the violence, much of it against them. He did not mention the groups on the Left either.

They were there. Admitted the *New York Times*, "Groups that identify as anti-fascist . . . have been physically confronting neo-Nazis, white supremacists and, in some cases, speakers who merely challenge the boundaries of political correctness on college campuses across the country."[63] During the Trump presidency, Leftist groups—many of them openly Marxist or Maoist—have generated almost all the ideological violence. Typically, the media pretend not to see them. From the perspective of these groups, everyone on the right is a fascist or a white supremacist and deserves to be confronted.

Even mild-mannered conservative intellectuals like Ben Shapiro, an orthodox Jew who is not a Trump fan, have been target by violent protests. A month after Charlottesville, a Shapiro speech on the Berkeley campus led to nine arrests, four for carrying banned weapons, and one for assaulting a police officer. Two years later, numerous people were arrested protesting the speech of conservative author Ann Coulter at Berkeley. In Portland, Oregon, any number of conservative activists and media people have been assaulted by Leftist thugs. We are not supposed to notice this violence but Trump has.

Two days after Charlottesville, responding to the mounting hysteria that he was not explicit enough in condemning bigotry, Trump got more specific. "Racism is evil," he explained. "And those who cause violence in its name are criminals and thugs, including the KKK, neo-Nazis, white supremacists, and other hate groups, that are repugnant to everything we hold dear as Americans."[64]

The media still were not satisfied. Speaking to the media off-the-cuff shortly thereafter, Trump tried to explain what happened at Charlottesville:

> If you reported it accurately, you would say that the neo-Nazis started this thing. They showed up in Charlottesville. Excuse me. They didn't put themselves down as neo-Nazis. You had some very bad people in that group. You also had some very fine people on both sides. You had people in that group—excuse me, excuse me. I saw the same pictures as you did. You had people in that group that were there to protest the taking down, to them, a very, very important statue and the renaming of a park from Robert E. Lee to another name.[65]

Trump then spoke for a minute about the danger of allowing the American equivalent of the Chinese Red Guard to launch a cultural revolution here by purging from the public square Jefferson and even Washington for having owned slaves. He then returned to the question of who the protestors on the right were. "You had people—and I'm not talking about the neo-Nazis and the white nationalists. They should be condemned totally. You had many people in that group other than neo-Nazis and white nationalists."[66]

Trump does not always get straight to the point, but there was no mistaking his message. There were fine people on both sides, but those fine people did not include "neo-Nazis and the white nationalists." These people, Trump insisted, "should be condemned totally." The Democrats refused to abandon their "very fine people" lie. In fact, they rode it into the Trump's second impeachment trial where it was exposed for the cynical distortion it was.

For a while, the media went full bore in trying to paint Trump as an anti-Semite. What prompted the accusations—although the media never need much in the way of prompting—was a series of threats called into Jewish community centers. On February 21, one month into his presidency, Trump publicly denounced these threats, but that very denunciation gave the *New York Times* an excuse to remind its readers how Trump's campaign "drew the support of racist and anti-Semitic groups." For this reason, Trump was "willing to stay silent about such actions" if not "quietly condoning them."[67]

A week later, a *Times* article upped the smear level starting with its headline, "Threats and Vandalism Leave American Jews on Edge in Trump Era." At that time, the "Trump era" was five weeks old. No matter. Bomb threats and vandalism, the trio of reporters insisted, "stoked fears that a virulent anti-Semitism has increasingly taken hold in the early days of the Trump administration."[68]

The fact that Trump has a Jewish son-in-law, a daughter who converted to Judaism, and Jewish grandchildren did not factor into the *Times* thinking. Nor does the fact Trump has been, in the words of Lawrence Leamer in *Politico*, a long time "crusader against anti-Semitism." In a lengthy 2019 article, Leamer recounted how Trump "attacked the anti-Semitism of old Palm Beach."[69] This was not something new. In 1990, Trump told *Vanity Fair*, "I wouldn't join [the island's Bath and Tennis Club] because they don't take blacks and Jews."[70]

As Leamer reported, Trump grew up with Jews, went to school with Jews, vacationed with Jews, wrote glowingly about Jewish businessmen, and had many Jewish associates. In creating Mar-a-Lago, he succeeded in opening club life on the island to blacks and Jews. The *Washington Post* has something like twenty reporters assigned to the Trump beat. The *New York Times* likely has more. How all of these reporters could ignore this history to portray Trump as a supporter of anti-Semitism tells you just about all you need to know about the way the media work today.

Unfortunately for the *Times*, just a week after reporting Trump-inspired terrorism against Jews, the police arrested one of the culprits in the campaign of threats. He was a black Leftist who called Jews "filthy fascist appeasers" and argued that they "should be taken out along with Trump."[71]

In August 2019, *New York Times* editor Dean Baquet made the paper's Trump strategy shockingly clear. "We built our newsroom to cover one story, and we did it truly well," said the delusional Baquet at a large internal meeting. "Now we have to regroup, and shift resources and emphasis to take on a different story." The "one story" had just collapsed. That was the story of Russia collusion. That tale proved to be a hoax. What Baquet was telling his staff was that they would now gear up to create a new hoax, namely the idea that President Trump was a racist. "It is a story that requires deep investigation into people who peddle hatred," said Baquet, "but it is also a story that requires imaginative use of all our muscles to write about race and class in a deeper way than we have in years."[72]

In truth, there was nothing new about this strategy. The media falsely painted Trump as a racist, a xenophobe, and an anti-Semite from the day he announced for the presidency. When Trump wisely shut down China traffic at the dawn of the Covid-19 era, the Left, Joe Biden included, denounced Trump for his "xenophobia." No amount of contrary evidence was likely to persuade the media that what they were peddling was a hate-filled hoax.

The strategy remained viable only because the Republicans writ large allowed it. Weeks before the 2016 election, then–House Speaker Paul Ryan showed just how willing he was to play the media's game regarding then-candidate Trump. In a conversation with the entire Republican conference, Ryan gave us his "every man for himself speech," telling us he would neither defend Trump nor campaign with him.

The friction had been building for months. In May 2016, after Trump clinched the Republican nomination with a decisive primary win in Indiana, Ryan told CNN he was "not ready" to endorse Donald J. Trump for president. "I think conservatives want to know," said Ryan, "does he share our values and our principles on limited government, the proper role of the executive, adherence to the Constitution?"[73] Had Ryan said this months earlier when the outcome of the primaries was still in doubt, it would be one thing. But Trump was the presumptive nominee. And Ryan knew Trump's remaining opponent, Hillary Clinton, absolutely did not share "our values and our principles on limited government, the proper role of the executive, adherence to the Constitution."

What really bothered Ryan was Trump's style. Ryan objected, said the *New York Times*, to Trump's "outrageous remarks—insulting women, Hispanics and Muslims."[74] Yes, Trump could be a little crude, but his remarks were "outrageous" only to the people—virtuoso virtue signaler Paul Ryan included—who accepted the rules set down by Big Media,

For some months Trump and Ryan maintained an uneasy truce, but the release of the *Access Hollywood* tape in October 2016 gave Ryan all the excuse he needed to dump Trump. The video was shot in 2005 when Trump was arriving on the set of *Days of Our Lives* to tape a segment. The content is well enough known, but what set people off was Trump's comment to Billy Bush, "when you're a star, they let you do it." The "they" being the women in show business, and the "do it" meaning grab them in impolite places. This was as much a comment on the women in Trump's sphere as it was on Trump.

"I said it, I was wrong, and I apologize," said Trump immediately afterwards. "I've never said I'm a perfect person, nor pretended to be someone that I'm not."[75] That was all true enough. He also distinguished his behavior from that of Bill Clinton—a credibly accused rapist and a known serial predator, not to mention a travel buddy of Jeffrey Epstein on the "Lolita Express"—and Hillary Clinton, whom Trump accurately accused of having "bullied, attacked, shamed and intimidated [Bill's] victims."

Like most Republicans, I was stunned by what Trump said in the 2005 video. A rural Iowa guy, I never ran in the kind of circles Trump did and never hope to. That said, we were facing a watershed election four weeks later. I knew the way the media worked. I knew they used all their resources to find this tape and then drop it a month before the election in a classic October surprise. I knew had they found a comparable tape about a Democratic candidate, they would have buried it. Four years later, weeks before the 2020 election, Big Media and Big Tech conspired shamelessly to block much more damning evidence about the Biden family, Hunter Biden in particular.

I knew too if the media had their way, they would have anointed Hillary Clinton the next president of the United States. If she became president, we would have lost the Supreme Court for a generation. The pro-life cause would have been doomed. The government would have continued to grow beyond reason. Illegals would have flooded our borders, and Washington would have been sacrificed to the Clinton culture of corruption. In the first few months of the Biden presidency, we are seeing that scenario play out.

For me, supporting Trump was a no-brainer. For Paul Ryan, it was time to bail. The *Politico* headline said it all, "Ryan 'sickened' by Trump, joint appearance scrapped."[76] That joint appearance was to be a fall fest in Elkhorn, Wisconsin, weeks before the election. Wisconsin just happened to be a pivotal battleground state. Ryan was prepared to sacrifice Wisconsin to stay in the good

Rep. Michele Bachmann observes as King points out an inflatable raft manned by two "coyotes" ferrying a pregnant woman across the Rio Grande River during a Border Patrol shift change. Roma, Texas — November 21, 2014

graces of the Washington establishment. His need to seem respectable trumped the need to save Washington from the Clintons.

Vice presidential candidate Mike Pence filled in for Trump at the fall fest. The same establishment that chastised Trump for being sexually crude chastised Pence for being a prude. Pence represented the Trump ticket. So Ryan was still supporting the ticket, more or less, just not the presidential candidate. Ryan was not exactly a subject for an updated version of *Profiles in Courage*. This was not my idea of walking point. Rather, it was a textbook example of fragging a superior officer. This proved to be a frequent tactic used by Republican leadership as the drama unfolded.

Although Ryan withdrew from Congress after the 2017–2018 term, the style of leadership did not change. When the media and the Democrats came for me in 2019, I knew what I was in for.

Republicans did not stand together. Our current leadership team immediately caved to the media pressure and acted to validate if not initiate the false accusations made against me. I was removed so quickly from the committees on which I served I wasn't afforded any opportunity to present the facts. McCarthy still insists he believes in due process—a process I experienced to be more akin to that of Caligula than American jurisprudence.

The incident reminded me of a scene in the Bible, specifically John 11:48–53. Before proceeding, let me clarify I am in no way comparing myself or Donald Trump to Jesus. The Democrats may have thought Obama was the "messiah," but we Republicans knew Trump was definitely *not* the messiah, and Lord knows I am not. What I hope to show is how little human nature has changed over time.

In the scene from John, the chief priests and the Pharisees worried that if Jesus continued inspiring people as he had been, "The Romans will come and take away both our place and our nation." Caiaphas, the high priest, explained it would be better "that one man die for the people, not that the whole nation should perish." Rather than let the Roman authorities crack down on the nation, the chief priests and the Pharisees took business into their own hands, and "from that day on they made plans to put him to death."[77]

The Steering Committee is the House's Sanhedrin, and McCarthy serves as its *Nasi* or president. At a secret location, the January day McCarthy met with me, he made a no doubt extremely disparaging presentation to the Steering Committee calling for my political death sentence. This is not hyperbole. No one has ever been reelected once they have been stripped of their committee assignments. "What cancel culture is about is not criticism. It is about punishment. It is about making a person radioactive. It is about taking away their job," Bari Weiss told Bill Maher on his HBO show. Weiss added, "The writer Jonathan Rauch called it 'social murder.' And I think that's right."[78] Yes, "social murder" sounded just about right to me as well.

Only three others were subjected to this congressional humiliation before me. They were, to a man, convicted federal felons.

And then there is me, accused of no violation of law or rule but summarily pronounced guilty of a thought crime. There is no hard evidence of that "crime" save for the word of one reporter at what Trump accurately calls the "lying *New York Times*."

According to the *Nasi*, the secret Steering Committee voted unanimously to remove me from all my committees. The next day, McCarthy argued before the Republican Conference that I received "due process." He would later argue vigorously how Trump did not receive fair treatment or due process from House Democrats. I agree with that sentiment, but hypocrisy knows no bounds in Washington. Human beings have a nearly infinite capacity to self-justify. The proceedings of McCarthy's Steering Committee made Adam Schiff's basement bunker impeachment hearings look positively Solomonic.

And how did our Romans—the media/Democratic complex—respond to my sacking? As one might expect, they saw my impromptu execution as a sign of weakness to be further exploited against any Republican they chose, the president included.

As we navigated 2020, despite all facts to the contrary, the Democrats continued to play their cards with a heavy hand, the race card most diabolically. Joe Biden was one of the scores of Democrats who continued to insist Trump insinuated the white nationalists were "fine people." Biden, in fact, made the preposterous claim that Trump's response to Charlottesville inspired him to run for president.

"[Trump] said there were 'very fine people in both groups,'" Biden told fairgoers in Iowa two years after the event. "No sitting president has ever said something like that." On an earlier occasion, he claimed, "The President of the United States drew a moral equivalence between those who were spreading hate and those with the courage to stand against it."[79]

On the pre-Covid campaign trail, Biden went even further. Speaking at a predominantly black church in South Carolina—no worries about the separation of church and state on the Left—Biden said, "This president and his, the Ku Klux Klans and the rest of them, they think they've beaten us again. But they have no idea—we're just coming back."[80] Here, Biden shamelessly put the president and the Ku Klux Klan on the same team, all in Biden's alleged effort to "defeat hate."

No, what Biden and the rest of his allies have been doing for the last half century, if not longer, is to incite hatred and fear, all in an effort to scare blacks into voting Democrat. The clumsy Biden could not have made his strategy more obvious than he did in May 2020 when he told a black radio host, "If you have a problem figuring out whether you're for me or Trump, then you ain't black."[81] And Trump's the racist?

CHAPTER EIGHT

2002: HONORING THE GREATEST NATION

On Tuesday, January 15, 2019, Republicans leaders in the House got together with their Democratic peers and ginned up a gratuitous resolution denouncing white supremacy and white nationalism. The very morning the resolution was voted on in the House, January 15, Trip Gabriel and his editors published a lengthy piece assuring House members they should have no second thoughts about condemning me.

Headlined "A Timeline of Steve King's Racist Remarks and Divisive Actions,"[82] the article deserves an honored spot in a media time capsule showing just how thoroughly the *Times* corrupted the language by 2019. As the reader will see, none of my "racist" remarks had anything to do with black-white relations or really with race at all, at least as "race" has been traditionally understood. More perversely still, this whole article was entered into the Congressional Record by Rep. Bobby Rush, a former Black Panther. As they say, you can't make this stuff up.

On that same day, Brit Hume of Fox News stepped up and said about the "Timeline" piece what the House leadership should have said, namely that the racism charge leveled against me was "completely bogus." Hume told Martha McCallum, "[*The Times*] had a big piece that said, his long history of racist comments. I read every one of them. Some of them weren't even about race. Some were about Islam. Islam is not a race. It's a faith." Hume continued:

> *Many of them might be considered insensitive, but they weren't racist. Racism is a very specific thing. It means the belief in the superiority of one race over another. And it is taboo in the United States as well it should be. But we need to be careful flinging this term around because what happened to this tragically is this great triumph of the civil rights movement making racism indefensible and intolerable has been weaponized. And the term now, the adjective racist, is hurled around with abandon.*[83]

Before returning to the House resolution on white supremacy and my response to it, I would like to walk the reader through Gabriel's timeline. It will show just how the progressive activists have changed the rules in America without most people even noticing.

Usually, when Leftists substitute a phony word for a real thing, they do so to deceive their audience. So, for instance, rather than saying they are pro-abortion, which they are, they say instead they are "pro-choice" or in favor of protecting "reproductive rights." Rather than saying they support same-sex marriage, they say they support "marriage equality." They used to be gung-ho in their fight against "global warming," but when the temperatures flatlined, they renamed the crisis "climate change." That way, they were safe if the temperatures went up or down, if it rained too much or too little, if hurricanes happened or didn't happen, if sea levels rose or fell, or if any climate variable strayed from the norm.

"Progressive" is different. This word choice represented an honest relabeling. "Liberals" could have fixed values. They could believe in free speech, innocent until proven guilty, equal justice under the law, freedom of religion and any number of other historic American values. "Progressives" just believe in progress, and they get to determine what progress is, which just means "change" to whatever policies or Leftist dogma is seen to accumulate more power.

To understand them, it is essential to know the Congressional Progressive Caucus's website was originally managed by the Democratic Socialists of America (DSA). The now deleted opening statement read in paraphrase, "We are not Communists. We are socialists. Communists want to nationalize all real property. Socialists just want to nationalize the Fortune 500 companies and manage them for the benefit of the people affected by them."

Half the Democrats in the House are members of the Progressive Caucus. The Pelosi majority would gather at the cliff top of the abyss to Marxism, join hands, sing, "We Are the World," and gleefully leap off the cliff into the abyss. Republicans are more disciplined. They march off the cliff in orderly ranks. The Project Veritas videos on the Bernie Sanders campaign shed light on the progressive movement. A Bernie 2020 field organizer, Kyle Jurek, pretty well summed up the view on the hard Left about where progress can lead:

> *No matter what country and what laws were that exist, they're irrelevant to, there are things greater than those systems, right? There are things that are more important than the Rule of Law in the United States when it comes down to the existence of the human race.*[84]

Of course, not all progressives are as hardcore as Jurek but he was one of at least two Sanders field organizers who were caught on camera recommending gulags for "Nazis"—meaning every Republican—who needed to be "re-educated." As of this writing, no one on the Left or in the mainstream media has denounced these hate-spewing, violence-promoting radicals although their threats came to fruition in the Antifa/Black Lives Matter mayhem of late spring and summer 2020. Orwell may have said more than he knew when he wrote, "If you want a picture of the future, imagine a boot stamping on a human face—forever."[85]

Now I am a different story. You have to wait in line to get to denounce me. According to Gabriel, my offenses dated back to 2002. As a state senator I filed a bill requiring schools to teach that the United States "is the unchallenged greatest nation in the world and that it has derived its strength from . . . Christianity, free enterprise capitalism and Western Civilization." This is the quote as it appeared in the *New York Times*. I have the bill in front of me, which has long been known as the "God and Country" bill. Allow me to quote its actual language:

> *The rules of the state board shall require that schools and school districts emphasize throughout the educational program that the constitutional republic of the United States, of which Iowa is a vital constituent part, was founded upon the guarantees of freedom of religion, the Rule of Law, and equal justice for all, is the unchallenged greatest nation in the world, and has derived its strength from* biblical values *[italics added] and the forces and philosophies of free enterprise capitalism and Western Civilization.*

I am not sure where Gabriel found the word "Christianity," but I am guessing he thought it "divisive" and wanted to preserve the anti-Semitic race card. Although it is undeniable Christianity was and is a major component of our greatness as a nation, I typically use the phrase "Judeo-Christian" to describe our cultural roots as I did in 2012 on the floor of the House. "We derive our strength from free enterprise capitalism, Judeo-Christianity, Western Civilization,"[86] I said at the time.

In that same speech and Mr. Gabriel can check the Congressional Record from February 7, 2012, I made a case for the uniquely non-ethnic quality of the American people. "We may not look like anyone else," I argued, "but underneath whatever those looks might be . . . is an American vigor, an American personality, an American culture, a common sense of history, a can-do spirit." Now, I would ask Mr. Gabriel just exactly how is it racist or divisive to celebrate our common, non-racial culture?

If Gabriel knew his history, he would realize it was America's progressives who led the drive to limit immigration by race and ethnicity. Among the most prominent of socialist eugenicists was Planned Parenthood founder Margaret Sanger. "There is every indication that feeble-mindedness in its protean forms is on the increase, that it has leaped the barriers, and that there is truly, as some of the scientific eugenists [sic] have pointed out, a feeble-minded peril to future generations—unless the feeble-minded are prevented from reproducing their kind," Sanger wrote in her 1922 book, *Pivot of Civilization.*[87]

Famed progressive Supreme Court Judge Oliver Wendell Holmes Jr. agreed. "It is better for all the world," wrote Holmes, "if instead of waiting to execute degenerate offspring for crime, or to let them starve for their imbecility, society can prevent those who are manifestly unfit from continuing their kind."[88] Norman Thomas, six-time presidential candidate of the Socialist Party of America, found "reason for alarm in the high birth rate of definitely inferior stock." Celebrated union leader Samuel Gompers argued that the "persistence of racial characteristics—both mental and moral" made the assimilation of certain ethnic groups impossible.[89]

As a result of this shared anxiety, the Immigration Restriction Act was passed into law in 1924. It should be recalled the act was aimed at Europeans, specifically those from southern and eastern Europe, Italians and Jews most notably. Meanwhile, on the west coast, the McClatchy brothers—C. K. and Valentine, founders of the liberal media empire that bears their name—were also the founders of the Japanese Exclusion League.

In the rush to pull down statues and scrub people from history books, progressives or Leftists such as Sanger and Holmes and Thomas and Gompers and McClatchy always seem to get a pass. Even after the Nazis adapted the Sanger-inspired eugenics movement to their own monstrous ends, the "reproductive rights" crowd remains unapologetic about Sanger.

CHAPTER NINE

2005: ELEVATING THE ENGLISH LANGUAGE

In 2002, as Gabriel pointed out, I also served as "chief sponsor of a law making English the official language of Iowa." I authored the bill, hired a lobbyist, pushed it through the Iowa House and Senate, and Democratic Gov. Tom Vilsack reluctantly signed it into law. Vilsack ran for president unsuccessfully, but Barack Obama, apparently overlooking Vilsack's "racist" embrace of the English language, named him Secretary of Agriculture.

Iowa is now one of thirty-five states to recognize English as its official language. Those states include Hawaii and Illinois; the two states Obama has called home. Are their lawmakers racist as well? I wonder if Gabriel considers Teddy Roosevelt racist. In 1907, while president, he wrote, "We have room for but one language in this country, and that is the English language, for we intend to see that the crucible turns our people out as Americans, of American nationality, and not as dwellers in a polyglot boarding house."[90] Those are my sentiments exactly.

In 2005, as a Congressman, I further offended the sensibilities of the *New York Times* by introducing the English Language Unity Act, a bill designed to make English the official language of the United States. This was not the first effort by a member of Congress to make English the official language. In 1981, Republican

85

Senator Samuel Hayakawa of California—an immigrant and unlikely to be a white nationalist—introduced an amendment to the constitution known simply as, the English Language Amendment (ELA). Although the amendment did not pass, Hayakawa helped found an organization to keep the movement alive. Subsequent bills passed either the House or the Senate, but no bill passed both houses.

Had my bill passed, it would have required all official proceedings of the federal and state governments be conducted in English. It would have also required immigrants hoping to become citizens be tested on their ability to read and generally understand the English language and to understand our founding documents as well. I was able to recruit 163 other sponsors. Were all of them racist?

By making citizenship contingent on learning English, we were giving immigrants an incentive to learn what has become the world's common tongue and the international language of commerce. More than a billion people of all races and nationalities speak it. When a Korean pilot attempts to land at an airport in Kenya, both speak English. It is the only language they share.

Those who immigrate to the United States, Britain, Canada, Australia, New Zealand, or even Ireland (where both Irish and English are recognized as official languages) have a major advantage over immigrants to other countries. They and their children will learn and speak English as their primary language, giving them a clear advantage over non-English speakers. The English language gives access to more information and more knowledge than any other language—by far.

In my work in Haiti, from the elementary school students up to the president, I strongly encouraged everyone to teach and/or learn English. Haiti is the singular place in the hemisphere furthest from first-world status. Virtually all Haitians speak Haitian-Creole, which includes three dialects. The information base accessible through this language is dramatically smaller than through English. Imagine trying to make a success of yourself and your society if you were limited to the French-Creole language on the internet.

Now imagine giving access to all the world's knowledge to every impoverished child in every country. Education through English is the fastest and most effective route to first-world status.

Among those I consider America's "Three Wise Men," economist Thomas Sowell has observed how English provides a common medium of communication among peoples whose respective mother tongues are incomprehensible to one another. To learn Italian helps in Italy. To learn Swedish helps in Sweden. To learn English opens doors not just in the United States but throughout the world.

The progressive enemies of our civilization prefer instead for immigrant groups to hunker down in isolated enclaves speaking their native tongues to each other. The word "Balkanization" nicely describes this state of affairs. Anyone who knows anything about the history of the Balkans knows how well this scenario has played out.

Progressives demand that instead of immigrants adapting to America, America adapt to immigrant groups. Adaptation is more than a little difficult and expensive in a nation that is home to people who speak an estimated three hundred fifty languages among them. In the Washington D.C. area alone, there are some 168 languages spoken. More than one-fourth of the metro area residents speak a language other than English at home. Should we adapt to each of these groups? If we did, translator fees and paperwork would consume municipal budgets.

In November of 2002, when I was first elected to Congress, I had my staff set up a meeting with the leaders of the minority groups in Sioux City. There were fourteen around the table, and we had ninety minutes set aside. I opened by saying I didn't expect any of them voted for me but, regardless, I was their congressman. I told them I called for the meeting to let them know they would have my ear. I then offered to listen to them for the duration of the meeting.

After a short pause, their first words were, "We don't need no English only! We pay our taxes and you have to listen to us!" The meeting went downhill from there even to the extent I was told I needed to learn Central American dialects so I could better understand the culture and needs of the people of Central America.

I didn't comment at any point. I just listened as I said I would. At about the eighty-ninth minute of the meeting I said, "I have taken notes on all your statements. I have heard you, and we don't have time for me to respond to everything that's been said. Instead, I'm going to ask you one question. Please sit up on the front of your chairs. I'm going to say only one word, and I want you to express by your body language your opinion of this one word. Ready?" They signaled they were. I offered the one word.

"Assimilation!"

All fourteen minority community leaders, every one of them, threw themselves back in their chairs, swearing their contempt for the principle: "You're not going to take our culture!" "We are going to speak our language!" "You have to adapt to us!" Progressives have been fomenting this divisive style of "diversity" for a generation or more. As should be obvious from this example, diversity, as currently preached, is not our strength. Diversity can be converted into strength but only by effective assimilation, the glue once binding our nation. As Heather MacDonald said to me, "The Left has made assimilation impossible."

Not too long ago progressives sympathized with those who protested the compromising of our culture. Senator Barack Obama in his 2006 book, *Audacity of Hope*, wrote, "Native-born Americans suspect that it is they, and not the immigrant, who are being forced to adapt. In this way, the immigration debate comes to signify not a loss of jobs but a loss of sovereignty, just one more example—like September 11, avian flu, computer viruses, and factories moving to China—that America seems unable to control its own destiny."[91]

In 2006, Obama did not attribute this apprehension to racism. As he noted, "Many blacks share the same anxieties as many whites about the wave of illegal immigration flooding our Southern border—a sense that what's happening now is fundamentally different from what has gone on before." Blacks also feared and with good reason, this influx "threatens to depress further the wages of blue-collar Americans and put strains on an already overburdened safety net."[92]

The Left's relatively new strategy of isolating immigrants serves a couple of functions, none of them good. For one, it fosters a sense of marginalization and victimhood the Left can exploit for votes. For another, the exploitation becomes easier because these immigrants depend on the advice of politically compromised leaders who are happy to tell them how to vote. The politicians control not just their votes but their livelihoods, even their futures.

My other supposed offense in 2005—it actually occurred in 2007—was to sue the Iowa Secretary of State, Chet Culver, and his successor, Michael Mauro, for posting voting information on an official website in Spanish, Laotian, Bosnian and Vietnamese. As I noted at the time, the Code of Iowa, which I authored and spent six years shepherding into law, mandated all official government communications must be in English. According to Chapter 1.18 of the Iowa Code, "The English language is hereby declared to be the official language of the state of Iowa. All official . . . publications . . . shall be in the English language."

Mauro violated the law. When I asked him and Governor-elect Chet Culver to honor the law, they continued to ignore it. "Unfortunately we can see a pattern for those who hold the title as Iowa's chief elections officer," I said at the time. "Culver was in violation of the law, yet he refused to abide by the law. Mauro continues to be in clear violation of the law. However, neither of these officials is above the law." I won the lawsuit, and Iowa government was enjoined by the courts from further violation of official English.

If the media thought I would back down from my support of the English language after my 2019 political lynching, they were in for a surprise. Just a few weeks after my public rebuke I reintroduced H.R. 997, a bill making English "the official language of the United States." I had four original Republican cosponsors: Reps. Rick Allen of Georgia, Thomas Massie of Kentucky, Tom McClintock of California, and Scott Perry of Pennsylvania. I picked up twenty-two more. This took some courage on all their parts. Being associated with me in February 2019 was not necessarily a good career move. Any idea I supported was now tainted. That was part of my own leadership's plan, and it played right into the hands of the Democrats.

Yet, as the Democrats knew, the rationale for a legislated common language was stronger than ever. For one, the growing Hispanic presence represented the first real threat to a single language and common culture since German immigration threatened the status quo in the eighteenth century. For another, by encouraging assimilation, we discouraged separatist movements and their inevitable hostility to national ideals. As recently as twenty-five years ago, Canada faced a real threat of secession from the French-speaking separatists of Quebec. On October 30, 1995, with a 94 percent voter turnout, the Quebec independence referendum failed on a vote of 50.58 percent to 49.42 percent. It was that close.

A common form of communications currency unites a people. The inability to communicate divides a people. The Latin root of the word "diversity" is *diversus,* meaning "turning in opposite directions." Other words evolving from the Latin root include "different," "divisive," "divergent," and "divorced." In the United States, the English language promotes unity and, yes, "coexistence." Better still, there was nothing coercive about my legislation. No one was *required* to learn English. All requirements were directed at governmental bodies. As a side benefit, this was one of the rare bills that actually had the potential to save the government money.

"The most unifying force in the history of the world has been a common language," I said upon introducing the bill in the previous Congress. "Almost without exception, every nation state, including the Vatican, has at least one official language—except the United States." The English Language Unity Act required all official functions of the United States to be conducted in English. It also mandated officials to encourage the use of English and make it easier for people to learn. Having learned the language, they could better understand our founding documents in English, a required first step to becoming naturalized.

I suppose I should have been relieved the media paid almost no attention to the reintroduction of this bill. The BBC did note I submitted a version of this bill every year since 2005 and all failed to become law. This was true enough, but what was not true was the BBC's insinuation this legislation was "driven mostly by hostility towards immigrants and their languages and cultures." For its inside scoop on the motives of the pro-English movement, the British media turned to America's foremost smear merchant, the Southern Poverty Law Center. "These reactions against people who speak Spanish are probably not new," the SPLC's Heidi Beirich told the BBC. "But Donald Trump unleashed feelings that were not expressed publicly so often before."[93] Yes, of course, it was Donald Trump's fault once again. Even the British could play that game.

CHAPTER TEN

2005: DEFENDING AMERICA'S INTELLECTUAL PROPERTY

In 2005, I listened in dismay to the testimony of those Americans whose patents, trademarks, and copyrights were stolen by China. After meeting with several of these people and talking the problem through, I set up a trip to confront the intellectual property pirates.

I was to visit five cities in China. In the first two cities, I heard the same spiel: The Chinese government was working on the problem; fines were levied; prosecutions were imminent. "Who's in jail now?" I asked. "What are the amounts of the fines? Who gets the money?" No one had answers. The truth was if a state-owned enterprise did pay a fine to the state, that was just money being shifted from China's left pocket to its right.

At each of the first two cities, after we finished our shark fin soup, the host walked around the table with a glass of wine in hand. He toasted each of us with a challenge to chug our glass with the Mandarin word for "bottoms up." Said the host cheerfully, "Ganbei!" We were expected to empty our small glasses while he touched his to his lips. Was this a toast to Chinese piracy? Or was it just faux diplomacy to distract us from noticing the theft of our intellectual property?

Beijing was the third of five cities on the tour. As I sat at the diplomatic table, the spiel began. To no one's surprise, it was almost identical to the first two cities. I decided I didn't need to hear it again and leaned back in my chair with my BlackBerry. I sent a request to Washington: "Draft a bill that requires the U.S. Trade Representative to conduct a study to determine the value of U.S. intellectual property rights pirated by the Chinese. Then require a duty applied to all products imported from China in the amount of their theft, plus an administrative fee. Distribute the proceeds to the rightful intellectual property rights holders." This was a self-enacting, self-enforcing, no-net-cost bill designed to shut down Chinese IP theft. It was a simple solution to a complex problem, but good ideas don't move in Washington without vested interests pushing them, and good ideas rarely appeal to vested interests.

I suspect the Chinese hacked my email but I didn't care. When I returned home, I introduced the bill and accumulated a respectable number of co-sponsors on the merits of the idea. That is until Hollywood and Nashville pushed back, killing the initiative. Had my colleagues been paying attention to the Chinese theft and had they looked to the taxpayers and not to K Street for approval, we might have solved the Chinese IP theft problem well before Donald Trump took office.

Despite the pushback, I re-introduced the bill in every Congress since then so it would be ready when America got ready. Today, U.S. intellectual property is infused into the Chinese economy at a value of more than six hundred billion dollars a year. The Chinese have been using state-sponsored stolen American creativity for free. The goal of this asymmetric warfare is to position China as the dominant world power at our expense and at the expense of Western Civilization. The fear of being called a racist or a xenophobe has silenced far too many of my colleagues.

When I proposed the bill, it made too much sense for the *New York Times* to attack me. After the Gabriel article in January 2019, however, it was open season on yours truly. In August 2019, at an Iowa town hall meeting, I criticized China for its brutal mistreatment of the Uighurs, a predominantly Muslim ethnic group. The *Times* found my attack newsworthy because in listing the ways the Uighurs were being abused—women sterilized, children abducted, populations forced into camps—I noted the Chinese were "trying to force the Muslims to eat pork."

In that Iowa is by far the nation's leading pork-producing state, I added as a comic aside, "That's actually the only part of that that I agree with, is, everybody ought to eat pork . . . you can't be truly happy without bacon." The joke police at the *Times* thought that comment worthy of an article in their august publication. Its unintentional punch line read, "Mr. King, already under siege for his history of racist remarks, drew yet another unwelcome spotlight on himself while breathing new life into a worn Islamophobic riff mocking some Muslims for abstaining from pork."[94] Where to begin?

CHAPTER ELEVEN

2006: DEFINING EVIL

In speaking to a gathering of those opposed to illegal immigration in Las Vegas, I said, "We have a slow motion holocaust on our hands." I was referring to the thousands of deaths caused by criminal aliens in the United States. Trip Gabriel linked my comment to the "Hatewatch" posted by the notorious SPLC slander artists who, in turn, fed off the outrage expressed by the Anti-Defamation League, a Left-leaning Jewish operation only a shade more fair than the SPLC.

Shortly after my speech, ADL's director, Abraham Foxman, sent me a letter saying it was "inappropriate and insensitive" for me "to suggest that the conduct of undocumented individuals in America in any way resembles the systematic, genocidal actions taken by Adolf Hitler and the Nazi Party." Of course, I never said or even implied such a thing. I responded that I used the word "holocaust" in a generic sense, meaning a great destruction, and that I was in no way referring to the *Shoah*, as the Nazi-era Holocaust is known in Hebrew. I have been to Auschwitz and Birkenau, guided by a survivor. I was fully educated before I arrived and the experience was still transformative.

As with all other dictionaries, the Merriam-Webster dictionary distinguishes between "holocaust" and "the Holocaust," the latter being listed third among its definitions. The generic "holocaust" refers to destruction or slaughter on a mass scale.

The Left uses the word "holocaust" to suit its own needs and always with impunity. I remember once listening to NPR and hearing the announcer talk soberly about a "dolphin holocaust." Google "polar bear holocaust," and you may get as many as three thousand hits, the first in the queue being a short video titled, yes, "Polar Bear Holocaust." Even more effectively, the Left has crudely appropriated a word directly related to "the Holocaust" to silence those who challenge the Left's all-but-religious belief in "climate change."

In 2007, a year after I was rebuked for using the word "holocaust," popular liberal columnist Ellen Goodman wrote, "I would like to say we're at a point where global warming is impossible to deny. Let's just say that global warming deniers are now on a par with Holocaust deniers, though one denies the past and the other denies the present and future."[95] There was no liberal uproar, just the opposite. Soon enough "denier" had become the term of art on the Left. Before long, Obama himself was using the word, as he did in a 2015 speech in Alaska, a state that might actually welcome a little global warming.

"We know that human activity is changing the climate," said Obama. "So, the time to heed the critics and cynics is past. The time to plead ignorance is surely past. The deniers are increasingly alone, on their own shrinking island."[96] With Obama's blessing, "denier" joined the long list of one-word slurs—"racist," "sexist," "Islamophobe," "homophobe," "xenophobe"—designed specifically to shut down debate. "The Revolution will be complete when the language is perfect," said Orwell. It amazes me as I write this that weak-kneed Republicans allow the Left to get away with "perfecting" the language.

In his critique, Gabriel challenged not just my use of the word "holocaust" but my numbers as well. I attributed twenty-five deaths a day to criminal aliens. Calling my numbers "unsupported and illogical," Gabriel hammered me over my calculations and cited a *Washington Post* article as his source.

The *Post* headlined its June 2018 article, "The original source for Trump's claim of 63,000 immigrant murders? Bad data from Steve King in 2006." In fact, Trump was responding to an attendee at an event who offered the number sixty-three thousand as those killed by illegal aliens since 9-11, and Trump did not challenge it. This same number was raised earlier at a March 2018 roundtable by Mary Ann Mendoza, whose son Sgt. Brandon Mendoza, was killed in 2014 by a drunk driver. The driver, admitted the *Post*, was "an immigrant in the country illegally who had had previous charges against him dismissed." The *Post*, in turn, traced the 63,000 number back to a blog post of mine from May 1, 2006.

On May 1, 2006— "International Worker's Day" on the Communist calendar—there were marches all across the country demanding amnesty and more for illegal aliens.

Amnesty advocates seldom confess their advocacy. Karl Rove and others pioneered the redefinition of the word in order to justify their attempted circumvention of the Rule of Law. For the purposes of this discussion and, I hope, an accurate and objective national definition of the destructive policy, I offer the definition I have used for more than two decades of public service: immigration *"Amnesty" in the United States is a pardon for immigration law breakers, coupled with the reward of the objective of their crime.* It is the legal equivalent of catching a bank robber on the steps of the bank with a sack full of stolen U.S. currency and saying to him, "I understand why you wanted the bank's money. Go forth on your merry way and you can keep the loot."

At the time I wrote the following:

> *What would that May 1st look like without illegal immigration? There would be no one to smuggle across our southern border the heroin, marijuana, cocaine, and methamphetamines that plague the United States, reducing the U.S. supply of meth that day by 80%. The lives of 12 U.S. citizens would be saved who otherwise die a violent death at the hands of murderous illegal aliens each day. Another 13 Americans would survive who are*

*otherwise killed each day by uninsured drunk-driving
illegals. Our hospital emergency rooms would not be
flooded with everything from gunshot wounds, to anchor
babies, to imported diseases to hangnails, giving American citizens the day off from standing in line behind
illegals. Eight American children would not suffer the
horror as a victim of a sex crime.*

In 2003, as a Member of the House Judiciary Subcommittee
on Immigration, I began to hear testimony from "expert" witnesses.
Invariably, Democrats would put up a witness to testify as to how
many "migrants" died in the Arizona desert in their attempt to steal
into the United States. These are tragic stories, but when I began to
ask this question of all the witnesses, I was thinking about the
legions of illegal aliens who did not die in the desert. I was thinking
about a family friend whose son was murdered by an illegal alien
and all the other sons and daughters, mothers and fathers killed by
illegal aliens. And so I asked, "How many Americans died at the
hands of those who did make it through the desert?"

Of course, none of these expert witnesses knew the answer,
nor had they given it any thought. After several similar hearings,
I found a witness who did have an answer. Mike Cutler is a former
INS (Immigration and Naturalization Service) agent with years of
hands on experience in the front lines. Mike is also a particularly
glib and nimble verbal image artist. When I asked him how many
Americans had died at the hands of those who did make it through
the desert, his first sentence was the same as the others, "I don't
have the answer to that."

Mr. Cutler's second sentence was a stunner, one that galva-
nized my own thinking, "But I can tell you it is in multiples of the
victims of September 11th!" Shortly thereafter, I commissioned
the first of three GAO studies to look into the question. All supported Mr. Cutler's claim. Today, I believe I have lowballed my
estimates of the loss of life in America at the hands of illegal aliens.

Rather than address the larger truth behind my assertions, the
Post's Philip Bump challenged the way I calculated my numbers.

To my critics, Bump and Gabriel included, I say, "What are your numbers? Cite your studies. Let me see your data and calculations." If my critics were to actually get into the arena, and subject themselves to similar scrutiny, I would easily prove their politically correct numbers to be ridiculously irrelevant. A review of the April 2005 Government Accountability Office (GAO) study showing that 28 percent of the inmates in our federal prisons were criminal aliens should be evidence enough. From there the math is easy.

Calculating the numbers of deaths caused by murder by DWI, vehicular homicide, negligent homicide, reckless driving, and especially drug overdose is an inexact science. Attributing those deaths to illegal aliens is more challenging still especially since so many crimes go unsolved. In 2011, I cited the GAO to the effect that there have been 25,064 homicide arrests of criminal aliens between 1955 and 2011. That is at least twenty-five thousand or so homicides that did not have to take place. By enforcing our immigration laws effectively and efficiently, we can save thousands of lives. Immigration law requires deportation of all who are unlawfully present in America. Every crime committed by an illegal alien is 100 percent preventable. Simply deport the deportables, and the problem is solved.

The GAO does not say how many killers were not arrested. For those indifferent to lives lost, we spend roughly $1.4 billion federal tax dollars per year incarcerating criminal aliens.[97] State expenditures are much higher. The Texas Department of Public Safety does a particularly good job tracking and posting the crime committed by illegal immigrants. The numbers are, to say the least, troubling. Lest I be accused of exaggerating, allow me to quote the Texas report on this subject:

Between June 1, 2011 and December 31, 2019, these 211,000 illegal aliens were charged with more than 333,000 criminal offenses which included arrests for 606 homicide charges; 37,128 assault charges; 6,309 burglary charges; 41,605 drug charges; 495 kidnapping charges; 17,475 theft charges; 26,354 obstructing police charges; 1,826 robbery charges; 3,974 sexual assault charges; 5,253 sexual offense charges; and 3,371 weapon charges.[98]

We are talking here about eight-plus years in one state. Each year, on the average, illegals committed seventy murders and nearly five hundred sexual assaults. Murders usually get counted, but in a community undeniably wary of law enforcement, sexual assaults do not. The *Post's* Philip Bump, like many on the Left, takes great glee in challenging me and others who have said that illegal immigrants commit more crime on average than American citizens, but whether they commit more or less is a question that does not concern the scores of people who are murdered and the thousands of girls who are assaulted every year by illegal aliens. Besides, without knowing specifically how many aliens there are in the population, we cannot accurately compare their crime rate to the crime rate of the legal citizens in the areas they inhabit.

In January 2019, President Trump tweeted: "23% of Federal inmates are illegal immigrants. Border arrests are up 240%. In the Great State of Texas, between 2011 & 2018, there were a total of 292,000 crimes by illegal aliens, 539 murders, 32,000 assaults, 3,426 sexual assaults and 3000 weapons charges. Democrats come back!" The *New York Times* responded critically to the tweet, saying the federal numbers were "exaggerated" and the Texas numbers "omitted important context."[99] The media would much rather quibble about numbers than address the slow motion holocaust for which illegal immigrants are responsible.

Deadlier than murderers and drunk drivers are drug dealers. Accidental drug overdose is now America's leading cause of death for those under fifty. More people are dying annually from overdoses than from guns, car accidents, murder, or AIDS. More Americans, in fact, are dying each year from a drug overdose than died in the entire Vietnam War.

There is a lot of blame to go around. The drug companies deserve their share, and the users deserve the lion's share, but there is no denying the role of Mexican cartels in fueling the epidemic.

In the last five years, more than three hundred thousand Americans have died from drug overdoses. The number of those who have died from heroin overdoses just in the last five years exceeds seventy thousand.[100] (The number would be higher still were it not for the widespread use of the antidote Naloxone.)

The great majority of America's heroin, as well as much of its methamphetamine and synthetic opioids, comes across our southern border, and none of it comes across legally. According to multiple drug enforcement interviews and Congressional testimony, 80–90 percent of the illegal drugs consumed in America comes from or through Mexico. When I ask what would happen if all illegal aliens woke up tomorrow morning in their home country, drug enforcement tells me that it would immediately halt virtually all illegal drug trade in America. The illegal drug distribution chain is largely comprised of illegal aliens, and virtually every chain has at least one illegal alien link.

In his acclaimed book *Dreamland,* Sam Quinones, a fluent Spanish speaker, shows how heroin makes its way north from rural Mexico to small-town America. According to Quinones, the cartels focused on cities and towns without an established drug trade. "They used customer service," said Quinones. "They deliver just like pizza delivery, and it really appeals to this new class of addict who were white, really kind of unfamiliar, maybe, a lot of times with the drug world."[101]

On the Mexican end, the cartels exploit young and impoverished men to deliver the drugs, not overly caring whether these "mules" get busted. There are always more young men willing to replace them. This commerce costs lives and erodes communities on both sides of the border, and the American Left remains largely mum about it.

Curiously, progressive politicians talked more about the issue when it was less of a lethal threat than it is today. "Folks, I voted for a fence," Joe Biden told a South Carolina Rotary in 2006. "I voted, unlike most Democrats—and some of you won't like it—I voted for seven hundred miles of fence." The reason why he wanted a fence? Said Biden, "[It] does not have anything to do

Steve King shouldering a 75-pound pack of marijuana that was carried across the border and through the desert by one of hundreds of backpacking smugglers or "burros." Bisbee, Arizona — July 31, 2019

with immigration as much as drugs. And let me tell you something folks, people are driving across that border with tons, tons, hear me, tons of everything from byproducts for methamphetamine to cocaine to heroin and it's all coming up through corrupt Mexico."[102]

The elites can take issue with the word "holocaust" if they want or quibble about just how many people have been killed as a result of illegal immigration, but those who have lost a loved one to murder, vehicular homicide, or heroin have no use for quibbling. To my critics, again, what are your numbers?

CHAPTER TWELVE

2006: BUILDING
THE WALL

In 2006, I alarmed the *New York Times* by presenting a model of a wall that might be built along the border with Mexico to discourage illegal immigration. On an earlier visit to that border, I came to the conclusion we could not stem the flow of illegal immigration until we built a wall. So I designed one and presented my design on the House floor.

For the media elite, it seemed odd, almost comic, that a congressman was prepared not just to talk about building a wall but to actually build one. It would not have seemed funny if they knew anything about my background. In fact, as I told President Trump's chief of staff, Gen. John Kelly, the company I founded in 1975, King Construction, could build a mile a day if given the go-ahead. I was not angling for the work. I just wanted to show that the job could be done.

My path to Congress was an unlikely one. When I started college in the late 1960s at Northwest Missouri State in Maryville, Missouri, I knew I wanted to get a broad education. I studied math, physics, and chemistry, and then settled on biology. I always loved hunting and fishing, the outdoors in general, and I was still the boy who roamed the woods of Coon Grove when I was home.

I decided the one job best suited to my interests was a forest ranger, ideally in Montana. I earlier applied to become a smoke jumper out of Missoula. I didn't get the job but I loved the state. When I wrote a letter to its forestry service, I learned that to have a realistic shot at the forest ranger job I needed to be a resident of Montana and have a degree from a Montana university. With my dream seemingly beyond reach and disillusionment setting in, I shifted gears.

After my junior year, still undecided about my future, I found a summer job working in the construction industry. My job was on the crew breaking out old highway paving. After it was broken up with a huge drop hammer and pushed up into a pile, my job was to climb up into the piles with a cutting torch and cut the tangled rebar so the rubble could be loaded into trucks. Being the "mountain goat" was hard and dangerous and not exactly the objective of my long-term career goals.

The work ethic my father instilled in me, however, served me well. The bosses appreciated my efforts and put me to work on an old dump truck and then on a loader. A huge opportunity presented itself when the company owner, knowing of my fascination with Alaska, chose me to work up there. Green and Groesbeck had a contract to build six hundred miles of right of way, a road and work zone running the length of the Trans-Alaska Pipeline from Fairbanks, north to Milepost Zero at Deadhorse. To put this job in perspective, the town of North Pole, Alaska, is *south* of Fairbanks. At the time the job paid $9.75 an hour, plus overtime, mileage, meals, and room. Just the wage translates today into more than $65 an hour.

The work schedule was seven days a week, twelve hours a day, with periodic R & R back to the lower forty-eight states with travel on the company dime. There would be no skipping out of the contract because management withheld a percentage of your pay to ensure you came back. True, the work was cold, hard, and dangerous. But the money was too good to turn down and good enough to get young men to give up their guns, gambling, whiskey, and women for two years—all of which were prohibited. I calculated if I did two years in Alaska, I would come back, after taxes and expenses, with a hundred thousand dollars in the bank. Not many twenty-two-year-olds could match that, degree or no degree.

Plus, I have always been an adventurer. I read Jack London's *Call of the Wild* and several other similar books, and Alaska just called out to me. Lacking direction and quickly running out of money for school, I decided to skip my senior year and head for the "Last Frontier." As the Johnny Horton song and John Wayne movie went, "Go north to Alaska, North, the rush is on!"

Except it wasn't. A lifetime outdoorsman, I believe in conservation as much as the next guy, but by this time the conservation movement had evolved from protecting the wilderness to sabotaging capitalism. In 1970, the same year as the first "Earth Day," environmentalists persuaded a judge to issue a temporary restraining order shutting the pipeline project down. The 1970s, you will remember was the decade of Arab oil boycotts and endless gas lines. The environmentalists could not have cared less. Our dependence on foreign oil scarcely fazed them. It took the 1973 oil crisis to overcome their resistance to the pipeline, but by that time it was too late for me.

In 1972, I married my lovely high school sweetheart, Marilyn. Needing to keep our marriage strong, I took a job closer to home as superintendent of a construction company. Younger than just about all the workers, I needed to show these guys, all of them tough and seasoned, I was going to work at least as hard as they did, even harder. That dynamic taught me a lot about leadership.

The early 1970s were a rough time to start a marriage. We moved several times and finally found our way to rent a small one-bedroom farmhouse. The company I worked for sold out, but I got a decent-paying job as a dozer operator. Unfortunately, it did not pay enough to send Marilyn back to college to finish her degree. Instead, she worked as a waitress at a steak house for tips and $1.25 an hour, and we struggled along, slowly slipping into debt.

In early 1974, the call came. The pipeline project was a go. I rushed home to tell Marilyn I was heading to Alaska, and I still remember her response. She simply asked, "You like being married?" Marilyn has a way of making decisions instantly, without the pretense of deliberation. I thought she might have been bluffing, but I was unwilling to take the chance, so I will always wonder. I decided staying married was more important than going to Alaska. That very short negotiation sealed my fate. Whatever I was going to accomplish, I was going to accomplish as a blue-collar, family guy in Northwest Iowa. God and Marilyn knew what was best for us.

For all the geographical limits my choices imposed upon me, I was not going to limit myself intellectually. I continued my work in the building trades during the day and I educated myself at night. I read Adam Smith's *Wealth of Nations*, all 1,057 pages, slowly enough to absorb the message. Often I would fall asleep and wake in the morning with a book on my chest. During the day, while building terraces, I reflected on what I read the night before. I never stopped reading and ruminating: history, politics, science, economics, theology, the Bible.

I was hungry to learn it all, that giant, multidimensional spreadsheet called "life." It was not enough for me to be an observer. To make a difference, to fulfill my destiny as a man, I realized I had to participate, to make waves, to strive. So one night after work, I interrupted Marilyn as she was preparing dinner, and said, "Guess what?"

"What?" she said in her flat and bored way.

"Today, I'm a man," I said.

"You've been one for a while," she said. "What else is new?"

"A man takes charge of his destiny," I said. "That's new. I recognize that. I am going to start a business."

For a young guy with no money and no real connections, this was a big step, but I was not going to let life pass me by. I refused to be one of those guys sitting on a rocker fifty years down the road, thinking about all the *woulda, coulda, shoulda beens* passing me by in life. I had to seize the day.

From that moment on, I started planning how I would launch this business. There was a beaten up old Caterpillar D7 bulldozer

I had my eye on, but I knew a negative net worth of five thousand dollars would not exactly make a loan officer smile. Even if I sold everything I had—my pickup, my chainsaw, and my shotgun—I would still have been deep in the red.

Local banker Leo Remmes believed in me. Yes, Virginia, there still are good Democrats. With loan approval in hand, I went across the river into Nebraska to write the check and drag that crippled relic out of the weeds. I arrived home at 1:30 a.m. on a typically steamy August night. The fan was blowing across Marilyn as I shook her awake to share the news.

"I have something to tell you," I said, "I just bought a dozer and started a business!"

"I have something to tell you," said Marilyn. "We're going to have a baby." And so it happened our family and our business began at the same time. Had I known Marilyn was pregnant I might not have taken the plunge, but now I was committed and I knew I had to succeed.

In truth, the dozer was a piece of junk, but after two weeks of welding on it, the parts hung together well enough to allow me to bid on a job. And so King Construction was born, a company whose name was a lot more impressive than its assets. At 7 a.m. sharp on Labor Day, 1975, I fired the dozer up, dropped the blade into the dirt, and started leveling off some ground for a future feedlot. At 10 a.m. the oil pressure gauge plunged to zero and my engine blew. Welcome, Steve, to the world of the entrepreneur!

As a one-man band, I wasn't just the dozer operator. I was the dozer mechanic. Truth be told, with this piece of discount junk, it was more important to be a mechanic than an operator. I borrowed a truck and hauled the dozer back to my front yard, stripped the engine down to the bare block, laid out all the parts, and still could not figure out what was wrong with it. Desperate, I called my friend Floyd Johnson, the neighborhood Cat mechanic. He came out on a Sunday on his own time. After examining all of the parts, he turned to me and said, "Here's your trouble right here." He showed me how the center main bearing had turned on the crankshaft and blocked all the oil to the engine.

Once I got the parts together and started reassembling the engine, it began to rain. The yard was getting sloppy and my tools were getting slippery, but I was determined to get the job done. Marilyn, bless her heart, came out to help me. She was a gamer. Four months pregnant, she stood on the tracks of the dozer, in the rain, with a seven-foot cheater pipe, torquing the head bolts on the D7. How could I not love this woman?

I suppose I could have taken a job with a paycheck and just chugged along. There were times along the way I wished I had. But once I committed, I did not have a fallback position. I had no choice but to solve whatever problems I faced. My advice to any young person starting out: make no provision for failure! If you fail, you should fall flat on your face. Put all of your energy, all your thoughts, all your focus into success.

If I was going to succeed, I had to take whatever I knew and turn it into something successful. Thanks to God and Marilyn, we pulled through, and today my oldest son, David, owns and manages the forty-five-year-old King Construction. It helps to start them young. David's first experience with heavy equipment was *in utero* while his mother torqued head bolts.

In reading a 2018 profile of my colleagues, I learned "the overwhelming majority of members of Congress have a college education. The dominant professions of members are public service/ politics, business, and law." Democrats lean heavily to law. In fact, every Democrat presidential nominee since 1984 went to law school as did every Democrat vice presidential nominee since 1976, except Lloyd Bentsen in 1988. For that matter, the last two Democratic First Ladies prior to 2020 were lawyers, as is Senate leader Chuck Schumer and his predecessor Harry Reid. I doubt if any of them could wield a cheater pipe as well as Marilyn. In fact, I doubt if any of them know what it is.

As for the media, I suspect when they hear the word "dozer" they think of a boring movie. When they hear "Cat" they think of a hipster. Today, most reporters are processed and packaged in liberal journalism schools and dispatched to the nation's newsrooms. These turn a degree to the left with every graduating class.

It didn't use to be this way. Reporters used to be regular Janes and Joes. Many had no college experience at all, but they had a much better feel for the struggles of real people than do the pampered inhabitants of today's newsrooms.

As to Trip Gabriel, I do not know much about his background, but I do know that before the *Times* assigned him to the racism beat, he edited the paper's Sunday and Thursday Styles sections. There, the *Times* tells us, "He introduced the Modern Love column and convinced the *Times* to employ a shopping critic." Presumably he did well enough there that the *Times* promoted him to a Peter Principle position in politics. Love and shopping wouldn't be my first choices to prepare a person for political warfare.

Here is the kind of question Gabriel was assigned to answer when he was the Styles editor. This is not a parody:

> *I am a recent college grad and would love to develop a business style to help me climb the corporate ladder. Toward that end I've been studying how successful men dress. There's this guy—a wildly eccentric Tuscan man, famed for strutting around Manhattan in $10,000 Italian suits while hobnobbing with billionaires who nosh in his restaurant at noontime. He also dons Lucchese cowboy boots almost every day. Is this the kind of style I can adopt and make my own?*[103]

I have a hard time relating to these kinds of anxieties. When I was starting a career in business, my only style worry was whether my welding burned enough holes in the sleeves of my shirt to necessitate cutting them off. And the problem's not just Gabriel. As far as I can tell, just about all the folks at the *Times* have lost touch with the common man. I do not expect them to know any more about building a wall than they know about why a wall must be built.

I know both ends of that question. "I want to put the wall in, and I designed one," I told my colleagues as I presented a small-scale model in 2006. I showed how we could create an efficient,

Second-term Congressman Steve King constructing a model border wall, during a speech, on the floor of the U.S. House of Representatives. Note the coil of "razor wire" on top of the wall—a subject of intense objection by open borders advocates. Years later "razor wire" adorned the perimeter barrier surrounding the U.S. Capitol Complex.—July 11, 2006

cost-effective, slip-form footing aligned flush with the desert floor. Then we bring in precast concrete panels, ten-feet wide, thirteen-and-a-half-feet tall.

I explained it would be essential to put wire on the top of the wall "to provide a disincentive" for people inclined to climb over. I mentioned too how we could electrify this wire with a non-lethal current, a deterrent sure to discourage the more ambitious border crossers. "We do that with livestock all the time," I added.

The beauty of this design, I continued, was it could be deconstructed as easily as it could be constructed. "If somehow they got their—they got their economy working and they got their laws working in Mexico, we could pull this back out as easy as we put it in," I made clear.

The built-in deconstruction potential made my intentions clear. The wall was a response to an existing set of conditions and not a permanent exclusion of a certain race of people. To help make his case that my presentation was racist and/or divisive, Gabriel made no mention of the deconstruction angle. That should not surprise anyone.

Gabriel did, however, take great offense at the electric wiring I proposed to put on the top of the wall while consciously skipping the part in which I said the current would be designed to discourage, not to kill. Just rereading this article makes me realize how routinely reporters distort the news. The title on the YouTube video of the presentation was "Rep. Steve King compares Mexicans to livestock."[104]

In 2017, when I reintroduced this model, the media had eleven years' worth of my comments from which to cherry pick. Here is how Hunter Walker, the White House correspondent for *Yahoo News*, characterized my presentation, "Steve King has a model of the border wall he wants to build to protect our 'superior civilization.'"[105] Using the tried and true tactics of the Leftist media, Hunter Walker mocked American civilization, implying it was inferior to that of Mexico and Central America. Does anyone suppose his disdain for our country will follow him to his grave?

Gabriel routinely referred to me as "a former bulldozer operator." And although I am proud to be one, I do not think Gabriel means the "bulldozer" label as a compliment. During the 2020 campaign, a CNN panel made clear just how deep is the contempt the media and the political class hold for ordinary Americans. The hilarity began when CNN contributor Rick Wilson said, "Donald Trump couldn't find Ukraine on a map if you had the letter 'U' and the picture of an actual physical crane next to it."[106]

Wilson is a Republican political strategist, a classic insider who has made a media career out of bashing Trump and other conservatives. He is also a cofounder of the notorious and now disgraced "Lincoln Project." As you might expect, he is no fan of mine. Five days before the 2018 election, he tweeted, "If Steve King isn't a flaming alt-right adjacent, Neo-Nazi coddling, xenophobic bigot

King, admiring a wall similar to his design. What is this wall doing here if walls don't work? Combined Forces Command - Camp Eggers - Kabul Afghanistan — November 27, 2006

. . . how can you tell?"[107] In the name-calling arena, Wilson can hold his own with the snarkiest of Left-wing trolls. I guess he wasn't too concerned about the Republicans holding the House.

Another panelist was Wajahat Ali, a Muslim lawyer, journalist, and, scarily, "a consultant for the U.S. State Department." Among his other accomplishments, Ali helped launch the anti-American network, Al Jazeera America. Here is what Ali wrote about me in August 2019: "Reminder we've had an open white supremacist in Congress for years: Steve King of Iowa. He admits to believing in the Replacement Theory which is the same ideology of the Christchurch and El Paso terrorists."[108] This is a theory I never heard of until it was assigned to me by the press a year earlier. I described what I saw while walking in Serbia and Croatia with the hordes of migrants who were pouring into Europe and after walking into several European "no-go zones." My experiences just didn't have the feel of a theory, conspiracy or not.

Hosting the panel was CNN's Don Lemon. Lemon majored in journalism at Brooklyn College and jumped right into the business without getting his hands dirty. This lack of real-world experience helps explain his goofy, on-air speculation in March 2014 that a *black hole* may have consumed Malaysia Airlines Flight 370. Lemon knew enough about human nature, however, to open a January 2018 show with the line, "I'm Don Lemon. This is CNN. And the president of the United States is a racist."

Lemon has a habit of cracking up over his own and his guest's witticisms. In 2019, he and guest Kamau Bell, a black comic, had a big laugh over a patently true comment of mine that all cultures are not equal. "He don't know he is being a racist," said Lemon in affected black slang.[109]

In January 2019, Lemon, Wilson, and Ali had a big laugh not just at Donald Trump's expense, but also at the expense of every American who supports Trump. With Lemon laughing hysterically, Wilson mocked "the credulous boomer rube demo that backs Donald Trump." Wilson then switched into what he imagined to be a rural white accent saying, "Donald Trump's the smart one, and y'all—y'all elitists are dumb!" While Lemon continued to laugh, Ali chimed in, also mimicking a rural white person, "You elitists with your geography and your maps and your spelling!"[110]

The truth of the matter is in every political knowledge survey I have seen, Republicans beat Democrats and do much better at identifying foreign countries on a map. This failure to understand Republican competence is not the problem here. The real problem is these are the people who get to call other people "racist."

Said Bell to this point, "The lucky thing is that you don't get to determine if you're racist. That's for other people to determine." Those "other" people include people like Bell, Wilson, Ali, and Lemon, people who have no problem mocking what they freely call "rednecks." These are the people who tell Republicans like Mitt Romney who it is they should denounce. Unfortunately, some Republicans listen.

CHAPTER THIRTEEN

2009: DEFENDING CONSTITUTIONAL GOVERNMENT

In 1998, as an Iowa state senator, I wrote some of the language and actually put the final edits in Iowa's Defense of Marriage Act. I believe our state's was the only Defense of Marriage Act whose language defined marriage as exclusively between one male and one female. Most states were using the language "one man and one woman." Sensing where the culture was heading, I did not want to later debate the definition of what was a man and what was a woman. I was right, by the way. Today, according to health-line.com, the Left has constructed as many as forty-six different genders. I could see the Left was hell-bent on desensitizing Americans not only to the sacredness of marriage but to simple facts of human biology.

There were those who questioned the need for the law, thinking the recorded six thousand–year tradition of male-female marriage immune to the Left's assault. These people were not paying attention to the relentless media propaganda campaign to break down resistance to same-sex "marriage."

In Iowa, progressives did not have to wait for public opinion to come their way. In 2009, the Iowa Supreme Court made their work easy. Indifferent to what Iowans thought, the court gave same-sex couples the legal right to marry. Among the most outrageous statements in *Varnum v. Brien* was this choice morsel declaring homosexuals have the right "to obtain for themselves and for their children the personal and public affirmation that accompanies marriage."[111] The right to "public affirmation!" I remember thinking, *Who else has the right to public affirmation?*

As to homosexuals, I believe their lifestyle is an issue between them and God. To make sure we understood each other, each year in the Iowa Senate we were called upon to talk with the lesbian lobby. Although these meetings were often contentious, I would not duck them. During one of these meetings, I asked the group to appoint a spokesperson so we might have a frank, one-on-one conversation. During that time, she said, "I know what I'm doing is against God's law, but that's between me and God." God love her for saying that because it clarified my convictions on the subject. Her behavior is not for me to condemn. But I will not support an activist court's decision sanctioning an imagined "right" to "public affirmation." Now, if I were to become convinced James Madison secretly inscribed special gay rights into the Constitution and we have just discovered them in this decade, I would be obligated to rethink my position.

Barring that discovery, I must ask, who, in all human history, has had a right to "public affirmation"? Not Jesus. Not Mother Teresa. Not Reverend Billy Graham. Certainly, not me. In fact, I seemed to have the opposite right, the right to be the target of relentless public criticism for having the moral courage to define our culture and to defend Western Civilization. No one has a right to "public affirmation."

Iowa is a wholesome state with strong families and good churches, but the Left got its way due to the Iowa Bar's exclusive grip on judicial appointments. For twelve years, 1999 to 2011, two Democrat Governors, Tom Vilsack and Chet Culver, chose the most liberal and activist judges from the list of three judges proposed by the increasingly liberal Iowa Bar Association for each opening. The unanimous 7–0 decision in *Varnum v. Brien* had less to do with the nature of the law than it did with the politics of the judges. These activist judges aligned their personal, political, and policy preferences with the conclusion they reached, and then rationalized their decision backward through the use of creative, if convoluted, legal jujitsu. Such was the judicial sausage making behind Iowa's same-sex marriage policy.

Still, the media accepted the Supreme Court's decision as if God appointed the seven wise people in black robes. Journalists refused to question the justices' reasoning or their rationale for the simple reason the decision fit the media's agenda.

I actually did see it coming but was unable to stop the judicial activism when it began. For far too long we left the Iowa judicial branch to its own devices. Like too much of government, it grew out of control without the blessing of Iowans or the watchful eye of voters. The judges proved again and again their willful determination to legislate from the bench. I held fast to the belief the Constitution means what it says and what it was understood to mean at the time of ratification by those who voted to ratify it.

After that decision, I wondered how far-reaching the current court could rule if left unchecked. The Iowa Supreme Court justices boldly claimed omnipotent power to imagine and confer constitutional rights that were—in their own words—"at one time unimagined." I argued the judges should be removed on that overreach alone. They somehow managed to find Iowa's Constitution unconstitutional. It was obvious they felt empowered and would continue to follow their whims in future decisions. They would stop, I was convinced, only if the voters threw them out.

On the matter of what the citizens of Iowa could do about their rogue judges, the retention vote was the only recourse. A congressman at the time, I made the case that when judges usurp the letter of the Constitution and the Code of Iowa to suit their tastes, they must be removed from office. The very fact the Iowa Constitution called for a retention vote on a general election ballot meant the citizens' right to check a runaway judicial branch was hard-wired into the Constitution.

The judges did not want to acknowledge that fact. They encouraged rubber stamp acquiescence from the citizens they wanted to rule. The creator of Iowa's same-sex marriage status,

District Court Judge Robert B. Hanson, revealed the political nature of Iowa's judicial system when he called opponents of his ruling "misguided." He continued to characterize a 'no' vote on judicial retention as "an abuse of the system."[112] Elitism and judicial arrogance were on full display.

The judges had so long controlled their own culture they openly considered our constitutionally granted right to vote them out of office abusive. Personally, I did not believe a judge should be allowed to remain on the bench who would turn thousands of years of law and human history on its head by discovering rights "at one time unimagined" in our Constitution. I encouraged my constituents to vote "NO" on all three judges then facing a retention vote. It was my sworn duty to uphold the Constitution. I also believed it was time to put the control of all three branches of government back in the hands of "We the People."

I went on the "Judge Bus Tour" with Tony Perkins, Connie Mackey (a verbal pugilist of the first order), Congressman Louie Gohmert, and others. We traveled all over Iowa and made the constitutional case that the court decision was out of bounds. If same-sex marriage was to be the law of the land, it had to be a legislative decision, not a Supreme Court decision. Former judge and now Congressman Gohmert made the most compelling case. He said, "When I was a judge, I wanted to legislate so I ran for Congress. As a judge, I honored my oath to the Constitution and refrained from legislating from the bench."

About twenty days before the 2010 election, I held a conference meeting with my campaign staff. Our polls showed me way ahead in my race, and other races were trending so quickly in our favor we couldn't keep up with the fast-breaking developments. It made no sense to spend any more money on campaign ads. I asked my staff where they thought we could best invest our campaign reserves.

Receiving no good answer, I said, "Let's go all in on the judges." Silence.

"We can't," said my chief of staff. "It's illegal."

"You have one hour to cite the statute that prohibits us from going against the judges," I responded. "In the meantime, we will buy all the radio ads we can in the state of Iowa." Three of us went to the KCHE radio studio in Cherokee, Iowa, to write and produce a radio ad to blanket the entire state.

The voters came through. In November 2010, three Iowa Supreme Court Judges—Chief Justice Marsha Ternus, Justice Michael Streit, and Justice David L. Baker—were booted off the bench by, on average, a 55–45 percent majority. This was the first time in Iowa history voters ejected Supreme Court justices.

The losing judges thanked those "who worked tirelessly over the past few months to defend Iowa's high-caliber court system against an unprecedented attack by out-of-state special interest groups." The "special interest groups" are the defenders of the most essential and successful institution in all human history, the nuclear family.

This case burned into my memory for one reason beyond the obvious, the insistence that homosexuals have the right to "personal and public affirmation." Although three of the seven judges were gone from the bench, their decision remains. The right to "public affirmation" still stands as judge-made law.

There was no denying that Christians and conservatives were under attack, especially if they were white and male and presumed heterosexual. I choose to be conservative and Christian but progressives use our Christianity against us. As they promote one assault on the culture after another—can pedophilia and polygamy be far behind?—they insist we Christians are trying to impose our values on other people. They twist the First Amendment of the Constitution in support of their argument, as though people of faith were uniquely prohibited from sharing their beliefs.

This is nuts. As John Adams said, "Our Constitution was made only for a moral and religious people. It is wholly inadequate to the government of any other."[113] Adams did not foresee the day when groups allegedly dedicated to protecting constitutional rights such as the ACLU would be debating whether they should defend pedophiles or child pornographers while refusing to defend Christian opponents of same-sex marriage. Unfortunately, ACLU leaders have lost the ability, if they ever had it, to draw logical, moral lines in which some behaviors are considered aberrant and unacceptable.

What the ACLU sees as "rights," homosexual marriage and abortion, for instance, are divorced from any concept of God and/ or Natural Law. The truth is certain behaviors do violate Natural Law. Moral relativists, however, don't care about truth, which is why I feel obliged to resist them wherever they strike.

This nearly constant conflict between morality and amorality calls to mind those immortal words of the Book of Wisdom which shed light on the motives of those who crucified Jesus and those who attack Christian values today: "The wicked say: Let us beset the just one, because he is obnoxious to us; he sets himself against our doings, reproaches us for transgressions of the law and charges us with violations of our training."[114] That about sums up the nature of the conflict. The forces of amorality are motivated to eliminate Christianity to remove all critics of their own wayward behavior.

CHAPTER FOURTEEN

2010: DEFENDING COMMON SENSE

In June 2010, while defending Arizona's immigration laws on the House floor, I said, "Profiling has always been an important component of legitimate law enforcement. If you can't profile someone, you can't use those common sense indicators that are before your very eyes." Having grown up in a law enforcement family surrounded by uniformed men and spending considerable time on the border riding with Border Patrol agents, I was speaking from firsthand experience. I also clarified the agents were "not discriminating against people on the sole basis of race."

Oddly, what Trip Gabriel found racist or divisive was my listing of the *non-racial* variables Border Patrol agents use to profile illegal border crossers. Here is what I said:

> *Those common sense indicators are all kinds of things, from what kind of clothes people wear—my suit, in my case—what kind of shoes people wear, what kind of accent they have, um, the, the type of grooming that they might have, there are all kinds of indicators there and sometimes it's just a sixth sense and they can't put their finger on it.*

Gabriel thought my comments sufficiently racist that they did not need any further clarification. The few who commented on my remarks at the time thought them stupid and funny. The most common response was to isolate one of the indicators and say something like what the *Huffington Post* did in its headline, "Steve King Says Illegal Immigrants Can Be Sussed Out by Footwear, Psychic Powers."[115]

Under pressure from my own party, I refused to back down. Yes, I had a few speaking engagements canceled but that is par for the course. No one, friend or foe, offered anything like constructive criticism of my remarks. There is none really. All law enforcement officers profile. They have to. Otherwise, they would be stopping no one or everyone. The most relevant variables are sex and age. After a violent street crime is committed, for instance, police will look much more carefully at men than at women and more carefully at young men than old men. Shouldn't they? In fact, if you took profiling away from the tools of law enforcement, you couldn't describe a criminal in any way whatsoever.

Over the years I have continued to defend profiling. "The fact that liberals have risen to attack me and call me names without rebutting my assertions concedes my point," I said at the time. "When they start calling you names, you know they've lost the argument."

In 2017, I found myself arguing the obvious with CNN's Chris Cuomo. Our talk about profiling was part of a larger discussion on Arizona's famed sheriff, Joe Arapaio. Days earlier President Trump pardoned Arapaio who was convicted on contempt of court charges. "Profiling is wrong," said Cuomo. "It is found wrong under the law. It is found wrong as a practice by the Justice Department. That is what they told Joe Arapaio he was doing and they said stop it."

"I don't agree," I responded.

"What don't you agree with?" said Cuomo who seemed shocked by my answer. I shocked him further by saying, "I don't agree that profiling is wrong."

For Cuomo this was heresy. I explained, "Racial profiling set by itself is wrong."[116] The same is true of ethnic profiling, but as one variable among many, either was permissible. If Arpaio's task was to round up illegal aliens near the Mexican border, how could he not factor ethnicity into the larger profile? I should have asked Cuomo what indicators he would look for if he were a border agent, but I am afraid he is too sensitive to answer. This is the same guy who, when called "Fredo," responded that Fredo was "like the n-word for us." No, Chris, "Fredo" is the universal word for an insecure, lesser brother.

CHAPTER FIFTEEN

2011: REVIVING A DYING CIVILIZATION

In 2011, I made a speech on the House floor opposing the contraceptive mandate in the inaptly named Patient Protection and Affordable Care Act, a.k.a., ObamaCare. Here is part of what I said, the part Gabriel reproduced in his "Timeline" article: "Preventing babies being born is not medicine. That's not constructive to our culture and our civilization. If we let our birthrate get down below the replacement rate, we're a dying civilization."

In reading the selection of this passage by the *Times*, I feel like I'm playing some version of "Where's Waldo?" Maybe I am being dense, but I do not see how it is divisive to encourage families to have children or to discourage governments from taxing its citizens to fund the eventual extinction of their civilization.

Still hard to understand? Taiwan has a total fertility rate of 1.0 babies per woman. At that rate, the population is reduced by roughly 50 percent every fifty-five years. Seven hundred years later, the last surviving Taiwanese woman would reach menopause. Of course, centuries before that date, their country and civilization will have collapsed. The U.S. total fertility rate is 1.73 babies per woman and the break even, no net loss of population, total fertility rate is generally considered to be 2.15 babies per woman.

I am not sure which part of that statement Trip Gabriel found racist and/or divisive. He offered no commentary at all as though my comment was sufficiently offensive and thus unworthy of explanation. I am not even sure where Gabriel found this quote as his article represents the rare time anyone in the media commented on it.

As to its racist quotient, I found a few pundits who were willing to interpret what I said to fit their preconceptions. One was a woman named Ajah Hales writing for an online publication with "Injustice" in its title. Not one for subtlety, Ms. Hales titled her article, "No Country for Old (White) Men."[117] She began the article with the following quote in large bold letters, "We must secure the existence of our people and a future for White children."

Hales then claimed these words "sound like a tweet written by US Representative Steve King or the current occupant of the White House." Apparently, she could not bring herself to utter Trump's name. But no, President Trump never said this and I never thought anything of the kind. The fellow who made this comment was David Lane, "a white identity extremist and terrorist."

I had never heard of the guy, but I was curious to know whom Ms. Hale was comparing me to. It turns out that in 1984 Lane achieved the notoriety he was looking for when he shot and killed Jewish radio host Alan Berg. That was thirty-five years prior to the article. Lane died in 2007, twelve years before Hales's article. This is how deep she had to plunge into the Southern Poverty Law Center's (SPLC) archives to find a suitable—in her mind—point of comparison.

According to the SPLC, "Lane first became disgusted with Christianity and bored with the idea of Jesus Christ while traveling from parish to parish with his adoptive parents. As a child, he was strangely obsessed with Adolf Hitler and National Socialism and often impersonated the flat-hand salute while playing World War II games with his brother."[118] Let's see, Lane hated everything I stand for—God, country, you name it. And Hales had the nerve to think I identified with him? These people are sick. They really are. We know the Lanes of the world are sick, but we need to recognize people like Hales are as sick and as obsessed as the Lanes are. They need help.

Yes, words do matter. That is essentially the theme of this book. In fact, I write this book in part to show just how routinely and purposefully the Left twists the words of its political foes to damage them and eventually silence them. Consider my quote at the top of the chapter, "Preventing babies being born is not medicine." As I noted, Gabriel added no commentary. That job was left to the caption writer. Beneath a photo of me holding about a six-foot length of the nearly half mile long Affordable Care Act, the caption reads, "Mr. King has rallied against contraception coverage, saying that birth control is 'not constructive to our culture and our civilization.'"

The *New York Times* is considered by many to be the "paper of record." I wrote and spoke a good deal about the legislative disaster known as the Affordable Care Act. In fact, no one has uttered the word "ObamaCare" into the Congressional Record nearly as many times as I have. I made it clear on any number of occasions, despite all the fiscal and policy problems surrounding the act, the most important reason for pursuing repeal is the law was blatantly unconstitutional. The individual mandate was offensive enough, but by imposing progressive rules and regulations on the private sector, the government was intervening in the personal lives of private citizens in ways that would have horrified our Founding Fathers.

On the House floor in the summer of 2011 I made my objections clear. When read in context you will see how willfully the *Times* caption writer misrepresented what I said:

> *We have people that are single. We have people that are past reproductive age. We have priests that are celibate. All of them, paying insurance premiums that cover contraceptives so that somebody else doesn't have to pay the full fare of that? And they've called it preventative medicine. Preventative medicine. Well if you applied that preventative medicine universally what you end up with*

is you've prevented a generation. Preventing babies from being born is not medicine. That's not—that's not constructive to our culture and our civilization. If we let our birthrate get down below replacement rate, we're a dying civilization.

The chart below shows the declining total fertility rate in the U.S. We are now below replacement, proving I was 100 percent right.

To read the caption, however, you would think I wanted to ban birth control because "birth control is not constructive to our culture and our civilization." How individual families handle their own reproductive plans is their business. I have never said or implied otherwise. No, what I clearly said is government policies encouraging birth control lead to below replacement birth rates.

As a champion of Western Civilization, I hope to see our culture preserved and strengthened. Japan and most European countries are now struggling with the demographic fallout following the failure of their citizens to have enough children to replace those who are dying off. No sane nation wants to see its civilization die. Even China had to abandon its one-child policy.

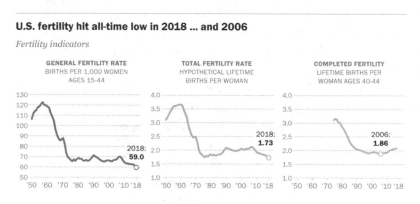

U.S. fertility hit all-time low in 2018 ... and 2006

Fertility indicators

Note: 2018 data are preliminary. Where necessary, TFR and completed fertility values are interpolated. Completed fertility data available from 1976 to 2016 only. All values based upon live births.
Source: Data for GFR obtained from National Center for Health Statistics and Heuser (1976); for completed fertility, U.S. Census Bureau, Current Population Survey; for TFR, National Center for Health Statistics.

PEW RESEARCH CENTER

In her 2011 *HuffPost* article covering my speech, Laura Bassett showed just how the media conspire to kill the messenger lest citizens begin to hear the message. The article began rationally enough. Bassett wrote that requiring health insurers to cover birth control, including abortifacient drugs, with no co-pays has "been controversial for a number of reasons, ranging from cost issues to moral objections." This is true. People voiced serious objections, as well they should have for both moral and fiscal reasons.

Yet when she came to summarizing my speech, Bassett waxed hyperbolic, if not hysterical: "Rep. Steve King (R-Iowa) expressed a fairly extreme concern on the House Floor Monday night about the expanded preventative health coverage: offering free birth control to women could eventually kill off the entire human species."[119]

HuffPost takes itself seriously. AOL owns the publication and uses its content in its news feeds. Millions of people are exposed to that content daily. There is not a hint of satire in Bassett's article, and yet she has me saying that offering free birth control could "kill off the entire human species." No, Angela, that won't happen if for no other reason than once a civilization starts to collapse, birth control will no longer be free.

It is axiomatically true that when a country imports even a single immigrant from a foreign culture, the foreign culture is imported along with the individual. It is also true a foreign born individual can effectively be assimilated into the larger culture. It is even truer their children and grandchildren increasingly adopt the ways of the host culture. But when the host country is replete with scattered and growing ethnic enclaves, the newly arriving immigrant generally migrates to an enclave of like kind.

The result is at best a delay in assimilation, at worst, the growth of permanent, isolated, ethnic enclaves. Ethnic "leaders" draw their power from the isolation and increasing dependence of those within the enclave. To sustain that power, leaders tend to ally themselves with external ideologues who reinforce their desire to remain separate and who demand the majority culture adapt to that separateness.

Each year, in America, we issue about a million green cards and abort about a million innocent babies, a one-for-one cultural exchange at the cost of our nation's soul. Add to that number the estimated 750,000 anchor babies born to parents here illegally and the annual influx of about a million or so new illegals. According to the most recently reported data, some 3.79 million American babies were born in the prior year, about three million total if you exclude the anchor babies.

Pick your number but, rounded to the nearest million, about three million people arrive each year who don't share our culture, which is only barely offset by the three million new American babies who may share our culture. This is still another one-for-one trade-off at the cost of America's cultural continuity. Add to this equation the millions of young Leftists churned out by our educational establishments who are taught to reject everything America stands for: our Constitution, the Rule of Law, free enterprise, freedom of speech, and Western Civilization writ large. To me, this looks like the formula for a declining civilization. Does this witches' brew call for moderation and silence? I don't think so. To remind you of the words of abolitionist William Lloyd Garrison, "I am in earnest—I will not equivocate—I will not excuse—I will not retreat a single inch—AND I WILL BE HEARD."

CHAPTER SIXTEEN

2012: FIGHTING FOR LIFE

For years, the Democrats and their media allies have been pushing the narrative, in spite of all evidence to the contrary; Republicans are waging a war on women. On one front in that war Republicans are allegedly trying to take away a woman's right to birth control. Given that an estimated 98 percent of sexually active women have used some form of birth control, this would not be a politically wise position. If, in fact, Republicans were seriously advancing a ban on birth control, the party would not survive the next election cycle.

The media want women to think otherwise. In a classic example, during the 2012 primary season, ABC moderator and former Clinton hack George Stephanopoulos asked Mitt Romney out of the blue, "Governor Romney, do you believe that states have the right to ban contraception? Or is that trumped by a constitutional right to privacy?"[120]

The question stunned Romney. He was not the most socially conservative candidate on stage nor the most constitutionally savvy. He handled the question as well as he was equipped to. "George, this is an unusual topic that you're raising," Romney answered: "Do states have a right to ban contraception? I can't imagine a state banning contraception. I can't imagine the circumstances where a state would want to do so." As Romney implied, the possibility was so far beyond the range of likelihood it was not even worth talking about.

Stephanopoulos persisted nonetheless and Romney responded, "George, I don't know if the state has a right to ban contraception, no state wants to!" Romney shot back. "The idea of you putting forward things that states *might* want to do, that no state wants to do, and then asking me whether they can do it or not is kind of a silly thing." Stephanopoulos was not put off. He kept demanding Romney give a yes or no answer and concluded saying, "I understand that, but you're still, you've given two answers to the question."

Unfortunately, the strategy worked. Many of the next day's headlines made Romney out to look confused and uncertain. "GOP debate: Mitt Romney grows foggy on contraception," said the *Los Angeles Times*.[121] *U.S. News and World Report* offered up the outrageous headline, "Mitt Romney and the GOP's War on Birth Control." What "moderates" like Romney discover—and then inevitably forget—is the closer they come to seizing power, the more likely the media are to treat them like conservatives. This means, of course, the media grant themselves the license to redefine everything a conservative says.

Having served as cannon fodder in the imagined "war on women" in April 2012, Mitt Romney should have been sensitive to other designated casualties later during that same election cycle. Spoiler alert: he wasn't. On August 7, 2012, Rep. Todd Akin, a good friend and fellow conservative from Missouri, won an upset victory in a tough three-way Republican primary for the U.S. Senate and turned his attention toward incumbent Democrat Claire McCaskill, a vulnerable two-term Democrat.

If "moderate" Republicans object to President Trump because of his allegedly lax morals, they object to people like Akin, a serious Christian and constitutionalist, for just the opposite reason. Akin takes his faith seriously. On the life issue, Akin has always been out front. When the March for Life is held each January, Akin has been there to greet the marchers.

Through his sheer straightforwardness, Todd Akin was the kind of congressman who made moderate Republicans uncomfortable. Until he ran for Senate, however, Akin did not pose enough of a threat to warrant the attention of the Left or of the Republican establishment. That all changed the moment he won the Senate primary. A father of six—two of them girls—Akin pasted a big fat "kick me" sign on his back.

On Friday, August 17, Akin sat down for an interview in the studios of a St. Louis-area TV-station. The interview was to be aired on a local Sunday show hosted by Charles Jaco, a predictably liberal reporter. Like me, Akin sensed the purpose of the interview was to trap him into saying something McCaskill could use against him.

Later, people faulted Akin as they faulted me for doing an interview with a suspected enemy, but Akin could not hope to win against a well-known politician like McCaskill unless people got to know him. In that regard, there is no medium like television. Plus, he had spoken enough about abortion over the years to anticipate the likely traps.

From the beginning of the interview, Jaco attempted to corner Akin on a whole variety of controversial issues and Akin maneuvered deftly around them all. Although Akin was as outspoken as anyone in Congress, he understood the current media environment has a low tolerance for candor.

With the phony war on women being reported as real by just about every media pundit left of Rush Limbaugh, Jaco tried to lure Akin into providing some evidence of his hostility toward women. Although a U.S. Senator has little input on the abortion question, Jaco asked Akin if there were any circumstances in which he thought abortion should be legal. Like almost all pro-lifers Akin believed an abortion could be justified to save a mother's life—a situation that almost never occurs in real life—so Jaco had to dig deeper if he hoped to do any damage.

He went for the most sensitive question of all. "What about in the case of rape?" said Jaco. "Should it be legal or not?" Akin chose not to duck this question. "If it's a legitimate rape," he said, "the female body has ways to try to shut that whole thing down. But let's assume that maybe that didn't work or something. You know, I think there should be some punishment, but the punishment ought to be on the rapist and not attacking the child."[122]

What's weird in watching this video from a distance is Jaco's response. In context, he thought Akin dodged the bullet. Jaco would be hard pressed to argue against punishing the rapist. He accepted Akin's answer without a challenge and moved on to the next question. "Let's go to the economy," said Jaco. The Left-wing blogs ridiculed Jaco for missing a career-making opportunity, but unlike the rest of the media he heard Akin's comment in context.

The Jaco Report aired on Sunday morning. Few watched, but it only took one observer from the McCaskill camp to ruin Akin's career. Within hours of the video's posting online, Twitter lit up. Leftist bloggers shared it with their allies in the major media, and even before the 5 o'clock news aired that Sunday, McCaskill was expressing her outrage on national television. "I was stunned by what he said and how he said it," said McCaskill. "But it opened a window into his mind and showed his beliefs. And I'm very familiar with a long list of items where Congressman Akin is outside the mainstream."[123]

Outside the mainstream? When you consider the "mainstream" condones the destruction in the womb of perfectly healthy unborn babies until the moment of birth—or even beyond—outside the mainstream is where any rational and moral person ought to be.

In his book *Firing Back*, Akin highlights one of the great ironies of his demise. The same people who were designating him the Osama bin Laden of the Republican war on women and demanding his withdrawal from the race were two weeks away from greeting Bill Clinton as a champion of women at the Democratic National Convention. Akin's sin was to make a comment about rape that was at worst a little awkward. Bill Clinton, on the other hand, was credibly accused of rape by at least two women and of sexual assault by many more. Lying about his conquests got Clinton impeached and disbarred. Yet, Hillary stood by her man, her power source. Had she unplugged from him, at the time, her political lights would have dimmed beyond recognition.

At that same 2012 Democratic Convention, the delegates honored the memory of a man whose sexual exploits rivaled those of Bill Clinton. Alone with a young staffer, driving off a bridge, he abandoned her to drown in his car. Unrepentant, Senator Edward Kennedy continued his well-documented lewd and lascivious behavior for years. In 1991, Kennedy took his son Patrick and his nephew William out drinking on a Good Friday night—sure, why not Good Friday?—in Palm Beach. The three inebriated fellows picked up a couple of young women and brought them back to Ted's mansion. When drunken Uncle Ted wandered without pants into the living room, one of the two fled in panic, leaving the other woman at the mercy of William Kennedy Smith whom she would accuse of rape. Since Democrats only "believe the woman" when a woman is accusing Republicans, the Kennedys hired the best lawyers for William and cheered when he was acquitted.

Ignoring the history of Clinton and Kennedy among others, the Democrats and their friends in the media demanded Akin withdraw from the race. If the Republican establishment forced Akin to withdraw, McCaskill would have won in a walk. I know rank-and-file Republicans well enough to understand how they would have reacted to some "safe" candidate hand-picked by the leadership. I came promptly to Akin's defense.

"Todd Akin is a strong Christian man with a wonderful family," I told CBS News. "I think this election should be about: How did Todd Akin vote? What did he vote for? What did he stand for?"[124] I argued how the Democrats were substituting personal petty attacks for policy debates and to focus on one single, easily misconstrued phrase was wrong. "He is my friend going in," I said, "and he will be my friend coming out."

The attack on Akin in 2012 almost perfectly prefigured the attack on me in 2019. The strategy was right out of the Saul Alinsky *Rules for Radicals* playbook: "Pick the target, freeze it, personalize it, and polarize it."[125] This has been effectively summarized in recent years as, "Cut off the support network and isolate the target from sympathy. Go after people and not institutions; people hurt faster than institutions."

To make Akin look like a callous buffoon, the media had to twist what he actually said. They made this job easier for themselves by attacking those like me who defended Akin. The day after Akin's statement and its distortions hit the press, I faced a press gaggle in LeMars, Iowa. There, a young reporter repeatedly posed a question. It was unintelligible to me in the noisy setting, but I could hear the word "rape." I gave a truthful and, I think, a deft answer: "That's nothing that's been brought to me in any personal way, but I'm open to discussion on the matter." The press turned that answer into, "Steve King Never Heard of Anyone Getting Pregnant by Statutory Rape."[126] If that were true, there wouldn't be millions of schoolgirls on contraceptives. There was no way to see that one coming!

Now, said *Politico*, I was "taking heat" over my own comments. "The liberal press and their allies have again twisted my words," *Politico* quoted me as saying, "I never said, nor do I believe, a woman, including minors, cannot get pregnant from rape, statutory rape or incest."[127] The fact is, though, that Akin never said a woman could not get pregnant from rape. He said, "The female body has ways to try to shut that whole thing down."

Akin might have spoken more artfully, but he has a case. Just google the phrases "stress" and "pregnancy," and you will see literally thousands of articles all making the same point: "stress can influence the chance of conception." Researchers disagree on the exact nature of the relationship between stress and pregnancy, but all seem to agree it has a negative effect. Akin seems to have overestimated the effect, but he knew even in an event as stressful as rape, stress does not reliably prevent pregnancy. His next sentence confirms as much: "But let's assume that maybe that *didn't work* or something." In other words, let's presume the stress of the rape did not prevent conception.

Akin was no fool. He had at least two young people conceived in rape working on his campaign. The final sentence in his notorious comment confirms his belief that a child can result from rape.

"You know, I think there should be some punishment, but the punishment ought to be on the rapist and not attacking the child." He acknowledged here that rape could result in a child.

Having picked the target, the Left's next step was to polarize it. The media long ago perfected this tactic: isolate some outspoken conservative and then find establishment Republicans to denounce him or her. The media did not have to look hard to find a candidate. In fact, they found *the* candidate, Mitt Romney, then as now a reliable squish. On that Sunday evening, Romney said, "Congressman's Akin comments on rape are insulting, inexcusable, and, frankly, wrong. Like millions of other Americans, we found them to be offensive."[128] Left unsaid by Romney or the *Post* is what made Akin's remark "offensive."

That did not much matter to those Republicans scrambling to distance themselves from Akin. Sen. Scott Brown of Massachusetts put out a statement saying, "Not only should he apologize, but I believe Rep. Akin's statement was so far out of bounds that he should resign the nomination for US Senate in Missouri." Sen. Ron Johnson of Wisconsin, who supported one of Akins's primary opponents, tweeted, "Todd Akin's statements are reprehensible and inexcusable. He should step aside today for the good of the nation."

Republicans could not volunteer fast enough for the Akin firing squad. "Over the next twenty-four hours, Congressman Akin should carefully consider what is best for him, his family, the Republican Party, and the values that he cares about and has fought for throughout his career in public service," said National Republican Senatorial Committee Chairman, Senator John Cornyn of Texas.[129]

If the *Washington Post* was willing to acknowledge Akin implied rape "rarely" resulted in pregnancy, the Democratic National Committee had no such scruples. The DNC promptly sent out an email blast claiming Akin "thinks that victims of 'legitimate rape' don't get pregnant because 'the female body has ways to try to shut that whole thing down.'"

We were polling my own very intense race the Sunday, Monday, and Tuesday of the Akin firestorm. Romney attacked Todd

Akin and I defended him. Both Romney and I saw our poll numbers drop twelve points overnight. Heads up, Mitt. Your virtue signaling at the expense of Todd Akin hurt all Republicans, regardless where we were on the political spectrum.

This was all unnecessary. Democrats handed Republican nominee Romney a huge opening and he should have charged in immediately. Akin wished Romney would have said the following: "A credibly accused rapist is giving the keynote speech at the Democratic convention in two weeks, and you want me to denounce a decent, God-fearing man for his inelegant comments about rape? No, not happening, and if the truth hurts, put some ice on it."[130] The "ice" is a reference to Bill Clinton's well-known final comment to his alleged rape victim, Juanita Broaddrick. Clinton's reported M.O. was to bite his victim's lip to subdue her. I believe Mitt Romney could have won the election in 2012, as I did, had he put the accusations against Akin into that context.

Akin apologized under duress, which he later conceded was a mistake, but he hung tough and refused to drop out. Running in a state growing redder by the year, Akin had a fighting chance. In fact, as the campaign came down to its final weeks, Akin narrowed the gap to within a few percentage points of McCaskill. Growing anxious, the McCaskill camp ran a TV ad so deadly, wrote Akin, "that it almost made me rethink who *I* was voting for." The ad featured Romney, Paul Ryan, John McCain, and a few Missouri moderates bashing Akin. The ad closed with a video clip of Romney standing next to Ryan and saying, "It was offensive. He should step out of the race." That ad was all it took. Romney carried the state by ten points. Akin lost by fifteen. His political career was finished.[131]

In 2020, for the first time in the March for Life's forty-seven-year history, an American president addressed the crowd. The five Republican presidents from Nixon to George W. Bush who had the opportunity to attend did not. In a *Washington Post* column, former Bush speechwriter Marc Thiessen expressed his wonder at Trump's gesture. In doing so, he expressed a truth rarely heard from someone inside the Republican establishment.

"While Republican presidential candidates couldn't win the nomination without declaring themselves pro-life," Thiessen wrote, "the GOP establishment not-so-secretly loathed pro-lifers. The prevailing attitude was: There they go again, making people uncomfortable by talking about abortion."[132]

On the subject of life, I have long been one of those people who make people uncomfortable by talking about abortion. For me the moment of enlightenment came when I saw my firstborn son more than forty years ago. As I held that nearly nine-pound, fresh-born miracle in my arms, I wondered at God's awesome creation. There was an aura about David that mesmerized me.

How, I wondered, could anyone take David's life during his first hour of breath? I wondered, too, how anyone could take his life the minute *before* he was born, the hour, the day, week, month, or trimester(s) before he was born. In a matter of seconds, I understood this profound miracle in my arms had a distinct beginning, a moment his miraculous life began. Sometime later, I began to contemplate when it was God placed David's soul into his being. I came to believe it was the moment of conception, more technically the instant of fertilization.

I had an unusual background for a pro-life congressman. I got involved in politics through my ownership of a construction company and my subsequent involvement with the Iowa Land Improvement Contractors' Association. My pro-life involvement came later. One day I was down in the state capital lobbying a state senator. I don't remember exactly the issue, but it was an unusual one in need of some explanation. As I was talking to the senator out in the rotunda, I saw his eyes glaze over like those of a dead fish. I realized I lost him. He was not listening to me. He was just marking time until I went away.

I thought about snapping my fingers in front of his face and starting my argument from scratch, but that would have done no good because the senator simply didn't care. I just stopped in midsentence, walked out of the capital, got into my old pickup, and drove home thinking about the people who represent us.

My issue, I saw, was inconsequential compared to the life issues then being debated, but many of our legislatures were no more attentive to life than they were to my issue. At the time I was working with Nancy Streck, a wonderful, glowing, fiery, red-haired Christian conservative with a marked-up, seriously worn-out Bible. She was watching what was going on in the state legislature and let me know about the parental notification bill then being reviewed in the Iowa State Senate. The bill required a "parent" be notified before the baby of a minor could be aborted. The bill did not require parental consent, just notification.

As the bill stood, it defined "parent" as an actual parent, a legal guardian, a grandparent, an aunt, an uncle, brother or sister in the whole or half blood. When I read the bill, it lit me up. I said immediately of the "definition" of parent, "They left out neighbor, friend, family cat, or family dog!" This was a life-or-death decision and yet we were prepared to condemn the unborn child of a minor with a certified letter to a half-sister in another state who might not have even met her pregnant relative and could have been a minor herself. So I wrote a letter and faxed it to my state senator, Wayne Bennett.

Bennett was in office twenty-three years by this time. In the letter, I asked Senator Bennett to support an amendment defining "parent" as either a parent or a legal guardian. Later that day and to his credit, Bennett called me. To his discredit, he told me he already voted against the amendment. Worse, he could not even rationally defend his decision. Like the eyes-glazed-over senator in the rotunda, I learned Bennett didn't care about or understand this profoundly moral issue, the rare issue in the Iowa legislature addressing the sacredness of human life and death. He told me, "That's not the people I vote with."

I knew right away we needed a new state senator. I approached a friend and asked if he would consider running. He said no but suggested I run. Other friends gave me the same response. *Why don't you run?* After several of these exchanges, I had an organically formed "kitchen cabinet" and eventually allowed its members to convince me I should be the candidate. In February 1996, I announced my candidacy and registered for the June primary. In the months to come I visited all fifty towns in the senate district and beat Bennett two-to-one in the primary and three-to-one in his home county. In November, I beat Democrat Eileen Heiden by a comparable margin, and my political career was born.

Throughout my career, the transgression that struck me as most offensive remained abortion. "Life" for me was and is the issue of issues. Our Founding Fathers recognized its importance. In the Declaration of Independence, they enshrined the "right to life, liberty, and the pursuit of happiness" as prioritized rights. They didn't pull those three rights out of a grab bag and randomly put them into the Declaration. They prioritized them because without life there is no other right. Yes, we have a right to liberty and the pursuit of happiness. Both are important, especially as the Founders envisioned "happiness," the freedom and even obligation to develop all our gifts to the fullest. But we cannot trample on someone's right to life to assure our liberty or happiness. Life trumps them both, always has, and always will. My close friend and glorious pro-life warrior, the late Henry Hyde, had this to say:

> *When the time comes, as it surely will, when we face that awesome moment, the final judgment, I've often thought, as Fulton Sheen wrote, that it is a terrible moment of loneliness. You have no advocates, you are there alone standing before God and a terror will rip through your soul like nothing you can imagine. But I really think that those in the pro-life movement will not be alone. I think there will be a chorus of voices that have never been heard in this world but are heard beautifully and clearly in the next world and they will plead for everyone who has been in this movement. They will say to God, "Spare him because he loved us," and God will look at you and say not, "Did you succeed?" but "Did you try?"*[133]

CHAPTER SEVENTEEN

2012: REBUTTING THE LEFT'S SLANDER

In 2012, I appeared on a panel at the Conservative Political Action Conference, CPAC, a mainstream event attracting Republicans of all stripes, including presidents. Also on this panel was Peter Brimelow, a man Trip Gabriel described as a "white nationalist." Appearing with Brimelow was offense number one for me. Before I get to number two, I should note Brimelow sued the *Times* for Gabriel's description of him as a "white nationalist" in the very January 15, 2019 "Timeline" article in which Gabriel also maligned me.

In an earlier edition, the *Times* apparently referred to Brimelow as an "open white nationalist" before performing what Brimelow calls "a stealth edit." In the five-million-dollar suit, Brimelow claims to have been "injured in his good name, fame, credit, profession, and reputation as a man, and in his various public and private positions, callings, and lines of endeavor, and has been held up to public ridicule before his acquaintances and the public, and to suffer the loss of prestige and standing in his community and elsewhere." Although an Obama-appointed judge dismissed the suit, Brimelow did not exaggerate the damage inflicted by this reckless labeling. I know exactly how he feels and then some.

A self-described "civic nationalist," Brimelow publishes a website called VDare.com, "the voice of the Historic American Nation." The site is named after Virginia Dare, the first baby of European descent known to have been born in North America. Although VDare is broadly anti-immigration, it is not absolutely so. Brimelow is an immigrant.

In the middle of the summer of 2020, during the presidential election, a fellow named Edwin Rubenstein wrote VDare's top article which dealt with immigrant population and worker displacement. According to the FBI, white nationalists "believe the white race is under attack from Jewish interests that dominate the government . . . act to the detriment of the white race."

Excuse me if I infer too much but I don't think it likely a fellow named Edwin Rubenstein would want to write for a publisher who believes Jews are a detriment to the white race. Nor would a white nationalist, as described by the FBI, want a noted economist like Rubenstein writing for his publication. I disagree with Brimelow on a number of subjects, but to stigmatize his publication's typically rational and well-researched articles as "racist" or "white nationalist" discourages debate and deserved a lawsuit.

CHAPTER EIGHTEEN

2012: SAYING NO TO MULTICULTURALISM

As to my second offense on the CPAC panel, I described multiculturalism as "a tool for the Left to subdivide a culture and civilization into our own little ethnic enclaves and pit us against each other." Again, Trip Gabriel offered no commentary as to why this passage is racist or divisive. To the readers of the *New York Times*, my offense is presumed to be obvious.

The critical word here is "tool." From the beginning, America has been a multicultural country. The earliest settlers came from Asia. Not to offend any young readers, but the various Indian tribes were not "native" to America. No one was. These early immigrants spoke hundreds of different languages and practiced nearly as many religions. The European settlers added a score of additional languages and even more religions. To be sure, not everyone came here voluntarily. A high percentage of early European settlers arrived as indentured servants. A very high percentage of Africans, almost all, arrived as slaves.

The West, of course, did not invent slavery. In fact, the word "slave" derives from the Muslim enslavement of the Slavic people of the Balkans in the ninth century. In some Muslim countries slavery is still practiced, and Muslims played a major role in the front end of the slave traffic to the Americas.

Our schoolchildren are repeatedly told about America's role in that traffic, but they are rarely told of the role Christians in England and America played in creating the world's first and most successful abolitionist movement. William Wilberforce, a devout Christian and the British father of that movement, spoke to the role of Christianity in shaping our consciousness:

> *Is it not the great end of religion, and, in particular, the glory of Christianity, to extinguish the malignant passions; to curb the violence, to control the appetites, and to smooth the asperities of man; to make us compassionate and kind, and forgiving one to another; to make us good husbands, good fathers, good friends; and to render us active and useful in the discharge of the relative social and civil duties?*[134]

Wilberforce was very specific about what he saw as his civic duty and who it was instructing him. Said Wilberforce, "God Almighty has set before me two Great Objects: the suppression of the Slave Trade and the Reformation of Manners." By "manners" Wilberforce meant religious discipline. His primary duty needs no explanation. Through Wilberforce's relentless efforts, Britain banned slavery in 1833 and freed more than eight hundred thousand Africans and their descendants enslaved in the various British colonies around the world.

Our progressive friends actually believe had they been born into a slave-owning society they would have been the first to arise and rebel. They kid themselves. As Wilberforce understood "the bulk of nominal Christians" lacked the will or the faith to do much beside talk. Thomas Jefferson, for all his virtues, was one such nominal Christian. Although Jefferson recognized slavery as a "moral depravity" and a "hideous blot," and although he made some legislative efforts to end it, his faith was not as strong as that of Garrison or Wilberforce.

To oppose slavery in eighteenth-century Virginia was like opposing abortion in twenty-first-century New York. Had Jefferson devoted himself to abolition, he would have effectively ended his political career. He would have had no more chance of securing the presidency in 1800 than an ardent pro-lifer would have of securing the Democratic nomination in 2020.

As the author of the Declaration of Independence, Jefferson helped create the world's first major multicultural country. Although English was the dominant language, there was no dominant tribe. Subsequent waves of immigration and the liberation of the enslaved made us progressively more multicultural, but given the limits of human nature, assimilation and acceptance rarely occurred without at least some friction. We were not a "perfect union," but we strove to be one and still do. As de Tocqueville reminds us, "The greatness of America lies not in being more enlightened than any other nation, but rather in her ability to repair her faults."[135]

For generations an ever-shifting multiculturalism was our reality. The "melting pot" was our goal. "E pluribus unum"—out of many, one—was our motto. Immigrants were not expected to abandon their faith or cultural traditions, but we expected our citizenry of whatever cultural background to understand and accept the concepts that made America great, the concepts embedded in our founding documents and forged by our history.

But then multiculturalism became a "tool," at the cutting edge of which is contempt for our heritage of Western Civilization. The Left wielded this "tool" not to pull America together but to pull us apart. As Christopher Caldwell notes in *The Age of Entitlement*, "The multiculturalism of the new century would steadily intensify the consciousness of racial differences."[136]

Designated minority groups were instructed to resist efforts at unification and reject our shared history. The members of these groups paid a price. "You are only a member of a recognize minority group so long as you accept the specific grievances, political grievances and resulting electoral platforms that other people have worked out for you," wrote Douglas Murray.[137]

These grievance groups had less interest in celebrating their own subcultures than they did in accusing those outside of their culture of "hatred." In the aftermath of the George Floyd death, every white person, including thinking liberals, was assumed to be guilty of hate and racism. Assimilation became a dirty word to the multiculturalist Left, but assimilation, not multiculturalism, not "diversity," is our true American strength.

In polite society, my position, which is still held by the majority of Americans, is now considered beyond the pale. This is a recent development. In 1960, a liberal icon did a radio ad for John Kennedy, then running for president. "Our nation enjoys its strength and its vitality because we are a melting pot," said Eleanor Roosevelt. "Because we have widely differing backgrounds, ideas, cultures that have merged and have made exciting the prospect our pursuit of happiness. We must not let ourselves become concerned with what particular wave of immigration brought our people here, or on what wave of immigration they will come in the future."[138] If there were a statue of Eleanor Roosevelt anywhere, it has probably been torn down by now.

Today, the University of Minnesota School of Public Health cites the phrase, "America is a melting pot," as an example of a "racial microaggression." I kid you not. Look it up. The University of Wisconsin gives its faculty the same advice: avoid saying "melting pot." The phrase is racist in that it suggests minorities have to "assimilate/acculturate to the dominant culture." To defend assimilation now is to provoke the wrath of America's elites. But the elites need to be provoked, and someone has to do the provoking.

The problem for provocateurs like Donald Trump and me is we are damned if we do and damned if we don't. In 2019, for instance, when Trump criticized "the Squad," the four radical congresswomen of various ethnicities, CNN's Chris Cillizza attacked him as a "racist." This much was expected. What was unexpected was the theme of Cillizza's attack as captured in the opening sentence: "Donald Trump wants to create an America that runs directly counter to the 'melting pot' principle on which the country has prided itself for generations."[139] Cillizza, missed the "melting pot" memo and, of course, committed a "racist microaggression." I have half a mind to report him to the SPLC's HateWatch. There is no hurry since there is no statute of limitations under the current cancel culture.

CHAPTER NINETEEN

2013: HONORING THE RULE OF LAW

Like many Americans, perhaps most, I opposed legal status for so-called "Dreamers" or more formally, Deferred Action for Childhood Arrivals (DACA). In summarizing my opposition, Trip Gabriel and the *Times* predictably twisted comments I made about these young people and then feigned outrage about what I allegedly said.

Before reporting what I said about illegal immigration, it might be helpful to review what others have said before me. In 1995, the chair of the U.S. Commission on Immigration Reform, former Texas Congresswoman Barbara Jordan, spoke for most Americans when she said, "For immigration to continue to serve our national interest, it must be lawful. There are people who argue that some illegal aliens contribute to our community because they may work, pay taxes, send their children to our schools, and in all respects except one, obey the law. Let me be clear: that is not enough."[140] Jordan, by the way, was a Democrat, black, and a very powerful speaker. I don't remember anyone criticizing her position.

President Bill Clinton certainly did not. In his 1995 State of the Union address, Clinton praised Jordan and expanded on her comments. He claimed Americans were "rightly disturbed" by the number of "illegal aliens" coming into the country. He claimed too they took away jobs from citizens and burdened taxpayers. "That's why our administration has moved aggressively to secure our borders."[141]

In 2005, Senator Barack Obama said, "We simply cannot allow people to pour into the U.S., undetected, undocumented, unchecked and circumventing the line of people who are waiting patiently, diligently, lawfully to become immigrants in this country."[142] In 2009, Sen. Chuck Schumer challenged the use of the word "undocumented workers" for undermining the fight against illegal immigration. "If you don't think it's illegal, you are not going to say it," Schumer said. "I think it is illegal and wrong, and we have to change it." At a campaign event in 2015, Hillary Clinton said, "I voted numerous times when I was a senator to spend money to build a barrier to try to prevent illegal immigrants from coming in. And I do think that you have to control your borders."[143]

As I mentioned earlier, progressives *progress*. If you don't progress along with them, depending on the issue, you become a racist, a sexist, an Islamophobe, a homophobe, a white nationalist, and ultimately, a white supremacist. In speaking with *Newsmax*, a conservative publication, I described many "Dreamers" accurately as kids "brought into this country by their parents unknowing they were breaking the law." I conceded some of them were likely valedictorians, "but for every one who's a valedictorian, there's another 100 out there who weigh 130 pounds and they've got calves the size of cantaloupes because they're hauling 75 pounds of marijuana across the desert."[144] The point was, if we grant a path to citizenship to the "Dreamers," many more drug smugglers than valedictorians would be legalized along with the rest.

At that time, Senator Dick Durbin was giving a floor speech nearly every week highlighting "Dreamers," often as valedictorians. My patience expired with Durbin's mischaracterization of the typical "Dreamer." I was also just back from a border trip. I have made many. The Border Patrol briefed me on the changes in the type of illegals they were apprehending. In the past, they said, a single agent could round up as many as seventy-five illegal aliens because they were docile and complied with authority.

This changed when more and more drug mules entered the scene and preferred to run or fight. The Border Patrol described the current breed of smugglers as weighing 130 pounds and carrying seventy-five pounds of marijuana on their backs. They said their muscle tone made them stand out in a group and showed me with their hands the size of their calves. I made the comparison to cantaloupes for alliterative, mnemonic purposes, and it was effective. It is a fact no meaningful amnesty has passed into law in the eighteen years of my watch.

For the nitpickers in the media, I would also add a real cantaloupe, not a muskmelon we typically see in the U.S., is about the size of a grapefruit or a softball. When sliced in half creating the profile of any human's calf, my wife's well-toned calves measure up to the description. (I actually measured her because I care about facts. I also raised a crop of real cantaloupes in the summer of 2019.) In any case, I reserve the right to criticize drug smugglers. My critics defended them.

Regardless, my cantaloupe remark was obvious hyperbole. I was making a rhetorical point. Leftists do this routinely when they speak of Dreamer valedictorians as though they were a regular feature of the American high school scene. They are not. It is just that when a Dreamer becomes a valedictorian, the media and Dick Durbin make sure the world knows about it. When a Dreamer is busted as a drug mule, a drunk driver, a thief, rapist or murderer, the media bury the story and almost never mention the perp's DACA status. Here are headlines the media prefer:

> *"Valedictorian declares she is an undocumented immigrant in graduation speech,"* CNN.

> *"Yale-Bound Valedictorian Comes Out as Undocumented in Emotional Speech,"* NBC.

> *"2 Valedictorians in Texas Declare Undocumented Status, and Outrage Ensues,"* New York Times.

These headlines were published during the 2016 presidential campaign. One of the valedictorians, who entered the country only six years prior, told a local ABC affiliate, "America can be great again without the construction of a wall built on hatred and prejudice." How about a wall built as a monument to national sovereignty and the Rule of Law? Another tweeted, "Valedictorian, 4.5GPA, full tuition paid for at UT, 13 cords/medals, nice legs, oh and I'm undocumented."

Katie Rogers of the *New York Times* expressed wonder that not everyone was celebrating the accomplishments of these young women. "Some observers," wrote Rogers, "saw the students' decision to express pride in being undocumented as an affront and criticized them on social media."[145] I don't blame the critics. American taxpayers rewarded these girls with a free education and now were about to send them to college free of tuition, and the girls expressed not a drop of gratitude. Rather, at least one of the two fully adopted the divisive Leftist talking points about "hatred and prejudice" in what amounted to a "Hillary for President" campaign ad.

One of the critics cited had a daughter who graduated with one of the Dreamers. It pained this Texas woman that the Dreamer bragged about "taking advantage of the system." Said the woman on Facebook, "I have never thought about deporting a child who graduated from a U.S. high school and fought against the odds to be successful. Until this moment." She added, "Something else that I have NEVER thought I would support until this moment is Trump and #buildthatwall."

Oddly, this is the kind of response Leftists hope to provoke. They thrive on division. They want to be able to brand their opposition as haters so the *Times* can run headlines like Katie Rogers's, "2 Valedictorians in Texas Declare Undocumented Status, and Outrage Ensues."

There are, of course, many more criminals among the Dreamers than valedictorians. According to data gathered in 2018 by U.S. Citizenship and Immigration Services, nearly 110,000 thousand of those who requested DACA status had arrest records for offenses such as assault and battery, rape, murder, and drunk driving. That figure represented 12 percent of potential Dreamers. Nearly sixty-eight thousand of those approved for DACA status were arrested prior to their approval. An incredible 218 of those requesting DACA status had ten or more arrests. Even more incredibly, fifty-four of those 218 had their status approved.[146]

When illegal aliens commit crimes, even horrendous crimes, their immigration status almost never makes the headline. In 2007, a half-dozen young illegals executed three black college students and sexually molested a fourth on a Newark, New Jersey, playground. A crime this appalling had the potential to drive a wedge between two of the major factions in the Left's multicultural coalition. The media did their best to keep the coalition together by not allowing the story to go national in any major way and also by keeping the immigrant status of the killers out of the headlines. I imagine most readers of this book will not have heard of this case. To get a sense of how the media reported it, I googled "Newark Playground Murders." Here are the headlines on the first Google page from the top:

> *"Chilling details emerge in Newark schoolyard murders"*
>
> *"Final defendant in '07 Newark schoolyard murders gets 195 years"*
>
> *"Survivor Recounts Horror of Attack in Newark Schoolyard"*
>
> *"Final Newark Schoolyard Slayings Defendant Convicted"*
>
> *"Witness: Machete used in NJ schoolyard killings"*
>
> *"Jury convicts first of 6 defendants in Newark schoolyard triple slayings"*

What the headlines have in common is none of them mentions the immigrant status of the killers. More than that, none of them mentions the race of the killers or the victims. I stopped searching after the fifth Google page without seeing any mention of the killers' immigration status or the race of either victims or killers. To put this in perspective, imagine how the media would have reacted if six young white men killed three promising black kids execution-style and slashed the fourth with a machete after sexually molesting her.

In the *New York Times* article cited above, "Survivor Recounts Horror of Attack in Newark Schoolyard," reporter Richard Pérez-Peña does not mention the immigration status of the killers. Not until the seventh paragraph of twenty does he share this bit of information: "Investigators have described Mr. Godinez, a native of Nicaragua, as a recruiter for MS-13, or Mara Salvatrucha, a violent street gang composed mostly of Central Americans." Even more impressively, Pérez-Peña fails to mention the race of the victims.[147]

I cannot say whether Godinez had calves the size of cantaloupes. That is rather beside the point. The point is, there are many more people like Godinez in America than there are Dreamer valedictorians, and the media routinely cover for the former and propagandize for the latter.

A *New York Times* article from 2013 makes an interesting point. Writes Juliet Lapidos, "If the Republican Party is split between those who support immigration reform, and those who don't, it is also split between those who realize the necessity, for their brand, of speaking sensitively and sensibly about the topic—and those who don't."[148]

I am reminded here again of William Lloyd Garrison's fiery denunciation of "moderation." How do you speak "moderately" about a schoolyard slaughter? How do you speak moderately about 68,000 criminal aliens—murderers and rapists among them—who do not need to be here? How do you speak moderately about the thousands of drug deaths every year from heroin hauled by illegal aliens across our southern border? I can't, and I won't. Yes, the Left is and remains the primary barrier to a better America, but the Left cannot prevail without the "center." They are both problems to be solved.

CHAPTER TWENTY

2015: WARNING OF THE ISLAMIC THREAT

Among the outrages Trip Gabriel cited in his "Timeline" article was my invitation to "far-right, anti-Islam" Dutch politician Geert Wilders to come to Washington. I appeared with him at the Capitol and once tweeted a photo with Wilders in front of a portrait of Winston Churchill. The *Times* took offense at all these gestures because Wilders reportedly said Islam was "not a religion" and the Koran was "worse than Mein Kampf." The actual quote was "worse than Mein Kampf when it comes to inciting hatred and violence." The *Times* edited the quote to make it sound more extreme and less defensible, but that's par for the course.

The *Times* was obviously counting on its readers to know nothing about Wilders's history. In truth, the courageous Dutch political leader knows a good deal more about hatred and violence than anyone in the *Times* newsroom. A self-declared "liberal," Wilders has publicly objected to the growing illiberal influence of Islam in the Netherlands. The price he has paid for speaking out has, unfortunately, confirmed his worst suspicions about the Islamic threat to free speech.

In 2004, Dutch police captured two grenade-wielding terrorists who threatened to kill Wilders and his political ally, Ayaan Hirsi

Ali, a native Somalian and former Muslim. That same year, a Muslim terrorist, Mohammed Bouyeri, killed Ali's partner in the making of a film called *Submission* about the suppression of women in Islamic culture, a subject with which Ali had brutal firsthand experience. The Dutch-Moroccan shot citizen Theo Van Gogh off his bicycle in Amsterdam and then stabbed a note into Van Gogh's chest threatening to kill Ali next. She eventually fled to the United States.

In 2008, Wilders produced a film titled *Fitna*, Arabic for "civil strife." The film frightened the Dutch government and the *New York Times* as well into a kind of resigned submission. According to the *Times*, the film paired "graphic images of terrorist attacks and death threats against Jews by Muslim extremists with verses of the Muslim holy book." Wilders argued the Koran inspired the violence. "Islam and the Koran are dangers to the preservation of freedom in the Netherlands in the long term," Wilders told reporters, "and I have to warn people of that."[149]

Not wanting a repeat of the worldwide violence following the publication of a cartoon showing an image of Mohammed with a bomb on his head, the Dutch government carried out a public relations campaign to distance itself from Wilders. The same campaign reminded people, not very convincingly, that Wilders lived in a country that guarantees freedom of speech.

The government used the word "guarantee" loosely. In 2016, Wilders was convicted of inciting discrimination and of insulting an ethnic group, namely Moroccans. Wilders posed this question at a public rally, "Would the Netherlands be better off with more or fewer Moroccans?" The crowd responded with, "Fewer. Fewer." Wilders responded, "We'll see what we can do about that." This statement brought hate speech charges against him after six thousand Moroccans went into protest mode.[150]

As Geert told me the day of his conviction for hate speech, "If I had picked a smaller group with fewer protestors, there would have been no charges filed." Said the judge in the case, "We state that you cannot offend groups of people." An attorney who brought the case against Wilders agreed, "The judge has ruled for the first time in the Netherlands that there are limits to what even a politician can say."

In its 2016 article on the case, the *Times* clearly favored the verdict against the "far-right" Wilders. In fact, the *Times* referred to Wilders as "far-right" in the headline, the photo caption, the lede, and the "correction." As late as 2010, however, the *Times* referred to Wilders only as "populist." As I could tell you from my own experience, the newsroom was weaponizing language to turn its political foes into pariahs. Bari Weiss's resignation letter merely confirmed what I already knew. "If a person's ideology is in keeping with the new orthodoxy, they and their work remain unscrutinized," Weiss wrote. "Everyone else lives in fear of the digital thunderdome."

Wilders remains active in Dutch politics, but he continues to receive death threats as a matter of routine and lives under constant surveillance. A permanent security detail of about six plainclothes police officers accompanies him wherever he goes, and he does not receive visitors unless they are cleared in advance. The state has had to provide him a secure house with a panic room. Wilders has said the cloud under which he lives is "a situation that I wouldn't wish on my worst enemy." Although Wilders doesn't sport a "coexist" bumper sticker on his bulletproof car, I am proud to call him a friend.

The tweet that troubled the *Times* has me shaking Wilders's hand in front of a portrait of Winston Churchill. The text reads, "Churchill looks over the shoulder of the world's leading voice against Jihad, Dutch MP Geert Wilders. @SpeakerBoehner."[151] The editors at the *Times* may have suspected we chose Churchill because of his prescient warnings about radical Islam.

Wrote Churchill more than a century ago: "The Mahommedan religion increases, instead of lessening, the fury of intolerance. It was originally propagated by the sword, and ever since its votaries have been subject, above the people of all other creeds, to this form of madness."[152] In June 2020, intolerance was on full display in London when vandals scrawled "was a racist" on Churchill's statue in Parliament Square. The statue is now boarded up. His granddaughter is left to wonder whether it might be safer if moved to a museum.

Dutch Parliamentarian and Party for Freedom leader, Geert Wilders and King stand before Wilders's prized portrait of Sir Winston Churchill. The Hague — March 12, 2015

CHAPTER TWENTY-ONE

2016: DEFENDING WESTERN CIVILIZATION

In July 2016, I offended the *Times* gang six ways from Sunday. My first offense, according to the *Times*, was to claim, "nonwhite groups haven't contributed as much as whites to civilization." Again, this was a distortion of what I said, but the conversation that produced it deserves attention.

At the time, I was participating in an MSNBC panel on the opening night of the Republican National Convention in Cleveland. I know, I'm crazy to give MSNBC a chance, but I do not believe in preaching exclusively to the choir. So I sometimes go where other Republicans fear to tread. As you might expect, the injection of race into the conversation came not from the right but from the Left, specifically *Esquire's* Charlie Pierce who is as pale as they come.

"If you're really optimistic, you can say this is the last time that old white people will command the Republican Party's attention, its platform, its public face," said Pierce, overlooking the fact the five final Republican candidates included two Hispanics, one black, and the son of an immigrant, that son being Donald Trump. By contrast, the six Democrats who took the stage for the televised debate in Iowa before the 2020 Iowa primary were all white and non-Hispanic. The final three candidates in that field were white men, the *youngest* among them being Joe Biden, aged seventy-seven.

"That hall is wired by loud, unhappy, dissatisfied white people," Pierce continued. "Any sign of rebellion is going to get shouted down either kindly or roughly but that's what's going to happen."[153] Had Pierce said the same about black people, he would have been booted from the network, and MSNBC would have taken virtue signaling bows in virtually every segment during the Republican convention.

In a vacuum, Pierce's comments could have been ignored, but I have long been engaged in ideological battles with the Left. I know, as did George Orwell, oppression starts with language. "'Don't you see that the whole aim of Newspeak is to narrow the range of thought?" Orwell wrote in his dystopian novel, *1984.* "In the end we shall make thoughtcrime literally impossible, because there will be no words in which to express it."[154]

On the Left today anything related to "white" is fair game. The Left's goal is to trivialize the Constitution and break down its restraints against government power. This begins by shaming white people into disowning their own history and traditions—the Confederate flag today, the American flag tomorrow. The Left is not about championing black people. The Left is about destroying the United States.

This mindless bashing of "old white people" was racism. There was no other word for Pierce's remarks. I saw no reason to tolerate them. It was the end of the segment, and Pierce's bigoted words had to be rebutted. "This whole white people business does get a little tired, Charlie," I answered calmly. "I would ask you to go back through history and figure out where are these contributions that have been made by these other categories of people that you're talking about. Where did any other subgroup of people contribute more to civilization?"

Moderator Chris Hayes tried to walk me into a trap. "Than white people?" he asked with a leer. I refused the bait. I never talk about racial superiority, but I do talk proudly about cultural superiority. The subgroup in question I specified not as white but "as

Western Civilization itself." I explained that Western Civilization was "rooted in Western Europe, Eastern Europe, and the United States of America, and every place where the footprint of Christianity settled the world."

As the *Times* conceded, "Frantic yelling ensued."[155] Black reporter April Ryan fanned herself as if she had a case of the vapors but made herself heard over the din, "What about Africa? What about Asia?" she shouted. If I had the time and space, I would have explained the northern rim of Africa and the western rim of Asia contributed substantially to the foundations of Western Civilization. Jesus came from an Asian country. Augustine came from an African one. Socrates came from a European country. Northern Europeans came late to the fruits of Judeo-Christianity and what we think of as Western Civilization.

Other parts of the world—Australia, Canada, the United States—came later still thanks to Christian missionaries and European commercial interests. There is not a country in the world that has not benefited greatly from the influence of the Judeo-Christian West. Western technology is also the science and technology of India, China, and Nigeria. China steals our secrets. We don't steal theirs. Not all of the encounters between the West and the East or the South were harmonious. Some were far from it. That said, no other culture—sorry, April, not in Africa or in Asia—can boast of a record anything like this.

True to form, the *Times* corrupted my comments by headlining its 2016 article on this televised dust-up, "What, Congressman Steve King Asks, Have Nonwhites Done for Civilization?"[156] Of course, I said no such thing, nothing close.

Gabriel also took me to task for defending my comments when challenged by the *Washington Post's* Philip Rucker. Here is the excerpt he apparently found racist or divisive: "The idea of multiculturalism, that every culture is equal—that's not objectively true, and we've been fed that information for the past 25 years, and we're not going to become a greater nation if we continue to do that."

Gabriel's "Timeline" article links to a 2016 *Washington Post* article by Amber Phillips. On the plus side, Phillips quotes my comments to Rucker at length. Here is what Phillips reported me as saying to Rucker:

> *Western Civilization is the most successful civilization the world has ever seen. And some of the reasons for that is it's borrowed the best of the cultures along the way, back to Mosaic law, the Greek age of reason, Roman law and the Roman order of government, and the Republican form of government, by the way that we're guaranteed in our Constitution. The foundation of our ideological thought is rooted in the enlightenment in Europe and then this country was born at the dawn of the industrial revolution. . . .*
>
> *The sum total that's been contributed by Western Civilization, it surpasses any other culture or civilization, partly because we borrowed from them along the way, and we're flexible enough to do that. And so I don't think we should apologize for our success.*[157]

What, you ask, did the ellipses leave out? It ignored my comment that there were elements of our cultural history "we're not proud of." Amber Phillips edited that out. She also omitted my introductory comments about why I chose to defend Western Civilization, namely because of Pierce's disparaging remarks about "old white people." If you'll note, nowhere in my defense of Western Civilization did I make any allusion to race, white or nonwhite. I never do when speaking of Western Civilization. I often say, "It's not about race. It's never been about race. Some see race as a marker but it is about culture and civilization. Western Civilization is a superior civilization and America is today the flagship of Western Civilization."

The headline of Phillips's articles suggests why the *Post* thought any of this exchange was newsworthy: "What Steve King's 'sub groups' musing says about the party of Donald Trump."[158] If, by the "party of Donald Trump," Phillips meant the Republican establishment, my "musings" say nothing at all.

Amber Phillips's follow-up comment is priceless. She complimented her "eagle-eyed colleague Philip Bump" for pointing out our society is shaped by numerous nonwhite societies, past and present." The "nonwhite" societies Bump cited include those in what are now Iraq and Syria. These are Semitic people just as Jews are. Obviously, Bump considers these people "nonwhite." I wonder if they do.

Whether they are white or not, Bump seems to have purposely missed my point. He saw the video of my conversation with Rucker. He heard me say, one reason Western Civilization has been so successful is because "it has borrowed from other cultures along the way." Bump isn't "eagle-eyed." That's laughable. He's downright myopic.

A middle-aged white guy of no distinguishing ethnicity, Bump defended cultures "outside of the Western world" in a way likely to embarrass the people of those cultures. Their specific inventions, Bump insisted, include: "the seismograph, the umbrella, gunpowder, stirrups, the compass."[159] Yes, the umbrella! Although the umbrella has independent origins in many cultures, the other "inventions" came from China.

No one denies that at one point China was more advanced than Europe. Confucius was sharing his timeless wisdom before Socrates and Plato were born, let alone Jesus Christ. China had cities of more than a million people when no city in Europe had as many as fifty thousand.

The Chinese have long been merchants and traders. In the early fifteenth century, a fleet of three hundred junks, commanded by Zheng He, sailed through the Straits of Hormuz and into the Red Sea. Zheng He also explored the east coast of Africa, landing in Malindi, Kenya, in 1416, fully eighty years before Vasco da Gama. But Emperor Yongle, third Ming emperor, died in 1424, and sea exploration died with him. By the beginning of the sixteenth century, anyone building a ship with more than two masts faced the death penalty. By the middle of the century, it was a crime to go to sea.

China turned inward at the time they were said to have the highest standard of living in the world. What the Chinese lacked was an adaptive, self-sustaining culture, a culture rooted in the Judeo-Christian concepts of responsibility for one's actions and equality under the law.

Over the past 500 years, if the world had to rely solely on China for useful technologies or cultural innovations, the entire planet would be third-world today. Two thousand years after the birth of Christ, most Chinese were living lives as oppressed and as impoverished as those of their ancestors who walked the earth when Christ did. The Chinese who lived better—the few with electricity, indoor plumbing, and automobiles among other amenities—were living off the successes of Western culture.

Japan was more backward still. In 1633, the Tokugawa Shogunate began issuing edicts establishing "sakoku" literally meaning "chained country" in order to preserve ruling dominance. He banned external trade fearing that new technologies and even Christianity could shift the balance of power. So for two hundred years, Japan remained stuck in time. When American Commodore Matthew Perry opened trade in 1853, Japan was still being ruled by feudal shoguns and was among the most isolated countries in the world.

Islamic people did make a great contribution to world culture. They preserved the classic Greek works housed in libraries in Mesopotamia, Egypt, Syria, and translated them into Arabic. They often commented on these works of science, philosophy, and mathematics among other forms of knowledge and sometimes elaborated on them.

Muslims also made their way to India. There they discovered the Indian numbering system, now called "Arabic numerals," which included the magic number "zero." Indians likely adopted the zero from Cambodia where the earliest evidence of it is found. The system liberated commerce in ways Roman numerals never could, and yes, Islamic people preserved it.

It was the Italians, however, who took these numbers to the next step. Italians introduced this system to the Western world, invented the revolutionary concept of double-entry bookkeeping, and gave the world the word *bank* from the Old Italian *banco*, meaning "bench or board." In fact, it was the Italians, the Medici in particular, who developed the whole concept of international banking.

Bump also cited the contributions of Arabic and Middle Eastern inventors and scientists as well as those who gave us "the numeric system that will be used to tally up the delegates to make Trump the nominee of King's party." Of course, I never denied any of this, but I understood the flow of civilization in a way Bump refused to.

In May 2019, I doubled down on my obvious point. "If we presume that every culture is equal and has an equal amount to contribute to our civilization, then we're devaluing the contributions of the people that laid the foundation for America and that's our Founding Fathers," I said at a town hall in Fort Dodge, Iowa. "It is not about race. It's never been about race. It is about culture." Once again, the media thought my comments newsworthy. Some samples:

> *"Steve King says all cultures do not contribute equally, to claim otherwise is to devalue the 'Founding Fathers,'"* Des Moines Register
>
> *"Steve King warns against presuming 'every culture is equal,'"* CNN
>
> *"Steve King: Presuming all cultures contribute equally to our civilization devalues the Founding Fathers."* Washington Post

There is an old campfire game we used to play. One person starts it by whispering a secret into the ear of the person next to him and then that person tries to pass the same secret to the person next to her. By the time the secret makes it around the campfire, it is usually unrecognizable. By the time my comment reached the *Post's* Colby Itkowitz four months later, it sounded something like this: "Rep. Steve King, who earlier this year was condemned by his Congressional peers for favorable comments about white supremacy, argued Tuesday that presuming all cultures are equal devalues the Founding Fathers."[160] "Favorable comments about white supremacy"?

Let me remind you what I said about white supremacy on the House floor the day after Gabriel's article came out. "I reject those labels and the evil ideology that they define. Further, I condemn anyone that supports this evil and bigoted ideology which saw in its ultimate expression the systematic murder of 6 million innocent Jewish lives." Favorable?

My critics were playing games here. They would not come out and insist all cultures were equal. That statement was too transparently false to defend. I would love to see their defense, say, of Taliban culture. Even the Left-wing British *Guardian* denounced the Taliban's "brutal, misogynist rule." Wrote the *Guardian* reporters, "They barred women from schools and most work, forced them to wear the all-enveloping burqa when they left home, and even policed their shoes and makeup."[161] For women who violated the rules, the punishments were severe to the point of death.

Frankly, an Afghan woman's life either before or after the reign of the Taliban was not much different. The producers of the Academy Award–winning documentary *Learning to Skateboard in a Warzone (If You're a Girl)*, explicitly describe Afghanistan as "one of the worst places in the world to be born a girl."

It would seem the Left are masters of what Orwell called "doublethink": the art of maintaining two conflicting ideas in one's brain simultaneously. On the one hand, progressives acknowledge the brutal sexism of the Afghan culture. On the other hand, they scold people like me who point out that the world's worst cultures for women are not *equal* to the world's best cultures for women.

Afghanistan is not unique. Women were and still are oppressed in many Muslim countries. Ayaan Hirsi Ali fled Somalia after her forced clitorectomy but before an arranged marriage. Taking refuge in the Netherlands, she thought she left hell for heaven. Dutch liberals often failed to see her point. Wrote Ali:

> *Many well-meaning Dutch people have told me in all earnestness that nothing in Islamic culture incites abuse of women, that this is just a terrible misunderstanding.*

Men all over the world beat their women, I am constantly informed. In reality, these Westerners are the ones who misunderstand Islam. The Quran mandates these punishments. It gives a legitimate basis for abuse, so that the perpetrators feel no shame and are not hounded by their conscience or their community.[162]

Hirsi Ali and I shared a stage presentation at CPAC one year, and she has been my guest speaker at my Conservative Opportunity breakfast. I want her voice to be heard.

The treatment of women is just one cultural variable out of many. I defy my critics to identify a single way in which Afghan or Somalian culture is equal to, say, that of the Netherlands or the United States. No, they won't defend those cultures. They won't say all cultures are equal. Instead, they ridicule me for walking point on one of their own causes. This strategy works only in an environment in which fear is rampant and logic taboo.

Fortunately for the rest of the world, Western Civilization has had an international outreach. It welcomed every culture that wanted to participate and, yes, even those that did not. Its hallmarks—the Rule of Law and individual freedom, restrained by a shared morality—elevated countries like India and Japan and even China to heights they had never achieved on their own. If proof were needed of our civilization's superiority, one need only compare the number of those fleeing *from* the west to the number of those fleeing *to* the west. Almost all migration goes one way—to the West.

CHAPTER TWENTY-TWO

2016: CALLING THE SUICIDE HOTLINE

Among the other sins I committed in 2016, at least as judged by the evolving standards of Trip Gabriel's "Timeline," was to tweet, "Cultural suicide by demographic transformation must end."

I tweeted the message during a meeting in Amsterdam. In the accompanying photo with me were Geert Wilders and Frauke Petry. The Dutch politico Wilders dominates every photo in which he appears. He is about half a foot taller than I am with a huge shock of blond hair making his visage loom large. Petry is petite and pretty and as un-Hitler-like as a human could be. At the time, however, she was the leader of the Alternative for Germany Party (AfD). To make her seem dangerous, Trip Gabriel dubbed Petry's party "far right." Petry's country being Germany, Gabriel felt free to insinuate Petry was something of a Neo-Nazi and I, by extension, a Nazi-sympathizer. I have heard this logical fallacy called *reductio ad Hitlerum*.

This allusion hinges on the Left's notion Hitler's National *Socialist* German Workers' Party was somehow right wing. Whenever I am compared to Hitler—and it happens—I have to wonder why someone who believes in Christ, in free enterprise, in our Constitutional Republic, who is a dedicated Constitutionalist, and who champions Israel can be seen as the political heir of an

King, then AfD (Alternative für Deutschland) party Leader Frauke Petry, and Wilders after an in-depth dinner discussion. The Hague — June 29, 2016

anti-Christian, anti-Semitic, anti-capitalist, anti-smoking, vegetarian socialist like Hitler. I am a dedicated and committed carnivore to boot, and I sometimes have a cigar while I mow my lawn. Hitler executed more than a thousand Catholic priests while he was executing six million Jews. Let us not forget the millions of Poles, Roma, Russians, and others he dehumanized and exterminated.

Anti-socialist Germans face even greater hysteria. The AfD prominently declares its position: "We are liberals and conservatives. We are free citizens of our nation. We are staunch supporters of democracy." The party's website lays out its program, which, of course, triggers the world's Leftists:

> *We maintain an open mind towards other nations and cultures, but wish to be and remain German at heart. Therefore, we shall continuously strive to uphold human*

*dignity, support families with children, retain our West-
ern Christian culture, and maintain our language and
traditions in a peaceful, democratic, and sovereign nation
state for the German people.*[163]

The AfD recently named a fellow with the conspicuously un-
German name of Tino Chrupalla as the party chair. East German
by birth, Chrupalla knows something about living under tyranny.
Although there is much the AfD and I agree on, I am sure there is
much we do not. That said, the AfD is Germany's leading opposition party. To denounce the AfD or even to ignore it on the say-so
of European Leftists is not something I am prepared to do.

Unlike the United States, Germany is staring down the barrel
of cultural suicide. Under the dubious leadership of Angela Merkel,
Germany accepted many more "refugees," real and pretend, than
it could possibly hope to assimilate. Many of these refugees arrived
with an indifference, if not downright hostility, to German language, culture, and religious traditions.

In 2016, for instance, an ISIS wannabe attacked a Berlin Christmas market, killing twelve and injuring fifty-five. Since that time,
the Federal Criminal Police have thwarted nine comparable
attacks. Even though Germany is not a devoutly Christian country,
Christmas markets are a deeply rooted tradition. Threatened
attacks on these markets strike at that tradition and make market-
goers apprehensive. Some of these markets have had to shut down.

Germany is in most ways more profoundly secularized than
the United States. The fact that in the Eastern half of the country
Christianity was suppressed for forty-four years after the fall of
Hitler did not help. Like secular liberals throughout the world,
German liberals have birth rates well below replacement. On average, non-Muslim German women have only 1.4 children per
woman against a replacement rate of 2.15, which is why the AfD
supports families with children.

In America, the problem is not as severe, but our birth rate has
been falling for the last thirty-two years and now stands at about
1.7 per woman. In every country in which the birth rate is below

replacement, even those without immigration like Japan, there are problems. These countries will lack an adequate workforce to take care of an increasingly elderly population. If the imported workforce disrespects the culture and the older people who created it, the problems are aggravated.

The cultures of Germany and Japan differ from our own, but neither remotely resembles the militant imperialistic cultures that led to World War II. We should trust them to deal with their own problems in their own way. As wise people everywhere know, any nation unwilling to fight to preserve its own traditions is doomed to lose them.

More than a decade ago, I was invited to deliver a keynote speech to a group in Germany. My subject was how Germans could best adjust to their declining birth rate and their contracting demographic pie. The audience expected me to promote immigration as a substitute for the missing German generations lost to abortion and a shrinking birth rate. Instead, I opened my talk with this quote from a 1911 speech then ex-president Teddy Roosevelt made before a group of liberal Christian theologians:

> *If you do not believe in your own stock enough to wish to see the stock kept up, then you are not good Americans [or Germans] and you are not patriots; I, for one, would not mourn your extinction, and in such event, I would welcome the advent of a new race [group of people] that would take your place, because you will have shown that you are not fit to cumber the ground.*[164]

In a 1905 speech on "American Motherhood," President Teddy Roosevelt declared, "no piled-up wealth, no splendor of material growth, no brilliance of artistic development" would benefit the nation unless its men and women were "able and willing to bear, and to bring up as they should be brought up, healthy children, sound in mind, body, and character." Of note, Roosevelt added, children should be "numerous enough" for the nation to grow.[165]

Roosevelt described this call to parental responsibility as "the most essential and the least pleasant truth that I have to tell you."[166]

I can assure you that the European audience did consider the statement unpleasant. Too bad Angela Merkel missed the "essential" component of Roosevelt's call to action.

France apparently has too. The country has many of the problems with immigration, legal and otherwise, that Germany does. In October 2016, Marine Le Pen, the leader of France's *Rassemblement National* (RN), tweeted a photo of the two of us with a message easily understood even by non-French speakers, "*Échanges très intéressants avec @SteveKingIA, membre du Congrès américain, au sujet de la France, de l'UE et des affaires internationales.*"[167] Yes, we had an interesting conversation about France, the EU, and international affairs.

Much as with Germany's AfD, the RN aspires to protect the culture and sovereignty of the nation it represents. The RN's philosophy is distinctly French. At the heart of that philosophy is a drive to localize both the economy and the politics in a country whose power is deeply centralized. That said, the RN is more statist and more green than, say, the Republican Party in America, but it is more openly pro-border and anti-immigration. The RN has reason to be more anti-immigration.

Many of the immigrants flooding the country would like to supplant French culture with their own. Some have resorted to terrorism to show their contempt. Just in the two years prior to my meeting with Le Pen, Islamic terrorists: attacked the offices of Charlie Hebdo, a satiric publication, and a Kosher market, killing seventeen; killed 131 Parisians in a series of coordinated attacks; and drove a truck through a Bastille Day crowd in Nice killing eighty-six and injuring more than four hundred others. In the major cities, terror has become routine. A few have immigrant-dominated areas where not just women but police fear to go, the dreaded "no-go zones."

When in France, I visited one of those zones. I wanted to understand the cultural climate that produces such venomous ideological hatred. Our U.S. Embassy, citing security reasons, refused to take me to the apartment in which a lethal terrorist plot was recently hatched. Not to be deterred, I hired a private car whose driver had the nerve to bring me to within two long blocks. He

Congressman King and Rassemblement National (RN) party Leader Marine Le Pen during an "interesting conversation about France, the EU, and international affairs." Paris, France—February 12, 2017

pointed down an alley and described which apartment the killers used. Escorted only by a U.S. Marine in a business suit, I started down the alley. My Marine escort, never short of courage but charged with the task of keeping me safe, said, "I don't think we should go, sir." To which I responded, "We came this far. I think we have to. Eyes front and walk with purpose." We continued on our way.

We did not go far before we faced a man openly urinating. We walked around him and then approached a rowdy cluster of about thirty young Muslim men cheering on a boxing match, gloves on. We had to walk through them, eyes front and with purpose. Unbothered, we continued to the corner just outside our objective.

I intended to shoot a video in front of the killers' apartment but thought better of it as I felt many sets of eyes on us and sensed the hostility behind those eyes. Instead, we walked one block away on a different street where I recorded a short video with the apartment in the background. From there, we took a different route out of the neighborhood and called our car. This was one of several terrorist-spawning, no-go zones I chose to visit. I saw others in Stockholm, London, Amsterdam, and Brussels.

Leftists do not like Le Pen's RN platform. By openly opposing the European Left, the RN has, not surprisingly, been deemed racist and fascist. The center right in France, much as it does in America, echoes the Leftist line to prevent its followers from straying to the RN.

Gabriel, of course, marches to the same beat as his Leftist European counterparts. In responding to my tweet, he dismissed the RN with the label "far-right" and suggested I was uniquely racist or divisive for being "the first elected American official to meet [Le Pen]." For the record, Le Pen received ten million votes in the most recent presidential election. In 2019, the RN beat President Macron's party in the European election vote. How, I wonder, can a media that insists all cultures are equal be so hateful and dismissive toward the law abiding, non-violent traditionalists of France who have rallied around Le Pen?

CHAPTER TWENTY-THREE

2017: PROTECTING A BEATING HEART

In January 2017, days after Trump's inauguration, I introduced the first "HeartBeat" bill at the federal level. If passed, this law would have banned the abortion of any baby with a beating heart, a phenomenon typically occurring about six weeks after conception. Although I understood the bill would have little chance, at least initially, of becoming federal law, I was more optimistic about its passage in individual states, beginning with Iowa.

In that same legislative cycle, I called my State Senator Jason Schultz and proposed we introduce my HeartBeat bill in the Iowa Senate. Jason took up the task. The Iowa Senate was absolutely stellar in its efforts, but the House was a different story. I spent seven weeks working the HeartBeat bill in the Iowa House. We remained three votes short of the fifty-one required for passage.

I was asked to turn the heat down and let House leadership and Governor Kim Reynolds work the bill. Throughout the entire seven-week process, I never picked up any signal that Reynolds was helping to nudge it along in any way. The legislative session was about to end, I feared, without House action on HeartBeat. I know what a "slow walk" looks like so I texted and called Governor Reynolds several times over a two-week period. The only response was an unkept promise to call back. Running out of time,

I sent her this text, "Governor, I musta missed your call. Can u try me again? Iowa House needs to move Heartbeat. I have been handling it delicately but now must talk to press . . . Thanks, SK."

Immediately, my phone rang and her first words were, "Steve! Are you threatening me?" We finally put the votes together for passage, again with the excellent help of many of the top pro-life legislators in both the House and Senate. In May, Reynolds signed into law the nation's strongest pro-life legislation. With their votes, the legislators heroically placed Iowa in the forefront of national efforts to protect innocent, unborn life from the abortion industry. Theirs was a deeply moral and principled vote. At the time, I praised Reynolds as "the most pro-life governor in Iowa's history." I have since lost some confidence in her motives.

For decades now, as the Todd Akin incident showed, rape and incest have caused Republican lawmakers political problems. In truth, though, rape and incest ought not be paired. If the incest occurs with a minor, that is rape. If the incest is between consenting adults, I do not know why the two partners should get an exemption from abortion laws.

The real issue is rape. For Democrats this is not a problem issue. Since they believe every woman is entitled to an abortion, they would certainly think rape victims are entitled to one as well. Those, however, who think an unborn baby deserves equal protection under the law have no moral or logical ground to exclude certain babies from protection. Who among us would vote for a bill that read, "All babies with a heartbeat are considered 'persons' under the law except for those conceived in rape or incest"?

As the Republican governor of Massachusetts, Mitt Romney supported abortion. As a candidate for president, Romney positioned himself as pro-life. An opportunist, he supported the "life" position only because a pro-choice Republican cannot win a presidential nomination. That said, in 2012 Romney was running ads saying he thought "abortion should be an option in cases of rape, incest or to save a mother's life."

In late October 2012, Indiana Senate candidate Richard Mourdock put Romney in a tight spot when he supported the position babies conceived in rape are entitled to the protection of the law. "Even when life begins in that horrible situation of rape, that is something that God intended to happen," said Mourdock. As in Akin's case, the media twisted Mourdock's words into some grotesque parody of what he actually said. The *Washington Post*, for instance, headlined his comments: "Indiana GOP Senate hopeful Richard Mourdock says God 'intended' rape pregnancies."[168]

Predictably, Romney ran from Mourdock almost as quickly as he had run from Akin. "Gov. Romney disagrees with Richard Mourdock's comments, and they do not reflect his views," a campaign spokeswoman told the *Post*. "The candidate supports abortion in cases of rape and incest, as well as to save a mother's life." This weak-kneed position impressed no one. Mourdock lost a winnable race. So did Akin. So did Romney, who contributed to all three losses.

My own views were challenged over time. I have always held to my conviction that all conceived babies have a right to life, and the vanishingly rare circumstances requiring an abortion to save the life of the mother are better not addressed by legislation.

Even after my public chastisement in January 2019, I was determined not to abandon the life issue. Once again, however, my plain speaking provoked the nation's army of Orwellian word twisters. In August of 2019, I made remarks at the Westside Conservative Club in Urbandale, Iowa, that sent the media atwitter. In response to a question, I was explaining my opposition to exceptions for rape and incest in anti-abortion legislation. "I'd like to think every one of the lives of us are as precious as any other life," I said in explaining my position. "That's our measure. Human life cannot be measured. It is the measure itself against which all things are weighed." If that wasn't triggering enough, my earlier comments certainly seemed to be:

> *What if we went back through all the family trees and just pulled those people out that were products of rape or incest? Would there be any population of the world left if we did that? Considering all the wars and all the*

*rapes and pillages that's taken place, and whatever hap-
pened to culture after society, I know that I can't certify
that I'm not a product of that. And I'd like to think every
one of the lives of us is as precious as any other life.*[169]

There should have been no confusion about what I said,
namely that if our forebears aborted the children of rape victims
or babies resulting from incest, we would have had a very different
history. The truth of history is politically incorrect. In any of our
family trees going back hundreds of generations, how likely is it
all babies were conceived by two unrelated consenting adults? Not
likely at all and completely implausible to anyone who simply
googles "child bride" to get a feel for the odds. Genealogists are
universal in affirming my statement. The members of the Westside
Conservative Club got my point. Predictably, however, the media
worldwide went nuts. Here are some sample headlines:

> *"Rep. Steve King says rapes, incest helped populate the
> world," Los Angeles Times.*
>
> *"Steve King: What About the Benefits of Rape and
> Incest?" Vanity Fair.*
>
> *"Steve King Discusses the Sunny Side of Rape and
> Incest," New York magazine.*

My favorite was this one: "Steve King Offers Passionate
Defense of Rape and Incest." This headline came not from some
silly Left-wing blog but from the allegedly reputable *New York*
magazine. Judging from the content of the article by Ed Kilgore,
the headline was *not* meant to be funny. Kilgore insisted my line
of reasoning, if followed, "would mandate the abolition of laws
against rape and incest as inimical to human survival."[170] He then
mocked the members of the Westside Conservative Club for not
being as alarmed as he was.

It is one thing for the media to betray their craft. It is another
thing for Republicans to betray their constituents. In consistently

fleeing from controversy, Republican leaders surrender the battle of ideas to our opponents who have proved themselves ruthlessly indifferent to the truth. When the media rushed to find Republicans willing to denounce me, they had no trouble rounding up the usual suspects.

"The Republican Party is the party of life—we're very proud of that," said Iowa Republican Party Chairman Jeff Kaufmann. If you expect a "but" clause to follow, you are right to do so. "*But*," Kaufmann continued, "in regards to the statements of population and where that population comes from, those comments are outrageous and that they are not reflective of the Republican Party of Iowa."[171] Kaufman had by then taken his lead from Reynolds.

One of my primary opponents at the time, U.S. Army Chaplain Jeremy Taylor, insisted, "I will be a champion for the unborn and

King and Rebecca Kiessling, president of www.SaveThe1.com during a press conference calling out Kevin McCarthy, Liz Cheney, Republican State Party Chairman Jeff Kaufmann, and the press for their admitted misquote and then willful mischaracterization of King's statement. Des Moines, Iowa—August 23, 2019 will fight for the right to life at all turns." This is one *turn* where I wished he took up the fight, but no, Taylor was worried that my "comments feed the Left."[172] My comments fed the Left only because people like Taylor added the necessary flavoring.

Not surprisingly, the response of my anticipated Democratic opponent, J. D. Scholten, was completely unhinged. "Yet again," said Scholten, "Steve King puts his selfish, hateful ideology above the needs of the people of Iowa's 4th district. Excusing violence— in any way—is entirely unacceptable."[173] Hateful? Selfish? What was he referring to? Here I was saying, "I'd like to think every one of the lives of us are as precious as any other life." And here was Scholten saying I was "excusing violence." For J. D. Scholten, tearing unborn babies limb from limb does not equate to violence.

Nor does it for Kevin McCarthy if the babies are conceived in rape or incest. He has argued that exceptions for rape and incest are "exactly what Republicans have voted on in this House. That's what our platform says."[174] It does not. Here is the 2016 Republican Platform:

> *Protecting Human Life*
> *The Constitution's guarantee that no one can "be deprived of life, liberty or property" deliberately echoes the Declaration of Independence's proclamation that "all" are "endowed by their Creator" with the inalienable right to life. Accordingly, we assert the sanctity of human life and affirm that the unborn child has a fundamental right to life that cannot be infringed. We support a human life amendment to the Constitution and legislation to make clear that the Fourteenth Amendment's protections apply to children before birth.*[175]

"I believe in exceptions for rape, incest and life of the mother, and that's what I've voted on," said McCarthy. For McCarthy, human life is apparently more sacred if conceived in mutual love or lust than if conceived in rape or incest. I wonder what he thinks about human life conceived in adultery? I would be willing to bet

McCarthy would rationalize another exception if confronted with such a reality. McCarthy does not appear to do much thinking. He complained on FOX News, "This isn't the first time I've had concerns with what Steve King has said."[176] It wouldn't be the last. Republican Conference Chair, Liz Cheney, born with a silver political spoon in her mouth and building a reputation as the Cersei Lannister (the cold, calculating, and ruthless character in *Game of Thrones*) of the House, tweeted: "Today's comments by [Steve King] are appalling and bizarre. As I've said before, it's time for him to go."[177]

Exactly one month after the January 6, 2021 Capitol incursion, the Wyoming GOP voted 56–8 to censure Cheney for her vote to impeach President Trump and called on her to "resign immediately."[178] Jesus made it clear in Matthew 7:1–2 (NLT): "Do not judge others, and you will not be judged. For you will be treated as you treat others. The standard you use in judging is the standard by which you will be judged." The Wyoming GOP made it clear too. Liz, "It's time for you to go."

To this day, I cannot fathom what is "appalling" or "bizarre" about defending the lives of the unborn? Ezekiel 18:20 (NLT) makes as much moral sense today as it did more than two millennia ago: "The child will not be punished for the parent's sins, and the parent will not be punished for the child's sins." Or, in the public words of this author, "Thou shalt not kill the child for the sins of the father or the mother. Thus sayeth the Lord and the Republican Platform." This is a commandment my critics need to take to heart if they are to be logically and morally consistent, not to mention supportive of their own party's platform.

To make a difference today, you have to walk point, walk through the fire, shoot and be shot at, and sound the alarm. If nothing else, I forced some Republicans to reflect on the rape exemption in their professed pro-life beliefs. My friends in Urbandale, Iowa, never suspected they would help make history, but they did. Said one of the club members to the *New York Times*, "You expect the Democrats to attack [King] but not the Never Trumpers, members of his own party."[179]

CHAPTER TWENTY-FOUR

2017: RESTORING OUR CIVILIZATION

In 2017, I sent the nation's race baiters over the edge when I tweeted, "[Geert] Wilders understands that culture and demographics are our destiny. We can't restore our civilization with somebody else's babies."[180] I had been saying this, specifically in regard to Europe, for years. Too many European countries were importing foreign workers because their citizens were not having nearly enough children to maintain viable population levels. As I mentioned earlier, the workers and refugees entering these countries too often had little respect for the culture of the host country.

In her memoir, *Infidel*, Ayaan Hirsi Ali documents the stubborn refusal of her fellow Somalians in the Netherlands to assimilate to Dutch culture. Instead of adapting, they tended to enforce among themselves an even stricter adherence to the worst elements of Muslim culture. Her feelings on this subject are worth hearing:

> *People accuse me of having interiorized a feeling of racial inferiority, so that I attack my own culture out of self-hatred, because I want to be white. This is a tiresome argument. Tell me, is freedom then only for white people? Is it self-love to adhere to my ancestors' traditions and mutilate my daughters? To agree to be humiliated*

and powerless? To watch passively as my countrymen
abuse women and slaughter each other in pointless dis-
putes? When I came to a new culture, where I saw for
the first time that human relations could be different,
would it have been self-love to see that as a foreign cult,
which Muslims are forbidden to practice?[181]

If all immigrants, or even most, were as appreciative and as adaptive as Ali, Europeans would welcome them, as would Americans. But in Europe, most are not. If proof were needed, Ali had to flee the Netherlands for the relative security of the United States after her creative partner was murdered and her own life was threatened repeatedly.

Not too long ago, William Grimes of the *New York Times* pictured Ali as heroic and called her memoir "brave, inspiring and beautifully written." In his 2007 review of *Infidel*, Grimes echoed Ali's concerns about "the dangers posed to the Netherlands by unassimilated Muslims." Wrote Grimes, Ali's warnings "made her Public Enemy No. 1 for Muslim extremists, a feminist counterpart to Salman Rushdie."[182] Rushdie lived for years in hiding after satirizing Mohammed in his book *The Satanic Verses*. Like Ali, he too was once a hero on the Left.

Although Grimes did not use the word "multiculturalism"— even in 2007, he did not dare—the philosophy Ali resisted was just that. "Ali warned the Dutch that their liberal policy of helping immigrants create separate cultural and religious institutions was counterproductive," wrote Grimes. "She deplored the crimes of violence against Muslim women committed daily in the Netherlands, to which the authorities turned a blind eye in the name of cultural understanding."

It did not take long for the American Left and the *Times* to turn on Ali. In 2014, after an uproar from American Muslims and their allies, Brandeis University abruptly canceled its plans to award this "notorious Islamophobe" an honorary degree. "We cannot overlook that certain of her past statements are inconsistent with Brandeis University's core values," said the university in a burst of fake piety.[183] The media did not lag far behind academia. Bari Weiss, who recruited Ali to write an op-ed for the *Times*, observed, "Op-eds that would have easily been published just two years ago would now get an editor or a writer in serious trouble, if not fired."[184]

In those seven years between the publication of *Infidel* and Ali's rejection by Brandeis, the worm turned. Activist Muslims insinuated themselves into the multicultural coalition and, by doing so, insulated themselves from criticism. As a result, the *Times* was reporting on Ali with nearly the same contempt it reported on me. The two reporters on the Brandeis story quoted one Ali critic after another but none in support of her. "She is one of the worst of the worst of the Islam haters in America, not only in America but worldwide," Ibrahim Hooper, a spokesman for the Council on American-Islamic Relations (CAIR), told the *Times*.

Conceding Ali's Muslim girlhood was less than ideal, they let Maya Berry, executive director of the Arab American Institute, explain why those experiences really did not matter. "She has her very real personal story, she has her views, and she's free to say what she'd like to say," Berry told the *Times*. "But for an institution like Brandeis to choose to honor someone like this is really disappointing."[185] At the same commencement, Brandeis was also scheduled to give an honorary degree to Jill Abramson, the *Times* executive editor. Coincidentally, the *Times* fired Abramson the week after Brandeis rejected Ali but before the ceremony. In bowing out, Abramson said not a word about Ali.

After my "babies" tweet shook up the Left, I appeared on CNN's *New Day* with Chris Cuomo to explain myself. I had no illusion about convincing Cuomo, but I hoped there were at least a few sane people in his audience willing to hear what I had to say. After reading the tweet, Cuomo said, "This is being condemned by many regions of American politics and citizenry. What did you mean?" I probably should have said, "Chris, many *regions* of politics and citizenry?" What did *you* mean?"

My goal, though, wasn't to hang Fredo for tripping on his words but to explain myself. "I meant exactly what I said as I always do,"

I replied. I explained how I had been making this pitch for the previous ten years, especially in those European countries with declining populations. "You cannot rebuild your civilization with somebody else's babies," I continued. "You've got to keep your birth rate up, and that you need to teach your children your values. In doing so, you can grow your population, you can strengthen your culture, and you can strengthen your way of life."[186]

In the American context, it's not about race. My image of America, as I explained patiently to Cuomo, was a picture of physically diverse peoples sharing a common culture. Cuomo did not want to hear what I was saying. "It seemed like you were doing the opposite," he said. "Like you were trying to say you're either white or you're not right." It "seemed" that way to him because it was what he wanted to hear.

To Cuomo's surprise I made a pitch for interracial marriage, a pitch not usually found in the white nationalist playbook. "If you go down the road a few generations, or maybe centuries, with the intermarriage, I'd like to see an America that is just so homogenous that we look a lot the same," I said. "I think there's far too much focus on race, especially in the last eight years. I want to see that put behind us." Cuomo continued to present my anti-racist views as racist, and I resisted. "It's the culture, not the blood," I told him. "If you could go anywhere in the world and adopt these little babies and put them into households that were already assimilated into America, those babies will grow up as American as any other baby."

I may have been the first American to be called a racist for advocating interracial marriage and adoption, but that is what happened. Some of my critics argued that since the majority of Americans are white, I was hoping intermarriage would eventually turn everyone white. That is how race-obsessed they are. All the usual suspects, including then House Speaker Paul Ryan, promptly denounced me. My critics no longer evaluated what I said. They simply rejected my words because I said them.

Nowhere did Trip Gabriel cite my advocacy for racial intermarriage as one of my racist or divisive statements. I write this not to thank him but to condemn his actions. He did not cite my promotion of intermarriage because, had he, it would have undercut his potential career-killing insinuation that I was a white nationalist or white supremacist. He clearly had access to this 2017 CNN interview when attacking me in January 2019. He had to balance my unequivocal public statement in support of interracial marriage against his twisting of my words in an unrecorded phone interview, and he put his finger on the "white supremacist" side of the scale. This grotesque character assassination passes for news at the *New York Times.*

On Breitbart radio, I defended my tweet endorsing Wilders in the Dutch elections. My defense apparently upset Gabriel. In his "Timeline" he quoted a lengthy excerpt without comment as though no comment were needed. I will let you be the judge:

> *We're watching as Western Civilization is shrinking in the face of the massive, epic migration that is pouring into Europe. That's the core of that tweet. They're importing a different culture, a different civilization— and that culture and civilization, the imported one, rejects the host culture. And so they are supplanting Western Civilization with Middle Eastern civilization and I say, and Geert Wilders says, Western Civilization is a superior civilization—it is the first world.*

CHAPTER TWENTY-FIVE

2017: NURTURING A MIRACLE

I was involved in one event in 2017 Trip Gabriel chose to ignore even though it had what might be thought of as a racial element. Gabriel ignored my involvement because the event spoke to the potential harmony among races when everyone pulled together. The event also spoke to the unique qualities of Western Civilization.

In the way of background, on Monday, May 8, 2017, I was traveling on a congressional delegation fact-finding trip through Greece, Italy, and the Balkans. While I was engaged in an intense conversation at an event hosted by the U.S. Embassy in Athens, my cell phone rang. I drew my phone from its holster expecting to decline the call.

My screen read "Steve Meyer." Dr. Meyer is a hunting buddy, a surgeon, a missionary, and an inspiration. He never calls for anything frivolous, and I answered his call immediately half expecting a request for a minor miracle. "You have heard about the awful bus wreck here in Tanzania," said the good doctor. I had not, and he filled me in on the heartbreaking tragedy that killed thirty-five of the thirty-eight bus passengers on a dangerous road near Arusha, Tanzania.

Steve told me, "I can't save them here in Tanzania." He wanted to fly the three surviving children back to Sioux City, Iowa, where we have the necessary medical equipment and where a team of volunteers would be ready. "Everything is set up to take care of them. All medical services will be donated," he continued.

Steve needed me to expedite the passports and visas and to find a medevac plane that could fly three critically injured kids, their mothers, and a doctor and nurse to Iowa. "They won't live much longer unless we can get them to Mercy Hospital in Sioux City," he pleaded. This, I knew, *was* going to take a minor miracle.

As Davy Crockett used to say, "Know you're right, then go ahead." I immediately employed some of the U.S. Embassy staff to chase down phone numbers and help make phone connections. My first effective call was to the U.S. Embassy in Tanzania where I spoke with Anthony Pagliai, the counsel general. Mr. Pagliai could expedite the visas if Tanzanian passports could be processed in time.

I had already called Lazaro Nyalandu, a mutual friend who was introduced to me years earlier by Dr. Meyer. Lazaro recently finished second as a candidate for president of Tanzania and was a minister in the government. Mr. Pagliai didn't sound like he completely bought my story that I was a member of Congress calling for help for three very badly injured Tanzanian kids. So I name dropped Lazaro and said he would be contacting Pagliai for visas as soon as Lazaro could get Tanzanian passports issued.

"We know Lazaro, he was the only candidate who returned our calls," said Pagliai.

Lazaro was key to getting the passports expedited for all eight who would make the trip and getting them to the U.S. Embassy. Pagliai impressed all of us with how quickly he expedited the visas. The easiest part was in motion.

Adding to the challenge was the logistical complications for me because I was soon back in the air on the way to Sarajevo. I was making calls in search of a medevac plane. I began calling every source I could think of, including the White House. I was encouraged by the responses I received from the Trump team but I couldn't get a "yes." In Bosnia, I employed the embassy personnel again in search of a plane.

Steve called me again to check on my progress and, I think, to reaffirm a sense of urgency. Still, the toughest link to forge in the chain of miracles was securing a plane. U.S. assets in that part of the world are thin, and we hold our military assets close to our troops to protect them. I received a return call from the White House and was asked the question, "Are the survivors U.S. citizens?" They were Tanzanian citizens; still God's children but at that moment, I knew we wouldn't get a military plane. It was a big disappointment, but I was glad I had other lines in the water. By then I made scores of calls and pushed out to many to do the same.

We then flew to Albania, arriving late. A few of us planned our strategy that evening, and I took up the search for a plane the next morning. Again, the U.S. Embassy stepped up to help, particularly Elizabeth Soderholm. By early afternoon, we set up a call with Reverend Franklin Graham, the stellar son of the late Reverend Billy Graham and president of Samaritan's Purse, an international relief agency.

I called Franklin at 4:00 p.m. Albanian time. He answered the call immediately and listened intently as I made my, by now, well-practiced pitch for a medevac plane. In little more than three minutes, Reverend Graham said, "We have a DC-8 that can be set up for them, and we'll fly the children and their supporting personnel to Iowa for you."

There it was! This was the "yes" I was working for. I found a plane on the tarmac in the Mid-East but the cost was $300,000. With that in mind, I said, "Thank you, Reverend Graham, but I don't know that I can raise the money." Franklin said without hesitation, "You won't need to. We will take care of it for you."

I should note the World Giving Index has rated America the most generous country in the world every year for the last decade. On this same index, six of the top seven "most generous" countries—the United States, New Zealand, Australia, Ireland, Canada, and the United Kingdom—have inherited the language and culture of our mother ship, England. This is something I think is worth bragging about and preserving. Not only is English the language of business, it the language of giving as well.

In the United States, a 2006 book titled *Who Really Cares* by social scientist Arthur C. Brooks examined the actual performance of liberals and conservatives when it came to donating their own time, money, and, literally, blood. Brooks's reluctant conclusion confirmed what I always suspected, namely that people who identify as conservative donate money to charity more often than people who identify as liberal. They even donate more money, despite having less of it, and a higher percentage of their incomes. Conservatives volunteer more time as well. Conservatives even give a lot more blood. These conclusions so surprised Brooks— even he had fallen prey to liberal propaganda—he double-checked his data.

Graham's words confirmed the chain of miracles was coming together. I said to Reverend Graham, "I will text you Dr. Meyer's cell and yours to him with a message to immediately call each other." Now the two of them would need to connect and work out the logistics. And I was on the way to the airport again on the "country-a-day" tour to Macedonia, then Kosovo, then Italy.

I was in Kosovo when I learned Reverend Graham and Dr. Meyer connected and the DC-8 would soon arrive in Tanzania to pick up the Miracle Kids and fly them to Sioux City. By my count, I worked through and with six U.S. Embassies just to forge my single link in the Meyer chain of God's miracles necessary to save the lives of the kids.

Upon my return to Iowa I couldn't wait to get to Mercy Hospital to meet the kids. It was an utter joy to see their faces and the light in their eyes. Little more than a week earlier they lingered at death's door. Their mothers by now understood their children were going to survive. Even with the language barrier, they left no doubt about their gratitude. You know when a Muslim mom can't stop hugging you.

Not all the news was good. Of the three children, there were twenty-five serious fractures among them: five of six arms were broken, as were four of six legs, two of three spines, and one of three jaws. I learned that the little girl, Doreen, was paralyzed from the waist down.

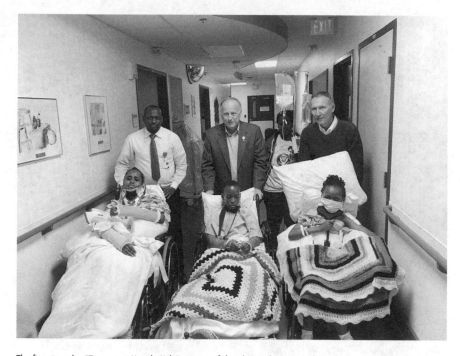

The first time the "Tanzanian Miracle Kids" are out of their hospital rooms and see each other. They don't yet know most of their friends are dead. (L–R) Sadia, Wilson, and Doreen. Rear (L–R) Tanzanian Dr. Elias Mashala, King, and Dr. Steve Meyer. Mercy Hospital, Sioux City, Iowa — May 20, 2017

Two weeks later, on a Sunday, I received another call from Dr. Meyer. I answered expecting to either hear bad news about one of the kids or a request for another miracle. Instead, he said, "I'm calling to tell you about another miracle. I went in to check on Doreen and teased her as I usually do and when I walked by her bed, she kicked me!"

"The neurologists think I'm crazy," Steve added, "but I know miracles. I know Doreen will walk again!"

Assuming the miracle for Doreen would come to pass, we began planning the return of the Miracle Kids to their home country. A few weeks later, we set August 18 as the date, and I set up a trip to multiple countries in Africa timed to be part of the welcome party in Tanzania.

Doreen, Sadia, and Wilson (L—R) backed by their mothers and Steve and Rachel King (granddaughter). TZ Miracle Kids rolled out to midfield to preside over the coin toss at the Sioux City Bandits indoor football game. They soon learned they were "adopted" by the entire Siouxland region. — June 12, 2017

The best place in the world to be on August 18, 2017, was on the tarmac at Kilimanjaro Airport when the Samaritan's Purse DC-8 touched down and rolled to a stop. My wife, Marilyn, and I, Steve and Dana Meyer, and Lazaro Nyalandu and his beautiful Miss Tanzania wife Faraja, shared in the utter elation of a nation as we celebrated together the joy of the Miracle Kids' homecoming. Sadia came down the long steps first to great cheers and tears of joy. Then the perpetually smiling Wilson made his way down the steps to set foot on his home country to even louder cheers. Then Doreen, the formerly paralyzed eleven-year-old, began making her shaky descent. All eyes were focused on her progress.

I'm sure many private prayers helped Doreen down the long flight of steps. As she descended, the cheers grew louder and louder as if the decibels would give her strength. Doreen finally set foot on her home turf to the loudest and most sustained roar from a

Back on the home turf at Kilimanjaro Airport, Tanzania. Here Dr. Meyer and King celebrate Sadia's first steps on the tarmac while surrounded by thousands of Tanzanians who turned out for the big day. Most never expected to see them alive again. Dr. Meyer and his wife, Dana, are profound believers in miracles. —August 18, 2017 crowd imaginable. She was then helped into a wheelchair and wheeled over to the celebration area.

Thousands of Tanzanians were dressed in their Sunday best for the occasion. The program included prayers and speeches. I kept mine short. There was a band and a group of Tanzanian women in long, beautiful, colorful dresses who wrote songs during the summer to welcome the Miracle Kids home. I couldn't understand the Swahili lyrics but the harmony was beautiful. They were the "Supremes" times two.

I looked at the program and saw the Tanzanian national anthem would be next. Thousands of Tanzanians sang proudly, loudly, and on key, from their hearts, of a country I was beginning to know and a people I just met.

Next up was our "Star Spangled Banner." I looked around to see how many Americans there would be to join us in our national

Doreen makes her shaky way down the long steps of Samaritan's Purse's DC-8. When she set foot on Tanzanian terra firma, an unbelievable roar went up from the crowd. Neurologists confirm her recovery was a miracle. Doreen, today, plays soccer with her friends.—August 18, 2017

anthem. We were only four. I leaned back to Dr. Meyer and said, "We're really going to have to belt this one out!" He agreed and we delivered.

I had never sung our national anthem with such pride as we celebrated the joy of serving God's Kingdom as Americans. That day, August 18, 2017, at Kilimanjaro Airport was our reward for answering God's call. I have been allowed the privilege of serving the greatest nation on the planet and been rewarded with a priceless memory. I have said, "If I am stricken by Alzheimer's and destined to lose my memories one at a time, let this cherished day in my memory be the last to go."

In the fall, Dr. Meyer asked me to say a few words at his annual auction, a fundraiser for his Siouxland, Tanzania, Educational, Medical, Ministries (STEMM). I only said it is a blessing

After the welcome home prayers, speeches, songs, and ceremony; friends of Dana and Steve Meyer with Steve and Marilyn King celebrate the afterglow. (Marilyn was in particularly good form:) Kilimanjaro International Airport, Tanzania — August 18, 2017

from God to have the rare opportunity to forge a link in the chain of miracles that saved the lives of the Tanzanian Miracle Kids. I didn't think my speech was that good but at auction, a dinner with Marilyn and me went for $20,000. Dana Meyer hugged me and said, "You've just built half an orphanage."

I forged only one or two links in the chain of miracles but had any link failed, all three children would be dead today. I can't help but ask, had the political lynch mob done their deed to me before the Tanzanian tragedy, would Reverend Graham have taken my call? If not, what chance would the kids have had? Dr. Meyer put the links together and was the linchpin of the entire life-saving effort. Reverend Franklin Graham was a most timely and essential link as well. We can't forget Kevin Nagaard, Manda Volkert, Jennifer Miley, and the other STEMM volunteers, who pulled the

Sadia, Wilson, and Doreen at the banquet for them at the Siouxland Tanzania Educational Medical Ministries (STEMM) facilities. Arusha, Tanzania—August 18, 2017

surviving children and thirty-five corpses out of the bus, prayed over them all, and who have been with them every step of the way.

Scores of lives were changed forever by this terrible tragedy. Given the gruesome scope of the loss of life and the injuries, the best possible outcome was realized. There is now a bright future as a result of the chain of miracles, shaped through His servants, by the hand of God. No "low' I have suffered as a congressman can ever match this "high."

CHAPTER TWENTY-SIX

2018: REDEFINING "MCCARTHYISM"

A 2010 *Washington Monthly* article smearing me for supporting Sen. Joe McCarthy begins with this sentence: "For the American mainstream, former Sen. Joseph McCarthy (R-Wis.) was a dangerous demagogue. His name is synonymous with witch hunts, smears, guilt by association, and the practice of destroying the lives of one's political rivals."[187]

When I read this today, I have to laugh. For the length of my time in Congress, especially these last four years, the "American mainstream" has relentlessly smeared me and painted me guilty by association to destroy my viability as a political rival. Joe McCarthy, by contrast, targeted only Communist subversives in government. They were real, and they were dangerous. If anything, as subsequent revelations show, McCarthy underestimated the problem, and he rarely, if ever, called someone a communist who wasn't. Anyone interested in a behind-the-scenes look at this era and issue should read *Witness* by Whittaker Chambers.

In his "Timeline," Trip Gabriel exercised no such restraint. Referring to a 2018 interview I did with a web publication in Austria, Gabriel wrote: "Mr. King demonstrates familiarity with the 'Great Replacement' conspiracy theory, also known as 'white genocide,' which posits that an international elite, including prominent Jews like George Soros, are plotting to make white populations minorities in Europe and North America."

In Serbia and Croatia, I walked and talked with migrants who were, day and night and horizon to horizon, streaming into Europe. You do not have to be a conspiracy theorist to recognize the most popular name for a newborn boy in England, as in much of Europe, is some variation of "Muhammad." You do not have to be a conspiracy theorist to understand those most at risk from Islamic dominance in Europe are Jews.

Consider the headline of this 2020 article from *Foreign Affairs*, the ultimate globalist publication: "A France Without Jews Is No Longer Unthinkable: Anti-Semitism Puts Pressure on a Community and a Cherished Idea."[188] The Jews in France worry far less about Neo-Nazis, as bad as they are, than they do about Islamic militants whose numbers are larger and growing.

The *Foreign Affairs* article begins, for instance, with a description of a lethal attack on a kosher market by terrorists claiming allegiance to ISIS. There are likely more such attacks on the way. In a 2005 Pew Research Foundation survey, 100 percent of Jordanians and 99 percent of Lebanese answered "Yes" to the question of whether they had a "highly unfavorable" view of Jews. Those attitudes have not softened since then and these people do not leave these views behind when they immigrate to Europe.[189]

Gabriel knew all of this or had no reason for not knowing. So what did he do? He made me sound like an advocate for some comic book anti-Semitic plot targeting George Soros. I will admit. I do have problems with George Soros, whose very name sounds like a Bond villain. I had problems with him long before I knew he had Jewish roots, roots he has largely severed if his hostility to Israel is any indication.

My problems stem from Soros's aggressive globalism and undisguised Leftism. According to the apolitical (non-governmental organization) NGO Monitor, the Open Society Foundations (OSF) Soros founded is known for its "often intrusive activities in both closed and democratic societies, including large scale funding of political NGOs." According to the OSF website, OSF is the "world's largest private funder of independent groups working for justice, democratic governance, and human rights." In the United States, the recipient of much of Soros's funding, the NGOs that OSF supports are inevitably Leftist and/or globalist, and often subversive.

The Center for Community Change is "dedicated to finding the [progressive] stars of tomorrow and preparing them to lead." The American Institute for Social Justice aims to "transform poor communities by agitating for increased government spending on social-welfare programs." Democracy for America is designed to "focus, network, and train grassroots activists in the skills and strategies to take back our country." Take back our country from whom exactly?

It was the media that made us aware of Soros's Jewish roots. They did so in order to stifle criticism of Soros as a Leftist mover and shaker. I would not be surprised if Soros was part of that awareness campaign. For sure he was involved in a 2016 Democratic confab that weaponized words like "white nationalist," "white supremacist," "Nazi," and "fascist."

I think Soros is evil and dangerous, and if he were my first cousin, I would still think he was evil and dangerous. But for Gabriel to condemn me for being "familiar" with a theory allegedly subscribed to by some unspecified anti-Semites does an injustice even to the Left's definition of McCarthyism.

To learn more about the "Great Replacement" theory, I turned to Google. When I did, the first thirty or so articles I found about the theory were written by some hack or other Leftist media outlets. All these articles were alarmist, if not downright scary, and untrustworthy. Gabriel's description of it as some unhinged "conspiracy theory" was something of a norm.

The French writer who coined the term "Great Replacement," Renaud Camus, describes the phenomenon very simply: "The Great Replacement is very simple. You have one people, and in the space of a generation, you have a different people."[190] Many neighborhoods throughout Europe, even cities, have witnessed rapid replacement. If the locals object to their disenfranchisement, the elites do not. In fact, they are quick to scold the locals for objecting.

Camus lost his standing among the elites for resisting the replacement. For many years, he had been celebrated in literary circles as a gay icon. Even more so than Jews, however, gays had reason to fear Islam, a religion notoriously intolerant of homosexuality. Camus saw what happened to his outspoken counterpart in the Netherlands, author and gay rights activist Pim Fortuyn. Living under constant threat, he was assassinated in 2002 by a Leftist whose goal was to stop Fortuyn from allegedly scapegoating Muslims.

Islamic takeover is not a real fear in the United States. I have attended thousands of conservative events nationwide and never been asked a single question about the Great Replacement. I would guess 95 percent of conservatives have no idea what it is.

Yet, in Europe the theory is better known because the threat is more imminent. For the most part, European nations have tribal origins. They have been able in the past to absorb limited numbers of immigrants because the immigrants have been largely willing to accept tribal customs and traditions, including Judeo-Christian values. They now face a new wave of immigrants eager to replace those traditions with their own. Here are some sample headlines from mainstream news sources reflecting the problem Europe faces:

> *"Germany Deports Islamic Radical"*
>
> *"France deports Islamist militants, imams amid crackdown"*
>
> *"Denmark wants to deport extremist imams"*
>
> *"Spain to deport MB Imam over extremist behavior"*
>
> *"Neutral Switzerland's Growing Islamist and Jihadist Challenge"*
>
> *"Austria to close seven mosques and deport imams in crackdown on 'political Islam'"*

"Cleric says some imams in Ireland hold extremist views"

"Sweden to deport two imams judged as national security threats"

"Radical Islamic cleric deported from Britain found not guilty of terror charges by Jordan"

The one European country refusing to play the multicultural game is Hungary. Among my many racist or divisive acts in 2017 was agreeing with a tweet by Hungary's Prime Minister Viktor Orban. Wrote Orban, "Mixing cultures will not lead to a higher quality of life but a lower one." Defying European orthodoxy, Orban hopes to build in Hungary a "constitutional order based on national and Christian foundations." He openly worries about a future in which "the whole of Europe has . . . submitted to Islam."

I met with Victor Orban in his formal office in Budapest. He has a mural of the history of Western Civilization painted all around him on the tall wall of his office. During an intense two-and-a-half-hour discussion, he took me on a tour of the mural. I found his intellect, his understanding of history, and his ability to understand the tectonic cultural shifts in Europe to be extraordinary. Orban knows he is defending Western Civilization, and he understands Soros. He understands Western Civilization and isn't afraid to make his points with clarity: "If somebody takes masses of non-registered immigrants from the Middle East into a country, this also means importing terrorism, criminalism, anti-Semitism, and homophobia." He is, in my opinion, the gold standard in leadership for our shared civilization.

Not coincidentally, according to Jewish political observer Daniel Pipes, "Hungary is the safest place in Europe in public for observant Jews."[191] Unlike much of the rest of Europe, Jewish institutions operate in the open here, and Hungary has the best relations of any nation in Europe with Israel. Although Hungarians almost uniformly reject Muslim immigration, they generally treat Muslim students, tourists, and residents with respect. Having regained their sovereignty just thirty years ago with the collapse

King and Hungarian Prime Minister Viktor Orban in his formal office. Orban's upper office walls are painted with a beautiful mural depicting an historically accurate continuum of Western Civilization. Budapest, Hungary —October 4, 2016

of the Soviet empire, Hungarians are not eager to lose it to Brussels or some international caliphate. As Pipes noted, Hungarians also saw the problems the rest of Europe was having with "polygamy, honor killings, rape gangs, partial no-go zones, Sharia courts, and parallel societies."

If Leftists really believed in multiculturalism, they would accept Hungarian culture as it is. They would not scold me and Orban for acknowledging the virtue of preserving that culture and the problems inherent in creating a parallel Muslim society within Hungary. Hungary is not America. Our culture is based on an idea, not a tribal affiliation.

Historically, we have been able to assimilate all peoples willing to honor that idea. For American Leftists to impose our values, more realistically *their* values, on a country like Hungary is the worst kind of cultural imperialism. A February 2021 headline in the *New York Times* speaks to the growing resistance to progressive exports even in a country like France, "Will American Ideas Tear France Apart? Some of Its Leaders Think So." The *Times* identifies those ideas as "out-of-control woke leftism," and among the leaders in question is French President Emmanuel Macron.[192]

CHAPTER TWENTY-SEVEN

2019: COPING WITH THE COLLABORATORS

There I was in the first full week of the 116th Congress, stripped of all my committees by the hand of Kevin McCarthy. K Street got the message from McCarthy, and PAC fundraising was shut off. My major donors were hounded to the ends of the earth. I was disparaged in nearly every media venue and shunned by many of my former political allies. There was no due process. In fact, there would be no venue in which to make my case.

McCarthy, the modern-day real McCarthyite, cowed the Steering Committee and the Republican Conference into stripping me of my committee assignments. Bari Weiss described well the kind of tactics McCarthy employed. "It's not just about punishing the sinner," Weiss told Bill Maher. "It's not just about punishing the person for being insufficiently pure. It's about this sort of secondary boycott of people who would deign to speak to that person or appear on a platform with that person."[193] The atmosphere was as toxic as I ever experienced. In the middle of all this madness, I did my best to keep my head, knowing it is impossible to reason with a lynch mob, especially when it's led by the sheriff.

There were colleagues who did stand up for me, and they know I know who they are. They will always have my gratitude. I will not name them here so I don't cause them any more retribution.

They paid a price from leadership and may never know how much it cost them.

I soon found myself with four primary opponents all intent on defeating me in eighteen months. The chorus began, "King was kicked off his committees. We have no seat at the table. He has lost the confidence of leadership." It is curious to me that throughout the entire primary campaign not one of my four opponents took issue with even a single vote of the thousands I cast in Congress. Neither did they disagree with any position I took on an issue. They only targeted my Achilles heel, the betrayal by my own Republican leadership.

At every Republican function in the thirty-nine counties of the Fourth Congressional District, the debate played out like a game of "King of the Hill." If any of my opponents were to succeed, he had to knock me off Capitol Hill. When you are the King of the Hill, everyone is trying to pull you down.

It is an axiom of human nature that children and adults will use whatever argument serves their purpose as long as it's effective and available to them. If I was golden on my votes and positions, I was vulnerable due to the withdrawal of my committee assignments, the political death sentence. My opponents would use this against me relentlessly and effectively. Again, McCarthy knew no one survives losing all his committees. It was becoming ever more evident he and Steve Stivers were planning this branding all along. To win in 2020, I knew I had to get my committee assignments back. So I set about playing the long game.

On March 6, 2019, I published a "Fact Check" document I made available to the public and all my colleagues, including the Steering Committee. "Fact Check" stands today as the definitive statement on my history of using language and on the falsehoods in the *Times* story. Over the span of two years, no press, politician, pundit, or constituent has made an argument against any of the facts or my rationale. They simply ignored the document.

My colleagues' blood was beginning to cool by the August break so I waited until September 2019. I had to find the right way to command my colleagues' attention, but the impeachment noise began that September and would continue until mid-February 2020. Now, my time was starting to get short. I was still strong in the polls but I knew while I toiled in Washington, four candidates were chiseling away at my reputation and my lead. That tag-team assault was bound to take its toll.

I pressed for meetings with McCarthy and with Republican Whip Steve Scalise. Each agreed to a meeting and told me so to my face. They assigned staff to set up the meeting during our conversations. Scalise was not to be taken at his word. He told his staff afterward to block any meeting with me. I have the emails. After persistent pressure, McCarthy finally consented to a scheduled meeting, set for Wednesday, January 29, 2020.

In the meantime, I spoke privately with President Trump. He seemed to understand but told me, "It's McCarthy's decision." Trump was right and I knew then the only alternative was to make my case to McCarthy. Trump also said, "I've never hit you." True, and he implied he wouldn't. As mentioned, Trump's statements have been far sharper than mine, and McCarthy has defended him, arguing for the due process he actively denied me.

In the McCarthy meeting there were four people in the room. We each brought our chiefs of staff into the conversation. I presented the arguments mostly from the "Fact Check" document. McCarthy asked if that document was available to him. Of course, it had been available for nearly a year. McCarthy wanted time to read and consider my document but made no argument against my points. This turned out to be a ploy to buy time. In the business, it's called "slow walking."

I expected an answer within a week to my request to get my committees back and my seniority restored. I let three weeks pass before texting McCarthy on February 18, 2020: "Kevin, just checking to see if my fact check document has risen to a priority for you. It will be three weeks tomorrow that we discussed my committee assignments. Time is running out. We can discuss by phone, if you prefer. Thanks, Steve King."

From that day forward, I sent twenty texts to Kevin, and I got three responses, all promises to call. I also made an uncountable number of calls, each time leaving a message. McCarthy did finally connect with me on Sunday, April 19. By then, according to our discussion, the only barrier to restoring my committees was the Steering Committee. McCarthy had to canvass its members to measure any opposition. I also knew this was a slow-walk tactic because McCarthy handpicks the committee.

Still, I had to play out the game. In that Sunday phone call we did reach an agreement. Since Kevin had two-and-a-half months to come up with an argument for why Gabriel and the *New York Times* were right and I was wrong, he surely came to the realization there was no such argument. His position was unsustainable in the light of day, so he had little choice but to agree with my position. Here is the transcript of the April 19, 2020, phone call.

> **King:** This is my understanding, and so that we understand each other, I'll ask you this way: Will you go to the Steering Committee and advocate on my behalf to restore me to all my committees?

> **McCarthy:** Yes.

> **King:** I don't need anything, Kevin, I don't need anything, and I don't need any retribution or anything of that nature. I don't need any compensation of any nature. I just need to just put things back to right. My constituents are suffering. So is the country.

> **McCarthy:** No, I appreciate that. That was one of the things that really helped me make the decision is when you told me that.

The next morning, I held a rare conference call with all my staff in Washington and Iowa to tell them McCarthy and I reached an agreement, and I expected to be restored to all my committees within a week or two at the outside. Everyone was happy this was coming to an end. The long game was paying off. Marilyn voiced serious skepticism about McCarthy's reliability, but I assured her his statement was too direct and definitive to be a lie.

Five days later I sent McCarthy this text:

> *Kevin, how did your discussions with Steering go? I would like to establish a unified message so I don't get out in front of your skis. I have a debate this weekend. The topic certainly will come up. I will tell them the truth, of course, but I want you to have had the chance to position yourself. A phone call will work. Thanks, Steve King*

Still no response. Multiple texts later, without response from McCarthy, I sent him this text on May 11:

> *Kevin, I will be called upon to make a public statement on committee assignments today at a TV interview and at a debate this evening. Is there anything you would like me to add or a statement you would like to make? Steve King*

No answer again. So that evening in debate, I said this in the context of what I just described as the long overdue exoneration of Michael Flynn: "On April 20, (actually April 19, my mistake), Kevin McCarthy and I reached an agreement that he would advocate to the Steering Committee to put all of my committees back, all of my seniority."

I continued, "When Congress comes back into session, when the Steering Committee can get together, I have Kevin McCarthy's word, and that will be my time for exoneration."

Each time I made a move on this subject, I was putting pressure on McCarthy. I was hoping to force his hand. It would not do to let this uncertainty ride through the June 2 primary election. McCarthy gave his word, and I was going to push him into either keeping his word or exposing his mendacity to the public.

I spent the week counting votes on the Steering Committee. The press had already found three "no" votes: Cheney, Stivers, and David Joyce. The two men were from Boehner's home state, and Cheney, the silver-spooned "Cersei," would have lynched Tom Horn if she lived in Wyoming a century earlier.

Those native to Wyoming—Cheney is not—know the Tom Horn story as part of their history. In the way of background, Tom Horn went to the gallows in 1903 after he was framed for the murder of a shepherd boy. Joe Belle, a crooked marshal, using a reporter positioned in a closet as his accomplice, questioned Horn while the reporter recorded Horn's denial which was, "Well, if I'da killed that kid, it'a been the best shot I ever made and the dirtiest trick I ever done."

Tom Horn was subsequently arrested for the murder of the shepherd boy. When the case came to trial in Cheyenne, the prosecutor asked the reporter, "Will you tell the court exactly what you took down at that time?" Testifying from his notes, the reporter replied, "The last thing Mr. Horn said before leaving Joe Belle's office was, 'When I shot that kid it was the best shot I ever made. The dirtiest trick I ever did.'" This willful misquote from a reporter sent Tom Horn to the gallows in Cheyenne where he was hanged on November 20, 1903. Some say it's irrelevant whether Horn was framed for the murder of the shepherd boy because Horn deserved to be hanged for other reasons.

I believe Liz Cheney feels that way about me. Horn and I were victims of a malicious misquote from a reporter. Tom Horn got due process, however rigged the trial. There would be no due process for me, and I would be hung out to dry. I was in good company. During the second impeachment, Donald Trump got the "Cersei" Cheney knife in his back as well. There was no due process in the House for him either.

I read the following on a tombstone in, as it happens, Tombstone, Arizona: "Here lies George Johnson, hanged by mistake. He was right, we was wrong, but we strung him up and now he's gone."

As I moved around and talked with the Steering Committee members, I soon learned McCarthy did not speak with any of them. When I came to that conclusion, I knew I had to lock in all the necessary votes and present my vote count to McCarthy. By the end of the week, I counted twenty-six "yes" votes, three "no" votes, and six "unknown" votes. It was clear a word from McCarthy as promised would have put me back on my committees, likely on a voice vote.

I was closing in, or so I thought. Then that Friday McCarthy held a press conference. A reporter asked a version of this question, "King says he has reached a deal with you and he will be restored to his committees and he will be exonerated." McCarthy said immediately, "I never said that." He went on to explain the Steering Committee would have to make the decision. He expected the committee would give me the same thumbs-down as before and even that vote would not come until the next Congress.

The only truthful part of the McCarthy response was he did not use the word "exonerate" in his discussion with me. That was the word I used in comparing my promised committee reassignments to General Flynn's expected exoneration. Now, McCarthy made *me* out to be the liar. Worse, he did this two weeks before the primary. Fragged by my own party leadership.

The Republican enemies of conservatism were lined up against me. The grievance groups I had been saying "No" to for years saw their opportunity. First came the Republican Main Street Partnership, a PAC formed to frustrate the conservative agenda in the House. As far as I know, I'm the first Republican to be targeted by the PAC. Its leaders are pro-amnesty, in favor of much of ObamaCare, and eager to deal with the Democrats. Boehner partnered with them in their efforts to thwart the conservative agenda. On the Hill, you don't have to say the group's name. The PAC is routinely referred to as the "RINOs." If you have read this far in the book, you already know RINO is an acronym for "Republican in Name Only." Many of the more aggressive RINOs were charging at this conservative for years.

Next came the U.S. Chamber of Commerce. The Chamber presented me with its "Spirit of Enterprise Award" every year I was in Congress. In 2019, three months after the Trip Gabriel flap, the Chamber CEO said in presenting me with the award, "By advancing good legislation, Rep. Steve King is helping businesses grow and thrive, keeping our economy strong, and promoting the free enterprise system that drives opportunity and prosperity."

Unfortunately, many of the U.S. Chamber's major donors demand cheap foreign labor. Conservatives quietly refer to it as the "U.S. Chamber of Amnesty." I have spearheaded every effort against amnesty and been successful every time. With my campaign shackled by the dissembling of the House leadership, these donors saw a chance to clear a path for more cheap foreign labor.

In the Covid-19 spring of 2020, with forty million Americans unemployed, the Chamber started running ads for one of my primary opponents, Randy Feenstra. What America did not need at this time—at any time—was the erasure of our borders, an erosion of cultural continuity, and a taxpayer subsidy to support the substandard wages usually paid to illegal aliens. I have long been a champion of free enterprise and have the Chamber awards to prove it, but I know free enterprise can only flourish when protected by the Rule of Law. So the U.S. Chamber of Amnesty and I parted company.

The lead Never Trump PAC was the Republican Jewish Coalition (RJC). Making the decisions at the RJC are its largest donors. One of them, an RJC board member, is hedge fund billionaire, Paul Singer, the top donor to Kevin McCarthy and the National Republican Senatorial Committee. Singer is also an LGBTQ funder and activist renowned for using his mega donor dollars to punish, silence, or sway Republican candidates and incumbent members of Congress. I suspect no one in Congress has a stronger record in support of Israel and President Trump than I do but like many PACs, RJC is commanded by donor checkbooks. Sometimes, it only takes one check. So, when the RJC attacks me, allegedly because I criticized George Soros, you are right to sense a hidden agenda.

Even more ironically, the next PAC to stand against me was National Right to Life Committee (NRLC), the self-proclaimed "oldest and the largest ProLife organization in the county." I don't doubt the group is old and large. I do question whether it is Pro-Life. When I recruited 174 co-sponsors for my HeartBeat bill, which had no exceptions for rape or incest, I started getting push-back from NRLC.

I spoke privately to each of my then leaders—Ryan, McCarthy, and Scalise—and pushed to get the bill through committee and on to the House floor for a vote. We more than qualified with 174 co-sponsors. Each of the three told me the leadership would not move ProLife legislation without the support of the top three ProLife organizations, namely Family Research Council, Susan B. Anthony List, and National Right to Life, collectively referred to as "The Holy Trinity."

The problem was National Right to Life. I did my diplomatic best with NRLC to make my case but reached an impasse. When that impasse became public in February 2018, *BuzzFeed* classified me among those "absolutists" who hoped to make abortion entirely illegal while the NRLC preferred an "incremental" approach. One of the NRLC's top priorities is the "Born Alive Act" which would make it illegal to kill a baby surviving abortion. My HeartBeat bill would save the lives of nearly every baby.

As much as I appreciate any ProLife allies, those who are not trying to eliminate *Roe v. Wade* are not really allies. If I'm walking point, these deeply entrenched incrementalists are leading from behind, way behind. Their stock in trade is raising money and trimming around the edges. Born alive legislation is all well and good, but in 2018, we had ProLife majorities in the House and Senate, a ProLife president, and an impending 5–4 majority on the Supreme Court. We should have been able to do much better.

Had the House alone passed the HeartBeat bill, that passage would have validated my deeply held conviction that babies conceived in rape or incest are as precious to God as my own grandchildren are to me. Unfortunately, nothing could convince NRLC the stars were aligning for a potentially successful challenge to Roe.

It became increasingly clear to me if we were ever to reverse Roe, we would have to challenge National Right to Life. NRLC published a tweet saying they did not *oppose* the HeartBeat bill, when in fact they did. A green light from them would have put my HeartBeat legislation on the House floor for a nearly certain passage. That's if leadership honored their word. To correct the record, I decided to use the best available tool, the truth. I went to the floor of the House and displayed a large poster with the tweet on it. I then drew a line through the word "oppose" and replaced it with "support," a much more honest description of the NRLC position.

Justice Clarence Thomas, my favorite of the nine justices on the Supreme Court, has a set of hooks outside his office engraved with this script, "Hang Egos Here." William Lloyd Garrison's statement was ringing in my ears, "I will be heard!" Forgive my immoderation but this was a time to be heard. My intention was to shame the NRLC onto the ProLife team. Instead, I ticked its leaders off royally. Truth has a way of upsetting people. Their bruised egos trumped National Right to Life's mission statement, which is to "protect innocent human life from abortion."

Leadership, starting with Speaker Ryan and probably Boehner before him, granted National Right to Life veto power over every

HR 490, the HeartBeat Protection Act had far and away more support in Congress than ANY other ProLife bill. ALL 129 other ProLife groups/leaders supported the bill. Only NRLC refused to support.

piece of ProLife legislation. It didn't matter to party leaders that 174 duly-elected members of Congress representing 124 million constituents wanted to see the HeartBeat bill passed into law or that we had the votes to pass the bill in committee and on to the floor. NRLC dug in and successfully blocked the bill with the active help of Kevin McCarthy. Given my experience, I am mystified to see McCarthy's signature on fundraising letters from the Susan B. Anthony List. Don't they know McCarthy was instrumental in killing the HeartBeat bill?

Add the gambling PAC to my growing group of powerful foes and you begin to see what I was facing in 2020, a firing squad of RINOs, globalists, elitists, amnesty advocates, NeverTrumpers, and "incrementalists." There was nothing bold about their collective agenda and little that was conservative. As an outspoken constitutional Christian conservative and an ardent defender of the Trump agenda, I reminded my opponents and my leadership of what they were not.

About two-and-a-half weeks before the June 2nd primary, I began to pick up information from the White House that Kevin McCarthy gained the trust of President Trump and Trump "outsourced" House race political decisions to McCarthy. That information was not particularly unusual or alarming until I heard from no less than five concurring sources, all in position to know, McCarthy was aggressively lobbying Trump to endorse Feenstra.

I decided not to take the issue to Trump given the pressure he was under managing Covid-19 response. I also ran the risk of stimulating an aggressive Stivers-like action from McCarthy. By now, I knew McCarthy and Cheney plotted against me for months. Cheney would have gladly shoved the stiletto between my ribs if given the chance. She is not bothered by blood on her hands. McCarthy is equally as devious and more adept. He prefers to manipulate his proxies to do his dirty work, believing he isn't leaving his DNA at the scene of the crime. In any case, Trump did not endorse Feenstra. That was one bullet dodged, but more were on the way.

CHAPTER TWENTY-EIGHT

2020: KEEPING THE FAITH

For several years I considered prominent conservative pundit Ben Shapiro a friend or at least a conservative brother warrior. Although smart and sophisticated, Shapiro has long lived in fear of the Left's broad, racist brush. For all his virtues, he has a knee-jerk impulse to virtue signal when an ally is accused of saying something that triggers the Left. Immediately after the Trip Gabriel fiasco in January 2019, I caught a Shapiro knee. Without knowing any of the facts beyond what Gabriel asserted, Shapiro tweeted, "Congress ought to vote to censure [King], and then he ought to be primaried ASAP."[194]

Not satisfied with the damage inflicted, Shapiro, the editor-in-chief of the *Daily Wire*, followed up with another tweet urging his followers to donate to Randy Feenstra's instantly concocted primary campaign. "Donate to his primary challenger, Randy Feenstra, here."[195] Shapiro tweeted, listing Feenstra's hastily constructed website. "I plan on doing so." Feenstra promptly thanked Shapiro in a tweet, arguing that King's "caustic nature has left us without a seat at the table."[196] Caustic? This was a new word in Feenstra's vocabulary. His handlers were already in charge.

Fast-forward only a year and a half. Now, Shapiro is tweeting another tune in response to a chart found in the "Whiteness" section of the Smithsonian museum's portal on race. The self-parodying chart describes fourteen categories of "white dominant culture, or whiteness." Shapiro said, accurately enough, the chart "suggests all pathways to success—hard work, stable family structure, individual decision-making—represent complicity in white supremacy."[197] Yes, Ben, we are all white supremacists now, including you.

In attempting to stereotype white people, the chart maker lists various attributes I have long been saying represented not "white culture"—there is no such thing—but American culture. What is more, many of these presumed character flaws I see as virtues. So do most thinking Americans. I tweeted at the time: "Setting up cultural conflict. The poster illustrates the 'Pillars of American Exceptionalism,' how to earn your keep, contribute to society, and make the world a better place. This is a direct attack on the first world; Western Civilization."[198]

In response to the Smithsonian exhibit, Donald Trump Jr. said almost exactly what I had been saying during my eighteen years in Congress and before. "These aren't 'white' values," said Trump. "They're American values that built the world's greatest civilization. They help you succeed here, no matter your color."[199]

The Smithsonian people feel otherwise. Let's start with the category "rugged individualism." Under this category are attributes like self-reliance, independence, and an urge to control one's own environment. The chart maker sums up these instincts in the dismissive axiom, "You get what you deserve."

Under family structure, the white male, we are told, wants a nuclear family with "2.3 children," a "subordinate" homemaker for a wife, and, bizarrely, a bedroom for every child. I should note if the chart people ever met Marilyn, they would know I did not choose a "subordinate" to be my wife. Does that make me less white? Oh, yes, the Smithsonian also instructs us the ideal white woman looks like "Barbie." Barbie? Is this whole thing a spoof?

These same white people, we are told, put an "emphasis on scientific method" and over-value "objective, rational linear thinking." Under the rubric "history," white people stress "Western

(Greek and Roman) and Judeo-Christian tradition." They also believe "hard work is the key to success." Ironically, the Smithsonian suggests all of the above are character flaws. If so, I wish more of us were flawed.

As should be clear even to Stivers and McCarthy, Western Civilization and traditional American culture are targets of the Left. This subversion wasn't coming from CNN or the Black Lives Matter website. It was coming from the *Smithsonian*. The source of the attack did not surprise me or Mark Steyn or others who have been trying to warn our allies. It did, however, seem to shock our self-assigned intellectual superiors.

The chart was originally designed in 1978. It was posted just *before* the George Floyd mania broke out across the country in a section titled "Talking About Race" that is as stupid and insulting as the chart, just not as obvious. For years this racist gibberish has been pushed down the throats of our students. And now it is being pushed down the throats of our athletes, our business people, even our military. Your recognition is welcome, Ben, I just hope it is not too late.

But it may be. "Make no mistake," said Donald Trump Jr. "Biden's radicals aren't coming for 'whites,' they're coming for the entire American way of life." He is right. In the months after Biden's move into the White House, even RINOs have been shocked by the Left's eagerness to erase American culture. We have now reached a pivotal point in our history. The death of George Floyd served as the catalyst for which Antifa and Black Lives Matter had long been planning. In the following violent spasms, our cities burned, our history was openly desecrated, and new grievances were generated by the day.

These grievances fed the rumbling appetite of mobs hungry for action after being locked down for months. Now conveniently sprung for the occasion, these young people showed the world just how deeply poisoned their minds have been by a crude and constant diet of Leftist dogma from kindergarten through college, then subjected to a globalist corporate multicultural imperium. Aiding and abetting the corruption of these young minds was a malicious

Leftist media, shamelessly censoring or trying to censor all but approved politically correct speech. So thorough has been the brainwashing, these youths have come to despise a civilization that, even by their own standards, is the fairest and most generous in world history. More perversely still, these self-designated "anti-racists" despise Western Civilization for its "whiteness." Ben Shapiro, at least, was catching on. In August 2020, he wrote:

> *Americans surrendered to the narrative promulgated for so long by those who seek to undermine American comity: that American history is not the story of moving toward the fulfillment of the promises of the Declaration of Independence but of the continuous, chameleonic perversion of bigotry; that America's founding ideas were lies, then and always; that only racial identity provides credence for talking about racial inequalities. The burden of proof has shifted to America's defenders.*[200]

For years, I was one of those defenders. I saw the onslaught coming when the Left hijacked Dr. Martin Luther King's "I Have a Dream" speech, and in the form of "affirmative action," promptly gave the color of one's skin priority over the content of one's character. I saw it coming when Lyndon Johnson's "War on Poverty" drove fathers out of the home and elevated "unwed mothers" to the heroic status of "single moms." I saw it coming when our universities eliminated inspiring courses on Western Civilization and replaced them with self-hating courses on race, gender, and Marx. I saw it coming when Ronald Reagan signed the 1986 Amnesty Act unaware of how the Left would use it to subvert the Rule of Law and reward illegal aliens. I saw it coming when each succeeding president turned a blinder and blinder eye to immigration enforcement until Trump forced those eyes to open.

I saw it coming when Nixon opened the door to China, and the Chinese absconded with our manufacturing and intellectual property. I saw it coming when the Left rejected the immutable binary nature of "sex" and replaced it with the mutable multiple choices of "gender." I saw it coming when advocates for "inclusivity" imagined new and more exotic "disadvantages" and rewarded the "marginalized" with a cornucopia of benefits, all at the expense of the deserving. And I saw it coming when Joe Biden agonized more over "intersectionality" points than merit in his choice of cabinet members and running mate.

Before 1973, I confess I did not see it coming that liberals would casually sacrifice sixty million babies, more than half of them girls, on the altar of feminism. Nor did I anticipate they would try to fill the demographic void with illegal aliens and their progeny. But I knew abortion was wrong. I knew it was wrong because the laws of Nature and of Nature's God tell us so, because the Bible and Jesus confirmed our instincts, because our Founding Fathers codified the right to life in the Declaration, because no cliché about "choice" or "reproductive rights" can replace reason and God's divine plan.

For years, I have been warning this day would come. Others have as well. Instead of heeding our warnings or even giving us a fair hearing, Republicans leaders, the high priests, handed us over to the Leftist mobs. Easier to appease the mobs, they thought, than to confront them. But now the mobs are at the gate, pitchforks in hand, and they will not be appeased.

Throughout these last few years, I have had to remind myself of what Jesus told us two millennia ago: "A prophet is not without honor, except in his hometown and among his relatives and in his own household."[201] Although I worry about the future of my country, I do not worry about my own. They can take my congressional seat—it belongs to Iowans—and even my reputation, but I have something they can never take away and that is my faith. Each morning, in prayer and meditation, I conclude my prayer with, "Lord, loan me the measure of your wisdom you would have me use this day to go forth and glorify you. And if you have room for an extra blessing, let me do so with joy."

God has given us all gifts. It is our duty to Him to develop them and use them for His Glory. Andrew Breitbart reminded us, "Walk toward the fire." And if you have the conviction to walk toward

After a year at home in Tanzania, the Miracle Kids returned to say thank you to Iowans for our hospitality and for the healing hands that saved their lives. This was the 26th event King planned and/or attended with them in the month prior to the 2018 election. Pictured: Sadia, Wilson, and by now a mischievous Doreen with King, friend Esther Maboir, and Dr. Meyer. Glen Oaks Country Club, West Des Moines, Iowa—November 1, 2018.

the fire, walk point. Someone has to. Walk *through* the fire, as I have, if you have to. Their bullets aren't real. You have no reason to fear man. Your only fear should be failing God. Draw your strength from the joy of the battle and leave the time and the place of His victory to the Lord.

> *A lie doesn't become truth, wrong doesn't become right,*
> *and evil doesn't become good, just because*
> *it's accepted by a majority.*
>
> —Booker T. Washington

APPENDIX

FACT-CHECKING THE *NEW YORK TIMES*: INTRODUCTION

The *New York Times* reporter Trip Gabriel, Rep. Kevin McCarthy, and many of the characters in this book now own the position; that the *New York Times* is gospel. In regard to the accusations made against me, the Latin maxim—*'actori incumbit onus probandi'*— applies. "He who asserts must prove." In every contest of logic, the burden of proof is on the accuser to produce evidence in support of his claim. In the case against me, there is no such evidence.

The *New York Times* and others have no facts supporting their claims. Their only remaining alternative has been to shift the burden of proof to the accused. An old trick—*argumentum ad ignorantium*—is the logical fallacy of putting the burden of proof on the person who denies or questions the assertion being made. This tactic requires the accused to prove a negative.

From philosophers to barflies, the argument has long been made that it's impossible to prove a negative. McCarthy reversed the burden of proof on January 14, 2019, when he gave me "one hour" to gather evidence in my defense. It took a while longer, but by March 6, 2019, my excellent communications director, John Kennedy, published a "Fact Check" document that did what many thought impossible: it proved a negative. It showed that what the *Times* had claimed could not be true. To date, and in the face of overwhelming media and public criticism, no one has rebutted one word of the "Fact Check" document. The evidence in this book, including and especially the "Fact Check" document, is seamless and air tight.

McCarthy knows he can't square this circle. I know he knows the truth. There are no arguments left for McCarthy. That's why he has to dodge and deceive. He knows he made a big mistake, and if he admits it, his career is in jeopardy. When that day comes, by the Grace of God, we can begin to restore integrity to the U.S. House of Representatives.

FACT CHECKING THE *NEW YORK TIMES* MISQUOTE OF STEVE KING

Presented in its original text

RELEASED: March 6, 2010, Washington, DC
UPDATED: February 3, 2020, Washington, D.C.

Congressman Steve King releases this memo as a service to the constituents of Iowa's 4th Congressional District. The memo lays out important information concerning the recent misquote of Congressman Steve King by the *New York Times*. King encourages interested parties to consider this important information as they form their opinions on the matter.

Allegation: In a quote attributed to him by the *New York Times*, King is alleged to have wondered when the phrases "White nationalist, white supremacist, Western Civilization" became offensive, suggesting to some that he does not view the first two terms as disparaging.

King's response: King has consistently disputed this interpretation, maintaining that he was simply trying to ask when the phrase "Western Civilization" had gained a pejorative connotation, an assertion that is supported by the remaining section of the *Times* quote. King says the conversation in which this quote is alleged to happen was about the Left's use of weaponized language: "We discussed the changing use of language in political discourse. We discussed the worn out label 'racist' and my observation that other slanderous labels have been increasingly assigned to conservatives by the Left, who injected into our current political dialogue such terms as Nazi, Fascist, White Nationalist, White Supremacist— Western Civilization, how did THAT language become offensive? Why did I sit in classes teaching me about the merits of our history and our civilization . . . just to watch Western Civilization become a derogatory term in political discourse today?"

Notably, none of the context of the discussion that spawned the "quote" was included in the *New York Times* story. This context would have added greater clarity to King's reported remarks, revealing that his intention was to question the inclusion of "WESTERN CIVILIZATION" alone as a pejorative.

Important Facts: No tape of the interview with the *New York Times* exists and the paper refuses to release the reporter's notes of the conversation. The content of the *Times* "quote" makes it clear that King was ONLY talking about "Western Civilization." The *quote*: "White Nationalist, white Supremacist, Western Civilization—how did THAT language become offensive? Why did I sit in classes teaching me about the merits of our history and our civilization?" NOBODY IN AMERICA EVER SAT IN A CLASS about the merits of White Nationalism or White Supremacism. The incorrect interpretation that has been given to this "quote" refutes itself based on the "quoted" sentence's own construction. Mark Steyn, hosting Rush Limbaugh's show on January 18, explains the *Times* game. Said Steyn: "He made a mistake, Steve King. He agreed to give an interview on national immigration policy to the *New York Times*. That's not a good faith interview request. They're only asking you, and he should know this, they're only asking you to stitch you up. To talk to you for three hours and get you to use one phrase in there that they can lift out and kill you with."

Steyn continues, "This guy, Steve King, was trapped, trapped! The words he said about 'when did that become controversial,' he meant the phrase 'Western Civilization.' He's not a white suprem-acist. He's not a white nationalist. It's all stupid talk. So you've just surrendered the phrase 'Western Civilization.' I don't get that. I don't see what's in it for conservatism in surrendering that phrase, in accepting the Leftist's view that the term 'Western Civilization' is beyond the pale."

Contemporaneous evidence supports King's version of story: In a *Christian Science Monitor* article published on January 15, 2019, five days after the *Times* story broke, King is quoted making a similar argument: "In a conversation with the *Monitor* just before the holidays, King defended himself against accusations of racism. The Left, he says, has weaponized terms like "racist," "Nazi," and "white nationalist," using them against anyone who dares to defend American values or the Constitution. "There are people that don't like America the way it is," he says, "and there are people that don't like America when she was at her best. They want to tear down the systems we have. I don't believe that. I think our Founding Fathers got it right." However, this *CSM* interview occurred prior to the release of the *Times* article and shows how King had been making a variation of this argument at the approx-imate time he spoke to the Times reporter. In this case, though, the CSM actually published it in the context in which it was made. It is clear that King was making a similar argument to the Times.

The quote in the CSM is the FIRST DOCUMENTED INSTANCE of Steve King ever using the phrase "white national-ist." This is an important point, because King has asserted, "That ideology never shows up in my head. I don't know how it could possibly come out of my mouth." A Lexis-Nexis search dating back to 2000 shows King has never used any of the following phrases: "white nationalism," "white nationalist," "white suprem-acist," or "white supremacy." In the same time frame, King is quoted 276 times using the term "Western Civilization."

Based on this data, it appears unlikely that King spontaneously used the phrases "white nationalist" and "white supremacist" in his discussion with the *Times* reporter, as they were never common elements of his speech. It suggests that King was repeating terms fed to him by the *Times*.

Steve King Quoted Saying "*Western Civilization*", "*White Nationalism*", or "*White Supremacy*"

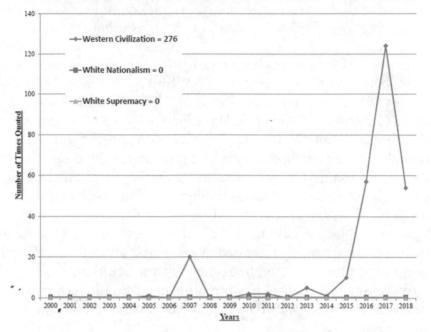

Source: Lexis-Nexis

The contention that King reacted to the Times reporter's use of the phrases "white nationalist," "white supremacist" and "western civilization" as pejoratives is supported by the body of the Times article itself. The article contains the following passage, likely written prior to the King interview: "Elected to Congress in 2002, Mr. King attracted the attention of hate-watch groups like the Anti-Defamation League as he spoke increasingly about preserving 'Western Culture' or 'Western Civilization.' The groups consider those buzzwords that signal support to white nationalists, along with an obsession with birthrates and abortion rates among different ethnic groups. "Doesn't it make more sense that the reporter asked a question in which "Western Civilization" was linked with the offensive epithets, and King responded by wondering how it came to be that the meritorious phrase "Western Civilization" became a similar pejorative? Certainly, the answer he is alleged to have given fits with this belief.

The point King was attempting to make about the Left's use of labels to smear conservatives, labels which now include even the concept of "Western Civilization" itself, is supported by Lexis-Nexis data.

Since 2015 there has been an explosive increase in the use of the labels "White Supremacist," "White Supremacy," "White Nationalist," and "White Nationalism." This squares closely with what Congressman King told Dave Price of WHO-TV regarding the phrase "White Nationalist": "It is a derogatory term today. I wouldn't have thought so maybe a year or two or three ago. Today they use it as a derogatory term, and it implies that you are a racist." In his statement, King was trying to put into words his entirely accurate observation that the term "white nationalist" has been weaponized by the Left against conservatives, and that its use in this form has markedly increased over the past several years. King's point about the increased frequency with which the weaponized term "white nationalist" has been injected into modern political dialogue is evident when data from a Lexis-Nexis News Database search is analyzed.

As King told Price, it has only been in the last "year or two or three" that the pejorative phrase "white nationalist" has gained purchase in the political debate as a weaponized term.

A follow up New York Times story about Steve King titled, "A Timeline of Steve King's Racist Remarks and Divisive Actions," was criticized by legendary journalist Brit Hume as being "completely bogus." This "completely bogus" story was written the next day by the same writer, in the same paper, on the same general topic, and could possibly be revealing of a bias regarding Congressman King.

The Congressional Record made the exact same error as the New York Times in transcribing King's 1/15/19 floor statement, when the transcriptionist left out a break between the words "white supremacist" and "western civilization." Video shows King intentionally inserting a break between those words, but the transcript does not reflect this. No one believes the Congressional Record was acting with animus. But their error did reveal how either a similar error, or an intentional misplacement of punctuation, could have

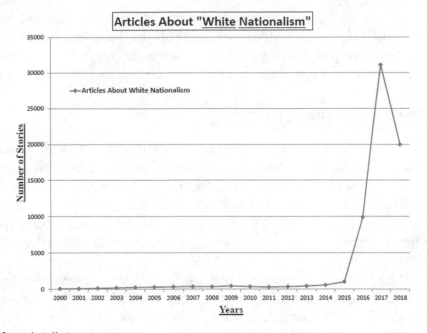

Articles About "White Nationalism"

Source: Lexis-Nexis

led to a botched quote in the times. Remember, King has always disputed the quote as it was portrayed in the *Times*.

King is insisting upon a correction in the Congressional Record so that it reflects the quote as he intentionally delivered it on the House floor. King's correction reveals that he was attempting to separate "Western Civilization" from the other two pejorative terms.

New York Times/Congressional record mistaken quote: "White Nationalist, White Supremacist, Western Civilization—how did THAT language become offensive? Why did I sit in classes teaching me about the merits of our history and our civilization?"

Corrected quote: "White Nationalist, White Supremacist—Western Civilization, how did THAT language become offensive? Why did I sit in classes teaching me about the merits of our history and our civilization?"

One misplaced hyphen in the *Times* story gave birth to a meritless controversy by falsely implying that Congressman King did not differentiate between the three phrases.

Steve King has no accusers. In the case of Brett Kavanaugh and the students from Covington High School, they had accusers whose claims could be rebutted. King has no accusers. No one has ever come forward to state that King has treated them improperly.

UPDATE ADDED FEBRUARY 3, 2020

Since the initial release of this fact check document, additional information has been revealed which further shows the extent to which a misquote in the *New York Times* was weaponized and used against Steve King. Further, this information also shows that Majority Leader Kevin McCarthy's unilateral decision to strip King of committee assignments was an unjust and unprecedented abuse of power.

The Left has weaponized the use of racially charged phrases to attack Conservatives. On November 14, 2016, *Politico* ran a story entitled, "Soros Bands With Donors to Resist Trump, 'Take Back Power'." The article discusses a three-day conference, beginning on November 13, 2016, in which "George Soros and other rich liberals who spent tens of millions of dollars trying to elect Hillary Clinton are gathering in Washington for a three-day, closed door meeting to retool the big-money left to fight back against Donald Trump."

King has frequently asserted that one of the strategies the activists attending the "Resistance" conference developed was the weaponization of new terminology spread through the media to malign conservatives, an assertion that the data corroborate. For example, Lexis-Nexis data show that the use of the phrase "White Nationalism" in the national media was virtually non-existent until November of 2016.

In fact, the spike in usage on November 2016 correlates perfectly with the "Resistance" gathering in the Mandarin Hotel. Note that the November spikes in usage of "white nationalism" correspond to the exact days (November 13–14–15) in which the Soros-led conference was being held and covered by the media.

Another indicator of the recent weaponization of the phrase "white nationalism" can be found in a study of the Congressional

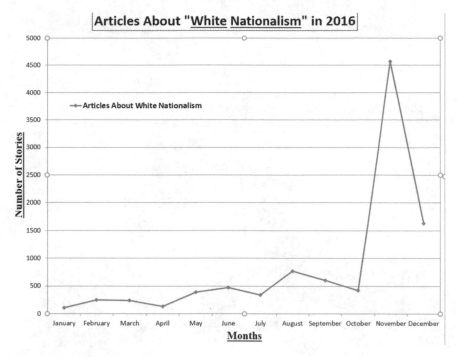

Source: Lexis-Nexis

Record. According to CRS, no Member of Congress has ever said, in their original words, the term "White Nationalist" on the House Floor prior to President Donald Trump being elected.

Kevin McCarthy's decision to remove King from all three of his committees for a misquote in the New York Times is unprecedented with no analogous case to Congressman King's. Apart from party switches or a decline in the level of party support, King is only the fourth Member in modern history, according to CRS, to be stripped of all committee assignments, and he is the only one who was removed from committees for a reason that has no basis in history, House or Conference Rules, or Federal law.

Conclusion: Congressman King was railroaded over a false quote. To believe the version of events relied upon by Kevin McCarthy to strip King of committee assignments, one must believe that an unreasonable but "sensational" interpretation, for which no evidence exists, is more likely to be accurate than a

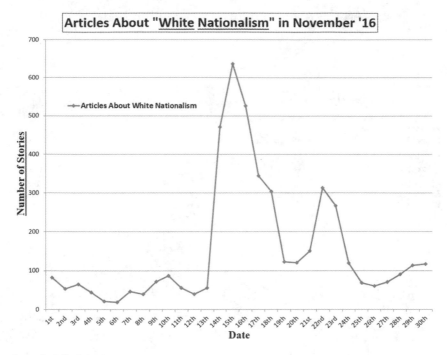

Articles About "White Nationalism" in November '16

Source: Lexis-Nexis

reasonable, "noncontroversial" interpretation which is internally supported by context clues and externally supported by data and other contemporaneous, published accounts. One must also believe that the *New York Times*, a hostile, liberal paper which has had other articles about Congressman Steve King written by the same author thoroughly debunked as "completely bogus," set aside its animus in this particular case.

Note: The online version of this document contains hyperlinks to source material. Parties interested in reviewing the links can do so at https://www.webharvest.gov/congress116th/20201021 094746/https://steveking.house.gov/media-center/press-releases/ memo-fact-checking-the-new-york-times-misquote-of-steve-king —which is hosting this document in an internet friendly version.

Addressed to the good people of Iowa's 4th Congressional District

Who is Steve King? We are here to stand by our friend and colleague Congressman Steve King. Steve is a visionary legislator, successful business man, a devoted Catholic and a father.

We have known Steve for over 25 years as man of principle who defends the US Constitution as written.

We all served in the Iowa Senate together. We all witnessed his courage and boldness in standing up for Iowa and western values. He stands for personal responsibility under the rule of law. He serves the people of Iowa with tenacity, defending them against an intrusive, over-taxing, over-regulating national government.

Steve's accomplishments cut across a wide range of issues; the defense of the unborn, insuring a safe work place, the dignity of marriage, and English as Iowa's official language. Now these Iowa values championed by Steve are no longer fashionable. President Reagan always remarked, "A man can do almost anything if he does not care who gets the credit" that is our friend Congressman Steve King.

Congressman Steve King has singlehandedly saved the lives of thousands of unborn Iowa children and his visionary "heartbeat bill" will save hundreds of thousands more.

A. Lincoln asked rhetorically, "What is conservatism? Is it not the adherence to the old and tried against the new and untried?" that is our friend Congressman Steve King.

Signed by our own hand,

Senator David Miller (ret.)

Senator Kitty Rehberg (ret.)

Senator Neal Schuerer (ret.)

1

Embassy of the Republic of Haiti
Washington, DC

AHW/BA/080/209-2020   Tuesday, June 23, 2020

The Honorable Steve King
2210, Rayburn House Office Building
Washington, DC 20515

Dear Representative King,

It is with deep sadness that I learned of the recent election results in the 4th District of Iowa after 24 years of selfless service in the United States Congress. Please accept my heartfelt thanks for your contribution to the Black community. Specifically, in 2002, as a Member of the Iowa State Senate, you proposed "An Act relating to the designation of a Juneteenth National Freedom Day" in the Iowa Senate, which was ultimately signed into law by Governor Vilsack.

Furthermore, I have had the pleasure of working closely with you to advance the interests of the Republic of Haiti, and I thank you for the many times you have helped the people of Haiti. You have represented the American people and the international community with great dignity and respect. I wish you much success in your future endeavors.

I avail myself of this opportunity to present to you, Dear Representative King, the assurances of my highest consideration.

Sincerely,

Ambassador Hervé Denis
Chargé d'Affaires

NOTES

1. Andrew Breitbart, *Righteous Indignation: Excuse Me While I Save the World* (New York: Grand Central Publishing, 2014), 209.
2. Thomas Babington, Lord Macaulay, "Horatius at the Bridge," Bartleby .com, https://www.bartleby.com/360/7/158.html.
3. Breitbart, *Righteous Indignation*, 209.
4. William Lloyd Garrison, "To the Public," *The Liberator*, January 1, 1831, https://www.pbs.org/wgbh/aia/part4/4h2928t.html.
5. New Hampshire Democratic Debate Transcript, February 7, 2020, Rev, https://www.rev.com/blog/transcripts/new-hampshire-democratic-debate-transcript.
6. Ibid.
7. Richard Goldstein, "Earl L. Butz, Secretary Felled by Racial Remark, Is Dead at 98," *New York Times*, February 4, 2008, https://www.nytimes .com/2008/02/04/washington/04butz.html.
8. Adam Clymer, "Robert C. Byrd, a Pillar of the Senate, Dies at 92," *New York Times*, June 28, 2010, https://www.nytimes.com/2010/06/29/us/ politics/29byrd.html.
9. Alan Blinder, "Was That Ralph Northam in Blackface? An Inquiry Ends Without Answers," *New York Times*, May 22, 2019, https://www.nytimes. com/2019/05/22/us/ralph-northam-blackface-photo.html.
10. John Fund, "Why Mama Grizzlies Run the Tea Party," *Wall Street Journal,* October 23, 2010, https://www.wsj.com/articles/SB100014240527023037 38504575568322608102424.
11. John Bowden, "Candace Owens tells Congress white nationalism not a problem for minorities in US," *The Hill*, September 20, 2019, https://thehill .com/homenews/house/462395-candace-owens-tells-congress-white-nationalism-not-a-problem-for-minorities-in.

12. Kenneth Vogel, "How Vilification of George Soros Moved from the Fringes to the Mainstream," *New York Times,* October 31, 2018, https://www.nytimes.com/2018/10/31/us/politics/george-soros-bombs-trump.html.

13. Steve Stivers, Twitter, October 30, 2018, https://twitter.com/repstevestivers/status/1057327397685653510?lang=en.

14. Rachel Bade and John Bresnahan, "Stivers 'could not stay silent' on Steve King," *Politico*, October 30, 2018, https://www.politico.com/story/2018/10/30/steve-king-steve-stivers-nrcc-949523.

15. Bret Hayworth, "Gov. Reynolds: Steve King must decide if his comments represent 'values' of Iowa 4th District," *Sioux City Journal*, November 13, 2018, https://siouxcityjournal.com/news/local/govt-and-politics/gov-reynolds-steve-king-must-decide-if-his-comments-represent-values-of-iowa-4th-district/article_466a5cfb-3659-5320-ad1f-6fd6954f0acd.html.

16. Trip Gabriel, "Before Trump, Steve King Set the Agenda for the Wall and Anti-Immigrant Politics," *New York Times*, January 10, 2019, https://www.nytimes.com/2019/01/10/us/politics/steve-king-trump-immigration-wall.html.

17. Alex Seitz-Wald, "Rep. Steve King: Immigrants are like dogs," *Salon*, May 22, 2012, https://www.salon.com/2012/05/22/rep_steve_king_immigrants_like_dogs/.

18. Glenn Thrush, "Mike Lee Suggests Trump Should Get a 'Mulligan' for Jan. 6 Speech," *New York Times*, February 9, 2021, https://www.nytimes.com/2021/02/09/us/politics/mike-lee-trump-mulligan.html.

19. Justin Wise, "GOP conference chair: Steve King's comments were 'abhorrent' and 'racist,'" *The Hill*, January 10, 2019, https://thehill.com/blogs/blog-briefing-room/news/424779-gop-conference-chair-steve-kings-abhorrent-and-racist-comments.

20. Aldous J. Pennyfarthing, "Liz Cheney tries to prove she can be just as racist and petty as Trump," *Daily Kos*, December 3, 2019, https://www.dailykos.com/stories/2019/12/3/1903330/-Liz-Cheney-tries-to-prove-she-can-be-just-as-racist-and-petty-as-Trump.

21. Eli Watkins, "Report: Top Republican's family netted government contracts through claim of minority descent," CNN, October 15, 2018, https://www.cnn.com/2018/10/15/politics/kevin-mccarthy-california-contracts-report.

22. Laurie Kellman, "Republicans slam Rep. King for what they call racist remarks," *Associated Press*, January10, 2019, https://apnews.com/article/da67550da63a45ac9b5c7d93d49c1f10.

23. Trip Gabriel, "Steve King's White Supremacy Remark Is Rebuked by Iowa's Republican Senators," *New York Times*, January 11, 2019, https://www.nytimes.com/2019/01/11/us/politics/steve-king-republicans-white-supremacy-.html.

24. Dave Dreeszen, "Steve King denies support for white supremacy after published quotes suggest otherwise," Associated Press, January 10, 2019, https://apnews.com/article/c6013fe63d044feb9e07e1af1d701d2d.

25. Erin Durkin, "Iowa Republican Steve King faces party action over 'white supremacist' remark," *The Guardian*, January 13, 2019, https://www.theguardian.com/us-news/2019/jan/13/iowa-representative-steve-king-white-supremacist-comment.

26. Robert Costa and Ed O'Keefe, "House Majority Whip Scalise confirms he spoke to white supremacists in 2002," *Washington Post*, December 29, 2014, https://www.washingtonpost.com/politics/house-majority-whip-scalise-confirms-he-spoke-to-white-nationalists-in-2002/2014/12/29/7f80dc14-8fa3-11e4-a900-9960214d4cd7_story.html.

27. Quint Forgey, "McCarthy: 'Action will be taken' over King's racist comments," *Politico*, January, 13, 2019, https://www.politico.com/story/2019/01/13/steve-king-racist-comments-republicans-house-1098731.

28. Cody Nelson, "Minnesota Congresswoman Ignites Debate on Israel and Anti-Semitism," NPR, March 7, 2019, https://www.npr.org/2019/03/07/700901834/minnesota-congresswoman-ignites-debate-on-israel-and-anti-semitism.

29. Susan Davis, "House GOP Leaders Move to Strip Rep. Steve King of Committee Assignments," NPR, January 14, 2019, https://www.npr.org/2019/01/14/685149580/gop-mulls-action-against-rep-steve-king-for-racially-charged-comments.

30. Bari Weiss, Resignation Letter, BariWeiss.com, https://www.bariweiss.com/resignation-letter.

31. Christopher Caldwell, *Age of Entitlement*: *America Since the Sixties* (New York: Simon & Schuster, 2020), 156.

32. Ben Rotherberg, Twitter, January 18, 2017, https://twitter.com/benrothenberg/status/821878343540740097?lang=en.

33. "An ESPN announcer has been removed from assignments after making a perceived racist comment during coverage," *FanBuzz*, January 24, 2017, https://fanbuzz.com/national/an-espn-announcer-has-been-removed-from-assignments-after-making-a-perceived-racist-comment-during-coverage/.

34. Ben Rotherberg, Twitter, January 25, 2017, https://twitter.com/benrothen berg/status/824462061115629569.

35. Trip Gabriel, "A Timeline of Steve King's Racist Remarks and Divisive Actions," *New York Times*, January 15, 2019, https://www.nytimes.com/2019/01/15/us/politics/steve-king-offensive-quotes.html.

36. "How identity politics drove the world mad," UnHerd, September 27, 2019, https://unherd.com/2019/09/how-identity-politics-drove-the-world-mad/.

37. Trip Gabriel et al., "Steve King Removed from Committee Assignments Over White Supremacy Remark," *New York Times*, January 14, 2019, https://www.nytimes.com/2019/01/14/us/politics/steve-king-white-supremacy.html.

38. H.Res. 789, January 10, 2020, https://www.congress.gov/116/bills/hres789/BILLS-116hres789ih.xml.

39. Ibid.

40. Brett Samuels, "Trump says he hasn't been following controversy around Steve King's white supremacy comments," *The Hill*, January 14, 2019, https://thehill.com/homenews/administration/425211-trump-says-he-hasnt-been-following-controversy-around-steve-kings.

41. H.Res. 41, January 15, 2019 - Rejecting White nationalism and White supremacy, https://www.congress.gov/bill/116th-congress/house-resolution/41/text.

42. Corinna Knoll, "How 2 Drifters Brought Anti-Semitic Terror to Jersey City," *New York Times*, December 15, 2019, https://www.nytimes.com/2019/12/15/nyregion/jersey-city-shooting-terrorism.html.

43. Michael Gold and Nicholas Bogel-Burroughs, "Suspect in Anti-Semitic Rampage in Monsey Is Eyed in Earlier Attack," *New York Times*, January 14, 2020, https://www.nytimes.com/2020/01/02/nyregion/monsey-hanukkah-stabbing-grafton-thomas.html.

44. Seth Frantzman, "Inconvenient antisemitism: daily attacks on Jews in New York," *Jerusalem Post*, https://www.jpost.com/opinion/inconvenient-antisemitism-the-daily-attacks-on-jews-in-new-york-612420.

45. Julia Ioffe, "How much responsibility does Trump bear for the synagogue shooting in Pittsburgh?" *Washington Post*, October 28, 2018, https://www.washingtonpost.com/outlook/2018/10/28/how-much-responsibility-does-trump-bear-synagogue-shooting-pittsburgh/.

46. "Steve King erupts at comparison to Pittsburgh suspect: 'Do not associate me with that shooter,'" CNN News, November 1, 2018, https://www.kbzk

.com/cnn-us-politics/2018/11/01/steve-king-erupts-at-comparison-to-pittsburgh-suspect-do-not-associate-me-with-that-shooter/.

47. Michael Calderone, "JournoList: Inside the echo chamber," *Politico*, March 17, 2009, https://www.politico.com/story/2009/03/journolist-inside-the-echo-chamber-020086.

48. Alex Pareene, "Journolist scandal: Liberals planned open letter," *Salon*, July 20, 2010, https://www.salon.com/2010/07/20/journolist_reverend_wright/.

49. Ben Smith, "Times ed board: McCain move 'racially tinged,'" *Politico*, July 31, 2008, https://www.politico.com/blogs/ben-smith/2008/07/times-ed-board-mccain-move-racially-tinged-010703.

50. Charlton McIlwain and Stephen Caliendo, "Mitt Romney's Racist Appeals: How Race Was Played in the 2012 Presidential Election," *American Behavioral Scientist,* November 4, 2013.

51. Aaron Blake, "George W. Bush's anti-Trump manifesto, annotated," *Washington Post*, October 18, 2017, https://www.washingtonpost.com/news/the-fix/wp/2017/10/19/george-w-bushs-anti-trump-manifesto-annotated/.

52. Roger Scruton, "How identity politics drove the world mad," UnHerd, September 27, 2019, https://unherd.com/2019/09/how-identity-politics-drove-the-world-mad/.

53. "VIDEO: Donald Trump Takes on Whoopi, 'The View' Over Obama's Birth Certificate," YouTube.com, May 28, 2011, https://www.youtube.com/watch?v=yfZixqYuL58.

54. John Carucci, "Bernie Sanders calls Trump a racist before Apollo event," AP, April 5, 2019, https://apnews.com/article/a4d684a28ae342bb97ff9cf464feec43.

55. "Full text: Donald Trump announces a presidential bid," *Washington Post*, June 15, 2015, https://www.washingtonpost.com/news/post-politics/wp/2015/06/16/full-text-donald-trump-announces-a-presidential-bid/.

56. Alexander Burns, "Donald Trump, Pushing Someone Rich, Offers Himself," *New York Times*, June 16, 2015, https://www.nytimes.com/2015/06/17/us/politics/donald-trump-runs-for-president-this-time-for-real-he-says.html.

57. Warren Fiske, "Tim Kaine falsely says Trump said 'all Mexicans are rapists,'" *Politifact*, August 8, 2016, https://www.politifact.com/factchecks/2016/aug/08/tim-kaine/tim-kaine-falsely-says-trump-said-all-mexicans-are/.

58. Mark Hensch, "O'Malley: Trump's immigration talk 'racist' and 'fascist,'" *The Hill*, January 11, 2016, https://thehill.com/blogs/ballot-box/presidential-races/265444-omalley-trumps-immigration-rhetoric-is-racist.

59. Alberto Martinez, "The media needs to stop telling this lie about Trump. I'm a Sanders supporter—and value honesty," *Salon*, December 21, 2015, https://www.salon.com/2015/12/21/the_media_needs_to_stop_telling_this_lie_about_donald_trump_im_a_sanders_supporter_and_value_honesty/.

60. Adam Liptak and Michael Shear, "Trump's Travel Ban Is Upheld by Supreme Court," *New York Times*, June 26, 2018, https://www.nytimes.com/2018/06/26/us/politics/supreme-court-trump-travel-ban.html.

61. George Orwell, *1984* (New York: Harcourt, 1949), 33.

62. Dan Merica, "Trump condemns 'hatred, bigotry and violence on many sides' in Charlottesville," CNN, August 13, 2017, https://www.cnn.com/2017/08/12/politics/trump-statement-alt-right-protests/index.html.

63. Farah Stockman, "Who Were the Counterprotesters in Charlottesville?" *New York Times*, August 14, 2017, https://www.nytimes.com/2017/08/14/us/who-were-the-counterprotesters-in-charlottesville.html.

64. Dan Merica, "Trump calls KKK, neo-Nazis, white supremacists 'repugnant,'" CNN, August 14, 2017, https://www.cnn.com/2017/08/14/politics/trump-condemns-charlottesville-attackers.

65. "President Donald Trump on Charlottesville: You Had Very Fine People, on Both Sides | CNBC," YouTube, August 15, 2017, https://www.youtube.com/watch?v=JmaZR8E12bs.

66. Robert Farley, "Trump Has Condemned White Supremacists," FactCheck.org, February 11, 2020, https://www.factcheck.org/2020/02/trump-has-condemned-white-supremacists/.

67. Julie Hirschfield Davis, "In First, Trump Condemns Rise in Anti-Semitism, Calling It 'Horrible,'" *New York Times*, February 21, 2017, https://www.nytimes.com/2017/02/21/us/politics/trump-speaks-out-against-anti-semitism.html.

68. Alan Blinder et al., "Threats and Vandalism Leave American Jews on Edge in Trump Era," *New York Times*, February 28, 2017, https://www.nytimes.com/2017/02/28/us/jewish-community-center-donald-trump.html.

69. Laurence Leamer, "How Mar-a-Lago Taught Trump to Play Politics," *Politico*, February 1, 2019, https://www.politico.com/magazine/story/2019/02/01/donald-trump-mar-a-lago-anti-semitism-town-council-palm-beach-politics-224537/.

70. Mark Seal, "How Donald Trump Beat Palm Beach Society and Won the Fight for Mar-a-Lago," *Vanity Fair*, December 27, 2016, https://www.vanityfair.com/style/2016/12/how-donald-trump-beat-palm-beach-society-and-won-the-fight-for-mar-a-lago.

71. Ziva Dahl, "Meet the Social Justice Warrior Behind JCC Bomb Threats," *Observer*, March 6, 2017, https://observer.com/2017/03/juan-thompson-anti-semitic-jcc-bomb-threats/.

72. Ashley Feinberg, "The New York Times Unites vs. Twitter," *Slate*, August 15, 2019, https://slate.com/news-and-politics/2019/08/new-york-times-meeting-transcript.html.

73. Jon Ward, "Why is Ryan opposing Trump?" *Medium*, November 10, 2016, https://medium.com/jon-ward/why-is-ryan-opposing-trump-1d1d7db84a01.

74. Jennifer Steinhauer and Alexander Burns, "Paul Ryan Says He Is 'Not Ready' to Endorse Donald Trump," *New York Times*, May 5, 2016, https://www.nytimes.com/2016/05/06/us/politics/paul-ryan-donald-trump.html.

75. "Transcript of Donald Trump's Videotaped Apology," *New York Times*, October 8, 2016, https://www.nytimes.com/2016/10/08/us/donald-trump-apology-statement.html.

76. Jake Sherman, "Ryan 'sickened' by Trump, joint appearance scrapped," *Politico*, October 7, 2016, https://www.politico.com/story/2016/10/paul-ryan-donald-trump-comments-women-wisconsin-229307.

77. John 11:48, ESV.

78. Joe Concha, "Bari Weiss rips cancel culture as 'social murder' on Bill Maher show," *The Hill*, August 1, 2020, https://thehill.com/homenews/administration/510115-bari-weiss-rip-cancel-culture-as-social-murder-on-bill-maher-show.

79. Shane Croucher, "Joe Biden Announcement Video Highlights Donald Trump's 'Very Fine People' Comment about Charlottesville Rally," *Newsweek*, April 25, 2019, https://www.newsweek.com/joe-biden-announcement-video-2020-trump-charlottesville-1405497.

80. Stephanie Saul, "Mentioning Trump and K.K.K. in Same Sentence, Biden Condemns Hate," *New York Times,* January 19, 2020, https://www.nytimes.com/2020/01/19/us/politics/biden-south-carolina-bernie-sanders.html.

81. Eric Bradner et al., "Biden: 'If you have a problem figuring out whether you're for me or Trump, then you ain't black,'" CNN, May 22, 2020, https://www.cnn.com/2020/05/22/politics/biden-charlamagne-tha-god-you-aint-black/index.html.

82. Trip Gabriel, "A Timeline of Steve King's Racist Remarks and Divisive Actions," *New York Times*, July 15, 2019, https://www.nytimes .com/2019/01/15/us/politics/steve-king-offensive-quotes.html.

83. Ian Schwartz, "Brit Hume on Steve King: Stop Hurling 'Racist' Around, The Term Has Been 'Weaponized,'" January 15, 2019, https://www .realclearpolitics.com/video/2019/01/15/brit_hume_on_steve_king_stop_ hurling_racist_around_the_term_has_been_weaponized.html.

84. "Bernie 2020 Field Organizer, Kyle Jurek: 'There Are Things That Are More Important Than the Rule of Law in the United States'; Declares That His Views Are Shared by Many Others In the Sanders Camp; Secret Service Notified Over POTUS Assassination Concern," Project Veritas, January 15, 2020, https://www.projectveritasaction.com/news/expose2020-part-2- bernie-2020-field-organizer-kyle-jurek-there-are-things-that-are-more- important-than-the-rule-of-law-in-the-united-states-declares-that-his-views- are-shared/.

85. Orwell, *1984*, 256.

86. Solutions for America; Congressional Record Vol. 158, No. 20, February 7, 2012, https://www.congress.gov/congressional-record/2012/02/07/house- section/article/H560-1.

87. Margaret Sanger, *Pivot of Civilization*, 1922, Chapter IV, http://groups.csail .mit.edu/mac/users/rauch/abortion_eugenics/sanger/sanger_04.html.

88. BUCK v. BELL, Superintendent of State Colony Epileptics and Feeble Minded, Supreme Court, Decided May 2, 1927, https://www.law.cornell .edu/supremecourt/text/274/200.

89. Daniel Okrent, *The Guarded Gate: Bigotry, Eugenics, and the Laws That Kept Two Generations of Jews, Italians, and Other European Immigrants Out of America* (New York: Scribner, 2019), 353.

90. Theodore Roosevelt, "English The Official Language," Bartleby Research, https://www.bartleby.com/essay/English-The-Official-Language- FCPD8F3B6R.

91. Barack Obama, *Audacity of Hope* (New York: Crown, 2006), 264.

92. Ibid., 263.

93. Beatriz Diaz, "'English Only': The movement to limit Spanish speaking in US," BBC, December 3, 2019, https://www.bbc.com/news/world-us- canada-50550742.

94. Catie Edmonson, "Steve King Back in Spotlight After Comments on Uighurs," *New York Times*, April 27, 2019, https://www.nytimes.com/2019/08/27/us/politics/steve-king-china-uighurs.html.

95. Ellen Goodman, "Global Warming," *Pittsburgh-Gazette*, February 8, 2007, https://www.post-gazette.com/opinion/Op-Ed/2007/02/09/Ellen-Goodman-Global-warning/stories/200702090178.

96. "President Obama rejects Keystone XL pipeline," CNN Wire, November 6, 2015, https://fox59.com/news/politics/president-obama-rejects-keystone-xl-pipeline/.

97. U.S. Government Accountability Office, https://www.gao.gov/products/gao-18-433

98. Crime in Texas, Texas Department of Public Safety, https://www.dps.texas.gov/section/crime-records-service/crime-texas.

99. Linda Qiu, "Explaining Trump's Tweet on Crimes by Immigrants," *New York Times*, January 12, 2019, https://www.nytimes.com/2019/01/12/us/politics/trump-illegal-immigration-statistics.html.

100. National Institute on Drug Abuse, https://www.drugabuse.gov/drug-topics/trends-statistics/overdose-death-rates.

101. "How Heroin Made Its Way from Rural Mexico to Small-Town America," NPR Interview with Sam Quinones, NPR, May 19, 2015, https://www.npr.org/2015/05/19/404184355/how-heroin-made-its-way-from-rural-mexico-to-small-town-america.

102. Andrew Kaczynski, "Joe Biden once said a fence was needed to stop 'tons' of drugs from Mexico," CNN, May 10, 2019, https://www.cnn.com/2019/05/10/politics/kfile-biden-drugs-fence-2006.

103. Talk to the Newsroom: Style Editor Trip Gabriel, *New York Times*, February 12, 2007, https://www.nytimes.com/2007/02/12/business/media/12asktheeditors.html.

104. "Rep. Steve King compares Mexicans to livestock," YouTube, February 20, 2008, https://www.youtube.com/watch?v=8F0la3Js9Mg.

105. Hunter Walker, "Steve King has a model of the border wall he wants to build to protect our 'superior civilization,'" *Yahoo News*, March 13, 2017, https://www.yahoo.com/news/steve-king-has-a-model-of-the-border-wall-he-wants-to-build-to-protect-our-superior-civilization-183248446.html.

106. Paul Bedard, "Liberal Media Scream: CNN ridicules Trump, supporters are 'boomer rubes,'" *Washington Examiner*, January 27, 2020, https://www .washingtonexaminer.com/washington-secrets/liberal-media-scream-cnn-ridicules-trump-supporters-are-boomer-rubes.

107. Rick Wilson, Twitter, November 1, 2018,https://twitter.com/TheRick Wilson/status/1058078917087629314.

108. Wajahat Ali, Twitter, August 7, 2019, https://twitter.com/wajahatali/ status/1159165264140865536.

109. "Don Lemon and W. Kamau Bell crack up over Steve King's comments," YouTube.com, May 31, 2019, https://www.youtube.com/watch?v=gRvJ1 E48ObM.

110. "CNN Condescension: Don Lemon, Rick Wilson and Wajahat Ali," YouTube, September 12, 2018, https://www.youtube.com/watch?v=JA-C8N8Q7lw.

111. VARNUM v. BRIEN, Supreme Court of Iowa, Decided: April 03, 2009, https://caselaw.findlaw.com/ia-supreme-court/1374250.html

112. Josh Nelson, "Gay marriage judge denounces ouster effort," *Courier*, September 22, 2010, https://wcfcourier.com/news/local/gay-marriage-judge-denounces-ouster-effort/article_598a75b8-c655-11df-9dfe-001cc4c002e0 .html.

113. From John Adams to Massachusetts Militia, October 11, 1798, https:// founders.archives.gov/documents/Adams/99-02-02-3102.

114. Book of Wisdom 2:12, 17–20, ESV.

115. Jason Linkins, "Steve King Says Illegal Immigrants Can Be Sussed Out by Footwear, Psychic Powers," *HuffPost*, December 6, 2017, https://www .huffpost.com/entry/steve-king-says-illegal-i_n_613014.

116. Ian Schwartz, "Rep. Steve King vs. Cuomo: Profiling Is Not Wrong; Difference Between Racial Profiling And Broader Profiling," *Real Clear Politics*, August 29, 2017, https://www.realclearpolitics.com/ video/2017/08/29/rep_steve_king_vs_cuomo_profiling_is_not_wrong_ difference_between_racial_profiling_and_broader_profiling.html

117. Ajah Hales, "No Country for Old (White) Men," *InjusticeMag*, December 29, 2018, https://aninjusticemag.com/no-country-for-old-white-men-dccc14fe5ed1?gi=38f599911eaf.

118. "About David Lane," The Southern Poverty Law Center, https://www .splcenter.org/fighting-hate/extremist-files/individual/david-lane.

119. Laura Bassett, "Steve King: Covering Birth Control Could Make Us a 'Dying Civilization,'" *HuffPost*, December 6, 2017, https://www.huffpost.com/entry/steve-king-free-birth-control_n_916519.

120. "Video Excerpt: Romney Quizzed On Contraception During Debate," KHN, January 8, 2012, https://khn.org/news/gop-debate-contraception/.

121. Robin Abcarian, "GOP debate: Mitt Romney grows foggy on contraception," *Los Angeles Times*, January 7, 2012, https://www.latimes.com/world/la-xpm-2012-jan-07-la-pn-mitt-romney-grows-foggy-on-contraception-question-20120107-story.html.

122. Todd Akin, *Firing Back* (Washington, D.C.: WND Books, 2014), 127–32.

123. Ibid., 132–33.

124. Katie Glueck, "King: Rape remarks out of context," *Politico*, August 21, 2012, https://www.politico.com/story/2012/08/king-my-rape-remarks-out-of-context-079955.

125. Saul Alinsky, *Rules for Radicals: A Practical Primer for Realistic Radicals* (1971; repr., New York: Vintage Books, 1989), https://www.openculture.com/2020/06/saul-alinskys-13rules-for-creating-meaningful-social-change.html

126. Dashiell Bennett, "Steve King Never Heard of Anyone Getting Pregnant by Statutory Rape," *The Atlantic*, August 21, 2012, https://www.theatlantic.com/politics/archive/2012/08/steve-king-never-heard-anyone-getting-pregnant-statutory-rape-incest/324450/.

127. Glueck, "King: Rape remarks out of context, "*Politico*.

128. Rachel Weiner, "Republicans condemn Akin's 'legitimate rape' comments," *Washington Post*, August 20, 2012, https://www.washingtonpost.com/news/post-politics/wp/2012/08/20/todd-akins-macaca-moment/.

129. Akin, *Firing Back*, 132–33.

130. Ibid., 130.

131. Ibid., 269–70.

132. Marc Thiessen, "At the March for Life, Trump will be greeted as a pro-life hero—because he is one," *Washington Post*, January 23, 2020, https://www.washingtonpost.com/opinions/trump-has-embraced-the-pro-life-movement-in-a-way-no-other-president-has/2020/01/23/d4ecab5c-3e11-11ea-b90d-5652806c3b3a_story.html.

133. "Thinking of those who were a 'voice for the voiceless,'" *Citizen's Voice*, November 13, 2016, https://www.citizensvoice.com/opinion/letters/

thinking-of-those-who-were-a-voice-for-the-voiceless/article_51e8550d-6cf0-53c3-a3cb-f5b826dc80c2.html.

134. William Wilberforce, GoodReads, https://www.goodreads.com/quotes/231539-is-it-not-the-great-end-of-religion-and-in.

135. Alexis de Tocqueville, *Democracy in America*, 1835, Book I, Chapter XIII, Gutenberg.org, https://www.gutenberg.org/files/815/815-h/815-h.htm.

136. Christopher Caldwell, *Age of Entitlement: America Since the Sixties* (New York: Simon & Schuster, 2020), 121.

137. Douglas Murray, *Madness of Crowds: Gender, Race and Identity* (London, UK: Bloomsbury Publishing 2019), 154.

138. Eleanor Roosevelt, JFK Campaign Ad, Eleanor Roosevelt Papers, https://www2.gwu.edu/~erpapers/mep/displaydoc.cfm?docid=jfk57.

139. Chris Cillizza, "Donald Trump's racist tweets show he doesn't understand America," CNN, July 15, 2019, https://lite.cnn.com/en/article/h_316f0544f0af5bc6ecd54d39c7b87b9c.

140. Brian Lonergan, "Barbara Jordan's wisdom is needed in today's immigration debate," *The Hill*, July 17, 2018, https://thehill.com/opinion/immigration/369153-barbara-jordans-wisdom-is-needed-in-todays-immigration-debate.

141. 1995 State of the Union Address, YouTube.com, April 11, 2012, https://www.youtube.com/watch?v=7hSBtgugeUk.

142. Dan MacGuill, "Did Barack Obama Express Opposition to 'Undetected, Undocumented, Unchecked' Immigration?" Snopes, August 2, 2018, https://www.snopes.com/fact-check/barack-obama-2005-immigration-quote/.

143. Jenni Fink, "RNC Cites Clinton, Obama, Schumer Immigration Quotes, Releases 'Illegal Immigration' Victims Video," *Newsweek*, January 8, 2019, https://www.newsweek.com/rnc-uses-clinton-obama-schumers-words-push-border-security-releases-video-1284059.

144. Jordan Fabian, "Steve King: For Every Valedictorian DREAMer, There Are 100 Drug Smugglers," ABC News, July 23, 2013, https://abcnews.go.com/ABC_Univision/Politics/steve-king-valedictorian-dreamer-100-drug-smugglers/story?id=19750985.

145. Katie Rogers, "2 Valedictorians in Texas Declare Undocumented Status, and Outrage Ensues," *New York Times*, June 10, 2016, https://www.nytimes.com/2016/06/11/us/2-valedictorians-in-texas-declare-undocumented-status-and-outrage-ensues.html.

146. USCIS Releases Report on Arrest Histories of Illegal Aliens who Request DACA, US Citizenship and Immigration Services, November 16, 2019, https://www.uscis.gov/news/news-releases/uscis-releases-report-on-arrest-histories-of-illegal-aliens-who-request-daca.

147. Richard Pérez-Peña, "Survivor Recounts Horror of Attack in Newark Schoolyard," *New York Times*, April 29, 2010, https://www.nytimes.com/2010/04/30/nyregion/30newark.html.

148. Juliet Lapidos, "Steve King Still Stands by 'Cantaloupe' Comments," New York Times, https://takingnote.blogs.nytimes.com/2013/08/12/steve-king-still-stands-by-cantaloupe-comments/.

149. Gregory Crouch, "Dutch Film Against Islam Is Released on Internet," *New York Times*, March 28, 2008, https://www.nytimes.com/2008/03/28/world/europe/28dutch.html.

150. Uri Friedman, "Should Calling for 'Fewer Moroccans' Be Considered Hate Speech?" *The Atlantic*, November 2, 2016, https://www.theatlantic.com/international/archive/2016/11/geert-wilders-free-hate-speech/506018/.

151. Steve King, Twitter, March 13, 2015, https://twitter.com/stevekingia/status/576481891009744896.

152. Winston Churchill, GoodReads, https://www.goodreads.com/quotes/122689-but-the-mahommedan-religion-increases-instead-of-lessening-the-fury.

153. Daniel Chaitin, "Panel erupts over Steve King's 'old white people' defense," *Washington Examiner*, July 28, 2016, https://www.washingtonexaminer.com/panel-erupts-over-steve-kings-old-white-people-defense.

154. George Orwell, *1984* (New York: Harcourt, 1949), 50.

155. Daniel Victor, "What, Congressman Steve King Asks, Have Nonwhites Done for Civilization?" *New York Times*, July 18, 2016, https://www.nytimes.com/2016/07/19/us/politics/steve-king-nonwhite-subgroups.html.

156. Ibid.

157. Amber Phillips, "Steve King: The idea that every culture is equal is 'not objectively true,'" *Washington Post*, July 20, 2016, https://www.washingtonpost.com/news/the-fix/wp/2016/07/20/steve-king-the-idea-that-every-culture-is-equal-is-not-objectively-true/.

158. Amber Phillips, "What Steve King's 'sub groups' musing says about the party of Donald Trump," *Washington Post*, July 19, 2016, https://www.washingtonpost.com/news/the-fix/wp/2016/06/22/what-steve-kings-fight-against-the-harriet-tubman-20-bill-says-about-the-gop-in-2016/.

159. Philip Bump, "Rep. Steve King wonders what 'sub-groups' besides whites made contributions to civilization," *Washington Post*, July 18, 2016, https://www.washingtonpost.com/news/the-fix/wp/2016/07/18/rep-steve-king-wonders-what-sub-groups-besides-whites-made-contributions-to-civilization/.

160. Colby Itkowitz, "Steve King: Presuming all cultures contribute equally to our civilization devalues the Founding Fathers," *Washington Post*, May 29, 2019, https://www.washingtonpost.com/politics/steve-king-presuming-all-cultures-equally-contribute-to-our-civilization-devalues-the-founding-fathers/2019/05/29/33b13490-8248-11e9-933d-7501070ee669_story.html.

161. Emma Graham-Harrison and Akhtar Mohammad Makoii, 'The Taliban took years of my life': the Afghan women living in the shadow of war," *The Guardian*, February 9, 2019, https://www.theguardian.com/world/2019/feb/09/the-taliban-took-years-of-my-life-the-afghan-women-living-in-the-shadow-of-war.

162. Ayaan Hirsi Ali, *Infidel*, excerpted in DavidFrum.com, https://davidfrum.com/article/infidel.

163. Alternative für Deutschland–Germany, https://www.idgroup.eu/alternative_fur_deutschland.

164. Realizable Ideals, the Earl Lectures, By Theodore Roosevelt, pg 54 https://books.google.com/books?id=xdUEAAAAMAAJ&pg=PA54&lpg=PA54&dq=Theodore+Roosevelt+most+essential+and+least+pleasant&source=bl&ots=3QlDXTdDVc&sig=ACfU3U1r4dx0h8h3e6H-Q2xz3pf7i1LdFg&hl=en&sa=X&ved=2ahUKEwiHns-io-3wAhW4AZ0JHWeGBqoQ6AEwFHoECBAQAg

165. Teddy Roosevelt speech, "On American Motherhood," 1905, https://www.bartleby.com/268/10/29.html.

166. Realizable Ideals, the Earl Lectures, By Theodore Roosevelt, pg 54 https://books.google.com/books?id=xdUEAAAAMAAJ&pg=PA54&lpg=PA54&dq=Theodore+Roosevelt+most+essential+and+least+pleasant&source=bl&ots=3QlDXTdDVc&sig=ACfU3U1r4dx0h8h3e6H-Q2xz3pf7i1LdFg&hl=en&sa=X&ved=2ahUKEwiHns-io-3wAhW4AZ0JHWeGBqoQ6AEwFHoECBAQAg

167. Marine Le Pen, Twitter, October 3, 2016, https://twitter.com/mlp_officiel/status/782940621204033536?lang=en.

168. Annie Groer, "Indiana GOP Senate hopeful Richard Mourdock says God 'intended' rape pregnancies," *Washington Post*, October 24, 2012, https://www.washingtonpost.com/blogs/she-the-people/wp/2012/10/24/

indiana-gop-senate-hopeful-richard-mourdock-says-god-intended-rape-pregnancies/.

169. Matt Stevens and Cheryl Gay Stolberg, "Steve King Asks If There Would Be 'Any Population' Left Without Rape and Incest," *New York Times*, August 14, 2019, https://www.nytimes.com/2019/08/14/us/politics/steve-king-rape-incest.html.

170. Ed Kilgore, "Steve King Offers Passionate Defense of Rape and Incest," August 14, 2019, https://www.thecut.com/2019/08/steve-king-rape-incest-abortion-comments.html.

171. Tess Bonn, "Iowa GOP chair calls Steve King's rape, incest comments 'outrageous,'" *The Hill*, August 16, 2019, https://thehill.com/hilltv/rising/457707-iowa-gop-official-calls-kings-rape-and-incest-comments-outrageous.

172. Kay Henderson, "Steve King criticized for his comments on rape, incest," Radio Iowa, August 14, 2019, https://www.radioiowa.com/2019/08/14/steve-king-criticized-for-his-comments-on-rape-incest/.

173. Stevens and Stolberg, *New York Times*.

174. Oliver Willis, "GOP leader doesn't even know his party's official position on abortion," *American Independent*, May 16, 2019, https://americanindependent.com/gop-leader-kevin-mccarthy-abortion-rape-exceptions-republican-platform/.

175. Republican Platform 2016, https://prod-cdn-static.gop.com/media/documents/DRAFT_12_FINAL%5B1%5D-ben_1468872234.pdf.

176. Stevens and Stolberg, *New York Times*.

177. CNN Transcripts, August 15, 2019, http://transcripts.cnn.com/TRANSCRIPTS/1908/15/nday.01.html.

178. Bob Brigham, Wyoming GOP demands Liz Cheney resign 'immediately' —and repay party for past donations: report," *RawStory*, February 6, 2021, https://www.rawstory.com/liz-cheney-2650346897/.

179. Stevens and Stolberg, *New York Times*.

180. Steve King, Twitter, March 12, 2017, https://twitter.com/stevekingia/status/840980755236999169?lang=en.

181. Ayaan Hirsi Ali, *Infidel* (New York: Simon & Schuster, 2007), 348.

182. William Grimes, "No Rest for a Feminist Fighting Radical Islam," *New York Times*, February 14, 2007, https://www.nytimes.com/2007/02/14/books/14grim.html.

183. Richard Pérez-Peña and Tanzina Vega, "Brandeis Cancels Plan to Give Honorary Degree to Ayaan Hirsi Ali, a Critic of Islam," *New York Times*, April 8, 2014, https://www.nytimes.com/2014/04/09/us/brandeis-cancels-plan-to-give-honorary-degree-to-ayaan-hirsi-ali-a-critic-of-islam.html.

184. Weiss, Resignation letter.

185. Pérez-Peña and Vega, *New York Times*.

186. Ian Schwartz, "Rep. Steve King vs. CNN's Cuomo: 'I Meant Exactly What I Said' about Western Civilization, Culture," RealClear Politics, March 13, 2017, https://www.realclearpolitics.com/video/2017/03/13/rep_steve_king_vs_cnns_cuomo_i_meant_exactly_what_i_said_about_western_civilization_culture.html.

187. Steve Benen, "Looking longingly to Joe McCarthy," *Washington Monthly*, March 12, 2010, https://washingtonmonthly.com/2010/03/12/looking-longingly-to-joe-mccarthy/.

188. Robert Zaretsky, "A France Without Jews Is No Longer Unthinkable: Anti-Semitism Puts Pressure on a Community and a Cherished Idea," *Foreign Affairs*, Febraury 4, 2020, https://www.foreignaffairs.com/articles/france/2020-02-04/france-without-jews-no-longer-unthinkable.

189. Pew Research Center, "Islamic Extremism: Common Concern for Muslim and Western Publics," July 14, 2005, https://www.pewresearch.org/global/2005/07/14/islamic-extremism-common-concern-for-muslim-and-western-publics/.

190. Roger Cohen, "Trump's Last Stand for White America," *New York Times*, October 16, 2020, https://www.nytimes.com/2020/10/16/opinion/trump-2020.html.

191. Daniel Pipes, "Hungary: Not Submitting to Islam," *Washington Times*, August 14, 2018, http://www.danielpipes.org/18477/hungary-not-submitting-to-islam.

192. Norimitsu Onishi, "Will American Ideas Tear France Apart? Some of Its Leaders Think So," *New York Times*, February 10, 2021, https://www.nytimes.com/2021/02/09/world/europe/france-threat-american-universities.html.

193. Joe Concha, "Bari Weiss rips cancel culture as 'social murder' on Bill Maher show," *The Hill*, August 1, 2020, https://thehill.com/homenews/administration/510115-bari-weiss-rip-cancel-culture-as-social-murder-on-bill-maher-show.

194. Andrew Egger, "Steve King's White Supremacy Comments Send Conservatives Running," *The Bulwark*, January 10, 2019, https://thebulwark.com/steve-kings-white-supremacy-comments-send-conservatives-running/.

195. Ben Shapiro, Twitter, January 10, 2019, https://twitter.com/benshapiro/status/1083392910375018496?lang=en.

196. Randy Feenstra, Twitter, January 10, 2019, https://twitter.com/randyfeenstra/status/1083413562020769792?lang=en.

197. Peggy McGlone, "African American Museum site removes 'whiteness' chart after criticism from Trump Jr. and conservative media," *Washington Post*, July 17, 2020, https://www.washingtonpost.com/entertainment/museums/african-american-museum-site-removes-whiteness-chart-after-criticism-from-trump-jr-and-conservative-media/2020/07/17/4ef6e6f2-c831-11ea-8ffe-372be8d82298_story.html.

198. Steve King, Twitter, July 15, 2020, https://twitter.com/stevekingia/status/1283487120913571840.

199. McGlone, *Washington Post*.

200. Ben Shapiro, "Americans in Surrender," *Jewish World Review*, August 5, 2020, https://townhall.com/columnists/benshapiro/2020/08/05/draft-n2573719

201. Mark 6:4, ESV